101 Coaching Sup(
Techniques, Approache
and Experime

This book locates 101 practical coaching supervision techniques in their theoretical context. It is organised into ten chapters, each reflecting a different philosophical basis for the coaching supervision work: Existential, Gestalt, Positive Psychology, Psychodynamic, Solution Focused, Systemic, Thinking Environment, Transpersonal and finally an Eclectic chapter.

With contributions and insights from leaders in the field, this book outlines the different philosophies and their principles and explains their application in practice. The book will help readers determine which technique to use and when, as well as offering a step-by-step guide to implementing or adapting it for their own work. With a breadth of techniques, the book will help all supervisors broaden their repertoire and ultimately become a better practitioner.

Accessible and practical, this book is a valuable resource for experienced and novice supervisors as well as their supervisees. It will inspire them to keep their supervision and coaching practices both current and fresh, offering a diverse range of techniques to experiment with.

Michelle Lucas is Director of Greenfields Consulting Limited, specialising in executive coaching, coaching supervision and the training of internal coaches, mentors and supervisors. She also supervises the MA Students at Oxford Brookes University, UK.

101 Coaching Supervision Techniques, Approaches, Enquiries and Experiments

Edited by Michelle Lucas

LONDON AND NEW YORK

First published 2020
by Routledge
2 Park Square, Milton Park, Abingdon, Oxon OX14 4RN

and by Routledge
52 Vanderbilt Avenue, New York, NY 10017

Routledge is an imprint of the Taylor & Francis Group, an informa business

British Library Cataloguing-in-Publication Data
A catalogue record for this book is available from the British Library

Library of Congress Cataloging-in-Publication Data
Names: Lucas, Michelle, 1965- editor.
Title: 101 coaching supervision techniques, approaches, enquiries and experiments / edited by Michelle Lucas.
Other titles: One hundred one coaching supervision techniques, approaches, enquiries and experiments
Description: 1 Edition. | New York : Routledge, 2020. | Includes bibliographical references and index.
Identifiers: LCCN 2019059030 (print) | LCCN 2019059031 (ebook) | ISBN 9780367481148 (hardback) | ISBN 9780367481155 (paperback) | ISBN 9781003038061 (ebook)
Subjects: LCSH: Employees—Coaching of. | Executive coaching.
Classification: LCC HF5549.5.C53 A12 2020 (print) | LCC HF5549.5.C53 (ebook) | DDC 658.3/124—dc23
LC record available at https://lccn.loc.gov/2019059030
LC ebook record available at https://lccn.loc.gov/2019059031

ISBN: 978-0-367-48114-8 (hbk)
ISBN: 978-0-367-48115-5 (pbk)
ISBN: 978-1-003-03806-1 (ebk)

Typeset in Utopia and Optima
by Swales & Willis, Exeter, Devon, UK

Printed and bound in Great Britain by
TJ Books Limited, Padstow, Cornwall

To all the contributors who made this book a reality – my heartfelt thanks for sharing your work so generously with our community. It has been both a pleasure and a memorable endeavour working with each of you.

Contents

Acknowledgments

I am grateful for all my colleagues and clients who have surrounded me with inspiration, encouragement and support to bring this book into being. There are however three people who deserve special recognition here:

To Claire Davey, independent executive coach and coach supervisor who provided a fresh pair of eyes to each and every one of the 101 techniques to help ensure they were accessible to our readers.

To Helen Robson, who reviewed the philosophical sections to help ensure we both honoured the voice of the Author while also offering the reader a sense of consistency throughout the book.

To Christine Mitterbauer, independent career coach (with extra-ordinary organisation skills!) who acted as the liaison point with all 41 contributors and who kept us on track throughout the project.

Thank you.

Note: Icons made by Freepik and Pixel Perfect from www.flaticon.com

Tables and figures

Tables

Figures

About the editor

Michelle Lucas is Director of Greenfields Consulting Limited, specialising in executive coaching, coaching supervision and the training of internal coaches, mentors and supervisors. She has a degree in Applied Psychology from UWIST and an MBA from Warwick Business School. Her early career was in Clinical Psychology before a 20-year career in fast-paced commercial organisations leading HR functions. Working independently since 2006, she is an Accredited Executive Master Coach and an Accredited Coaching Supervisor with the Association for Coaching. Having completed her training in both coaching (2009) and coaching supervision (2012) at Oxford Brookes University, she is now an associate lecturer and coach supervisor for their MA programme. She holds a voluntary role as the Supervision Education Lead for the Association for Coaching and co-facilitates their Global Co-Coaching Virtual Forum. She is also a member of the Association of Coaching Supervisors.

Michelle is an innovative practitioner interested in exploring atypical applications of coaching supervision. She is a confident and energetic speaker and has presented annually at the Oxford Brookes International Supervision Conference for seven consecutive years. She has written 15 peer-reviewed professional articles, and is a keen blogger. This is the third title she has written for Routledge, the previous books being collaborations with David Clutterbuck, Carol Whitaker and Tammy Turner.

She lives in Weymouth, Dorset, with her husband, Mark, stepson, Luke, and two dogs, Tia (a Chocolate Labrador) and Colin (a rescued Dachshund).

Contributors

Chapter authors

Julie Allan MSc CPsychol AFBPsS FRSA is an experienced coaching psychologist and executive coach as well as a supervisor and advisor on adult developmental processes. She has a journalistic background and has contributed articles, papers and chapters on gestalt, ethics, supervision, wisdom, metacognition and complexity, and co-authored *The Power of the Tale* book about story and narrative in organisations. Her early training with Petruska Clarkson laid the foundations for a holistic, enquiry-based approach that enables effective learning and leadership in challenging times.

Linda Aspey is an executive coach, supervisor, therapist and leadership development specialist with almost 30 years of experience in these fields. A qualified Time to Think Coach, Facilitator, Thinking Partnership Teacher and Time to Think Consultant, she is a member of the Time to Think Global Faculty, teaching, supervising and qualifying others in the Thinking Environment™ approach. A registered and accredited counsellor/psychotherapist, in 2010 she was awarded Fellowship of the British Association for Counselling and Psychotherapy for services to BACP, particularly in setting the BACP Coaching Division and launching its journal *Coaching Today*. Linda has a Master's in Strategic HR Management, and diplomas in Counselling, Integrative Supervision of Groups and Individuals, and Stress Management. Chair of the Coaching Panel at the New Entrepreneurs Foundation from 2012 to 2018, she is on the editorial panel of *Coaching at Work* magazine, and is an external examiner for the University of East London's Counselling and Coaching Psychology courses.

Professor **David Clutterbuck** is one of the earliest pioneers of coaching and mentoring. Co-founder of the European Mentoring and Coaching

Council, he is now one of its two special ambassadors, tasked with spreading good practice internationally. He is visiting professor in the coaching and mentoring faculties of Henley (Reading), Sheffield Hallam, Oxford Brookes and York St John Universities. Author, co-author or editor of some 70 books, his current projects include an ambitious plan to create five million school age coaches and mentors over a five-year period.

Hetty Einzig brings 25 years of psychology and executive coaching experience to global leadership development. A best-selling author, her career has spanned the arts, media, health, NGOs and strategy. She designs and delivers leader-coach and global corporate culture change programmes. Key focuses are women's leadership and regenerative coaching for contribution. She works systemically and holistically founded on a transpersonal approach informed by psychoanalytic depth. She teaches at the Irish Management Institute, and is the Editor of *Coaching Perspectives*, the AC global magazine. She holds a Master's in Psychoanalytic and Systemic Approaches to Consulting with Organisations from the Tavistock Centre (UEL), a Certificate in Coaching Supervision from Oxford Brookes, and a Masters in History of Art from the Courtauld Institute (UL). She is married with two millennial daughters.

Evan George is a Solution-Focused practitioner, and founding partner in BRIEF. In addition to working as a therapist and coach in London, his Solution-Focused teaching takes him across the world and he is a co-author of three books on the Solution-Focused approach. Evan has a particular interest in making change easier, and briefer, and in building engagement and co-operation with reluctant clients, a subject on which he is currently writing (www.brief.org.uk).

Dr **Carmelina Lawton-Smith** is a coaching and development specialist who combines her private practice with a consultancy role for Oxford Brookes University Business School. She specialises in management and leadership development together with one-to-one executive coaching. Her recent research interests have focused on leadership resilience and the assessment of coaching capabilities. As part of the International centre for Coaching and Mentoring Studies at Oxford Brookes University she delivers supervision and master-classes for coaches. She supports the teaching team on both the MA and the Professional Doctorate in Coaching and Mentoring Practice. She is a member of the British Psychological Society and the Association for Coaching. She writes regularly and is a member of the Editorial Board of the *International Journal of Evidence Based Coaching* and Consulting Editor for the

International Journal of Stress Prevention & Wellbeing. She has presented at a number of conferences and is a member of the Oxford Brookes University Supervision Conference Academic Board.

Professor **Ernesto Spinelli** has gained an international reputation as one of the leading contemporary trainers and theorists of existential therapy and, more recently, the related areas of coaching and facilitation. He is a Fellow of the British Psychological Society (BPS), a founding member of the BPS Special Group in Coaching Psychology as well as an APECS accredited executive coach and coaching supervisor. In 1999, Ernesto was awarded a Personal Chair as Professor of Psychotherapy, Counselling and Counselling Psychology. Ernesto is currently the Director of ES Associates, an organisation dedicated to the advancement of existential perspectives in therapy, coaching and facilitation through specialist seminars and training programmes. His most recent book, *Practising Existential Therapy: The Relational World*, 2nd edition (Sage, 2015) has been widely praised as a major contribution to the advancement of existential theory and practice.

Lynda Tongue is a management educator and coach. She runs leadership programmes in organisations and she also coaches on a team and individual basis, and is a coach and trainer supervisor. She is currently undertaking a large research project on leadership and TA. She is a teaching and supervising transactional analyst in the organisational field. She has delivered workshops throughout the UK, in the USA, Russia, the Ukraine, Romania, Spain, Prague and Poland. Also, she is Deputy Programme Director for the MSc in Professional Development (Developmental Transactional Analysis). As well as her TA qualifications, Lynda has a post-graduate Diploma in Training Management, a Diploma in Supervision and a BA (Hons). She is also a Neuro Linguistic Programming Practitioner and has been running her learning and development consultancy since 1991.

Maren Donata Urschel is an experienced systemic supervisor, facilitator and coach based in Berlin, Germany. She works face-to-face and virtually with individuals and groups. Maren, who was born in Heidelberg is fluent in English, German and Italian. She lived and worked in the UK and Switzerland for over 20 years before returning to Germany and settling in Berlin. She holds an MSc in Organisational Psychology from the London School of Economics and trained deeply in organisational constellations and systemic coaching. Maren contributed to the book *Systemic Coaching & Constellations* by John Whittington and leads the Coaching Constellations trainings and workshops in Germany which are designed for coaches, coach supervisors, facilitators and organisational consultants who wish to integrate a systemic perspective in their work. In her spare time, Maren enjoys playing the violin in symphony orchestras and chamber ensembles.

Dr **Alison Whybrow** PhD CPsychol, AFBPsS specialises in leadership coaching, senior team development and system change. At the forefront of the development of Coaching Psychology in the early 2000s, she has contributed papers, chapters and books on the subject of Coaching Psychology and, for many years, directed accredited programmes in coaching practice. In her work, Alison integrates a range of psychological and philosophical underpinnings, leadership frameworks and an ecological world-view. Gestalt is a core underpinning.

Technique contributors

Denise Yusuf is a Solution-Focused practitioner. She works predominantly with children and young people and is the co-author of a book, *Solution Focused Coaching with Children and Young People*. She is also an experienced supervisor working with highly experienced practitioners as well as with students on the BRIEF Diploma in Solution-Focused Practice. Denise is currently working on a book exploring Solution-Focused practice with children and young people across the world.

Fredrike Bannink is a clinical psychologist and lawyer, living in Amsterdam, the Netherlands. She is an international keynote speaker, trainer and author of more than 40 books. www.fredrikebannink.com

Dr **Henry Campion** is an experienced coaching supervisor, accredited with Oxford Brookes University and the Association for Coaching. He has worked as a doctor (including a psychiatric internship), a TV program maker, a senior BBC manager and an executive coach. He also holds a postgraduate diploma in Psychosynthesis (transpersonal) Counselling. Henry Campion is particularly interested in how insights from neuroscience can inform coaching and coach supervision. He has presented on attachment theory to the Global Supervisors' Network and the Americas Coaching SuperVision Network; and has contributed to a chapter on Neurobehavioural Supervision: Applied Neuroscience in the context of Coaching Supervision. His website is www.coachsupervisor.co.uk

Anne Calleja MSc, MAC, MBACP, NLPtCA, UKCP is a leadership coach, psychotherapist and supervisor. She works with chief executives, main boards of directors. their teams and also provides coaching and therapy supervision. She brings a blend of proven business acumen with counselling, psychotherapy and facilitation to give a unique and focused approach to executive coaching and Senior Team Development. Anne is a Master NLP Practitioner and Trainer. She works globally and is based in Oxford, UK. An accredited coach and coach supervisor with the Association for Coaching (AC), Anne is Chair of the Supervision Special Interest Group and actively involved in the engagement of those interested in developing strategy for coaching supervision. Anne also provides a counselling service for individuals seeking personal support.

Christine Champion founded acumen executive coaching in 2003, based in the City of London, and is a coaching supervisor on the Master's program in Coaching and Mentoring at Oxford Brookes University. A passionate and experienced, executive coach; her organisation is focused on the postmodern approaches drawn from Vertical Development approaches and how these can be applied in the development of leaders and coaches to be fit for the future in an increasingly, dynamic, uncertain and ambiguous world. The starting point for coaching is designed to increase self-knowledge, insight and awareness which in turn elevates levels of consciousness, enabling the individual to intentionally choose how to respond in different situations. This enhancement of consciousness moves the individual away from old habitual and learned responses to create and embed greater resourcefulness, agility and flexibility which is required for successful leadership in today's environments

Dr **Sue Congram** is an experienced leadership development consultant, in-depth executive coach and supervisor, Sue brings systemic, progressive and creative thinking to her work. Clients describe her as tenacious and inspirational, with an infectious zest for life. Sue works nationally and internationally, where she has gained a rich and varied appreciation of cultural differences and cultural belief systems that impact professional practices such as coaching and coaching supervision. Working in this field for over 30 years, her success is rooted in an ability to infuse logical processes with creative input that enables people to see situations in new and different ways. Her PhD research on the underlying influences of leadership (2013), led to co-founding the EB Centre for Engendering Balance in Leadership. As a respected author, Sue has published a range of books and papers on business psychology, management and leadership, organisational development, coaching, coaching supervision and diversity and inclusion.

David Crowe is an experienced accredited executive, career and personal development coach and trained coach supervisor. He works one-to-one with a range of people in the public and private sector in coaching projects in areas like business improvement, career change, retirement coaching and building confidence. David has worked in coaching practice for many years and is a full member of the Association for Coaching, an accredited Coach with the Association for Coaching and has a post Graduate Coaching and Mentoring qualification and Coaching Supervision training through Oxford Brookes University. He is an accredited Insights practitioner using the Insights personality traits framework. He is also a foundation trained counsellor and has done part of the integrated psychotherapy MSc training at Metanoia Institute. He has foundation training accreditation with the Institute of Group Analysis and familiar with different frameworks such as Neuro Linguistic programming (NLP), Transactional Analysis and mindfulness practice.

Claire Davey has worked in the UK and internationally as an executive coach, supervisor and development consultant for global organisations within professional services, the financial sector, education, telecommunications, the third sector and elite sport. Prior to starting CDPerformance Ltd she was Head of Coaching and Leadership Development at Deloitte where she pioneered systemic team coaching, experimented with external and internal supervision and was an early adopter of supervision on supervision. In her EMCC Governor role she continues to both innovate and challenge advances in the world of coaching and supervision. She completed her supervision studies with The Bath Consultancy Group, specialising in Transcultural Supervision and Supervising Teams and Organisations. Claire is now part of the supervision bench supporting those undertaking Henley Business Schools Professional Certificate in Supervision. She has an integrative approach to supervision that encourages enquiry and experimentation often through a creative approach and with ecology in mind.

Peter Duffell an experienced, board level, executive and personal coach and coach supervisor with 30 years of business experience before becoming a full time coach and supervisor. He worked at board level in senior roles with a number of global financial services organisations such as HSBC and UBS. He has many years of practical experience of coaching and mentoring individuals in a leadership capacity and has led a number of organisational and cultural transformations. Peter has an MA in Coaching and Mentoring Practice from Oxford Brookes University and is a qualified Coach Supervisor. Peter is currently the Governance Director on the Board of EMCC UK. He is a regular contributor to coaching industry periodicals, such as Coaching at Work – from whom he won Best Article award in 2017 for his work on emotion in supervision. Current interests include the impact of generational difference on supervision and impact of AI on coaching.

Angela Dunbar is a highly experienced coach, coach supervisor, author, trainer and Master NLP Practitioner. She is a lifetime fellow of the Association for Coaching, a former council member and accredited as both a coach and coach supervisor. In business since 1994, Angela coaches people on all aspects of their professional and personal lives, with a special interest in confidence, creativity and communication skills. Angela's passion is Clean Language, a powerful non-directive facilitation process that engages the coachee's non-conscious resources through the metaphors they use to describe their experience. Angela teaches 'Clean' techniques for coaches through The Clean Coaching Centre: www.cleancoaching.com. Angela has twice been nominated for the AC's coaching Honorary Award for 'Impacting the Coaching Profession' and holds a degree (first class) in Psychology. Angela's is author of *Essential Life Coaching Skills* (2009) and *Clean Coaching: The Insider Guide to Making Change Happen* (2016).

Marie Faire is co-founder and owner of The Beyond Partnership Ltd. As a coach, Marie has a reputation for being both supportive and challenging working with both individual executives and with teams. As a coaching supervisor she describes herself as relational and eclectic. She brings humour and compassion to her work and takes an integrative and relational approach, drawing on different psychological theories. She says she is a 'fellow traveller', working in partnership with her supervisees, for the benefit of them, their clients and the organisations within which their clients work. Following her first degree Marie has gained several post-graduate qualifications including a Master's degree (MA) in Management Learning. She is an accredited coach and coaching supervisor with AC. She is the lead trainer of an AC recognised coach training programme and has pioneered Coaching Supervision training in Turkey. Marie is an ANLP recognised 'Master' NLP trainer.

Liz Ford is an accredited master executive coach, Accredited Coaching Supervisor, facilitator and trainer with a passion for learning. She has a special interest in the training and ongoing development of coaches and enjoys working in partnership with them to foster potential, build belief and inspire excellence. Her areas of supervision expertise include; developing creative skills for coaching and supervision, providing external supervision for internal coaches, supporting coaches working towards accreditation and developing coaches in training. Her approach is reflective and imaginative using a variety of creative methods to aid exploration and learning including the outdoors, images, colour, metaphor, music and movement. When she's not working she enjoys walking in the hills, reading crime novels and listening to music. She also sings with a local choir and loves going to the theatre.

Dr **Damian Goldvarg** has 30 years of experience providing executive coaching, leadership training, and facilitation in over fifty countries. He is a Master Certified Coach and received his PhD in Organizational Psychology from Alliant University. He is an accredited coach supervisor (ESIA) and facilitates certifications in Professional Coaching, Mentor Coaching, and Coaching Supervision. He was the 2013–2014 ICF Global President. Damian published three books on coaching and several book chapters and received the Circle of Distinction award from ICF for his global contribution to the coaching profession.

Jackee Holder is London born and raised, and loves the diversity and richness of urban living. Her multi-layered portfolio includes her work as an executive coach, writer and published author, creativity coaching, and facilitation of leadership and well-being courses and workshops. She speaks at conferences and events, adding her voice to what feeds and nourishes our souls and spirits. A nature and tree lover, she brings the world of nature into her coaching and therapeutic work at every opportunity and sees that as the voice of her creative spirit at work. She is the curator and host of the online Paper Therapy course and is currently hard at work on her fifth book. Website: www.jackeeholder.com; Email: info@jackeeholder.com; Twitter: @jackeeholder; Instagram: @jackeehol

Charlotte Housden is an occupational psychologist, trained in coaching for transitions. She is also a photographer. Her current focus is running self-managed learning sets for the NHS and is an experienced and engaging facilitator and presenter. Charlotte Housden is photographer and occupational psychologist, which are two sides of the same coin. She helps drive change in a thinking, data-driven and word-based profession.

Diane Hanna has been a qualified coach and coach supervisor of 15 years, who spends her time coaching and supervising one-to-one and in a group setting. She is a lead tutor on a PGC in Business and Personal Coaching and Coaching Supervision on behalf of Barefoot Coaching Ltd and the University of Chester and is active in promoting good practice across the profession. She is accredited by the ICF at PCC level. Prior to working as a coach and coach supervisor Diane spent over 20 years in the corporate setting in various senior HR and Development roles and is a Fellow of the CIPD.

Andy King decided on a career change in 2007 and trained as a coach after a 30-year career in fashion retail when he had senior positions in many of the leading high street names. He believes he learnt more in those 20 days than the previous 30 years. He then developed his coaching business and continued to deepen his coaching practice, including adopting David Grove's Clean Language and Emergent Knowledge techniques. This led to him experimenting with different approaches to helping client's get out of their own way and access the information hidden under the surface of their system. In recent years he has co-developed a model around the art and science of having better conversations and uses it to facilitate teams to work together more effectively and make the whole greater than the sum of the parts.

Paul King is co-founder of The Beyond Partnership, a leading-edge people and organisational development company. Paul has been working as a coach, facilitator and consultant for more than 25 years, having previously worked for Deloitte and PricewaterhouseCoopers. He works with senior executives on organisational and personal issues and with private individuals and sports people. He is particularly known for his integral approach and his expertise working with the body-mind to help people become the best they can be. He has run somatic intelligence and leadership embodiment workshops for coaches, executives and others across Europe and in the Far East. His work brings a whole person, whole system approach to managing stress, developing resilience, raising performance and a creating a sense of wellbeing. Paul is a Master Practitioner and certified trainer in NLP, an Inner Game Coach. He is trained in Feldenkrais (movement re-education) and teaches Tai Chi workshops.

Tsafi Lederman is a coach trainer, supervisor, integrative arts, body-psychotherapist and group facilitator with over 25 years of experience. She specialises in integrative arts psychotherapy, gestalt and body-psychotherapy. She has a private psychotherapy and supervision practice in London. Tsafi is a senior lecturer, trainer and supervisor in the integrative arts therapy MA programme. She was also involved in developing, teaching and co-directing the Creativity & Imagination programme at IATE. In the past 12 years she has been involved in developing and teaching somatic coaching workshops through her work at Creative Expansion. Tsafi also runs workshops in counselling and communications skills for clinicians and therapists. Tsafi and Jenny Stacey are directors of Creative Expansion, a training organisation with a focus on somatic, embodied coaching and the creative arts. Creative Expansion has a strong track record of devising and delivering successful experiential courses about psychological issues that come up in coaching as part of professional and personal development. Recent course titles include: Body of Awareness, Shame and the Inner Critic, Holding the Mirror Up, Stories We Tell Ourselves (www.creativeexpansion.co.uk).

Lesley Matile has a passion for learning and development in her working life. She specialises in facilitating others to find the motivation and determination to harness their best personal attributes and skills to achieve the success and fulfilment they seek. As a coach, Lesley works principally in manufacturing, embedding coaching cultures through 'leader as coach' programmes and individual sessions in order to establish environments in which all can thrive. As a supervisor, Lesley enjoys supporting and challenging those who have a desire to help their clients develop and excel. She encourages supervisees to pay careful attention to the motivational elements of their coaching. She feels privileged to have worked with such a diverse range of clients.

Julia Menaul is an executive coach and supervisor at the practice she set up in 2001, Spark Coaching & Training. Julia started her career in retail before moving into management development for various private sector companies, a leading charity and the justice system. Julia is a Psychology graduate, an Accredited Professional Executive Coach with the Association for Coaching, and has post graduate diplomas in Executive Coaching (2000) and (CIPD) Human Resource Development. She has a Certificate in Supervision of Coaches, Mentors & Consultants from Bath Consultancy Group (2008) and ICF Accredited Diploma in Coaching Supervision from the Coaching Supervision Academy (2010). She is a Member of the EMCC, British Psychological Society, and Fellow of the Chartered Institute of Personnel & Development. As well as running a thriving group and individual supervision practice, Julia also sits on the Board of the Association of Coaching Supervisors.

Clare Norman's approach to coaching is simple, non-directive, client-centred, encouraging clients to work and think in an adult way with themselves and towards others. Having worked as an internal coach herself at Accenture, and having set up and provided thought leadership to a 650+ strong community of practice, Clare is familiar with the ethical dilemmas facing internal and external coaches. She is a certified coach supervisor, and supervises coaches to pay attention to what needs to shift in them in order to enable their clients to shift. She also mentor coaches those going for International Coach Federation accreditation and those wanting to be sharpen their edge in her 'lock-in'.

Helen Reuben is an experienced coach and coach supervisor. She trains and develops coaches on accredited programmes and master classes. A Master Practitioner of NLP and Hypnotherapist, Helen offers a variety of services to most sectors and at most levels. A passion for Helen is Transpersonal Coaching and 'Spiritual Intelligence'. She also trains in this area and feels that Transpersonal Coaching is a way forward for many coaches looking to develop their practice and effectiveness. Helen believes in all coaches having strategies and approaches to stay well and release their own personal blocks and diversions before engaging in a coaching sessions. Self-care is sometimes neglected even for the most experienced coaches she says.

Lily Seto, MA, PCC, ESIA, CEC, Certified Mentor Coach and has a Diploma in Coaching Supervision, has a thriving global leadership coaching and coach development practice and is the first Canadian to be awarded the European Mentoring and Coaching Council (EMCC) Supervision Accreditation (ESIA). Her clients come from the service, financial and business sectors, the Public Service, as well as Canadian Indigenous Communities. Her passion is to support organisations and leaders to step into their power. As an Associate Faculty of Royal Roads University, Lily teaches the *Intercultural Competence and Global Coaching* course in the Advanced Graduate Certificate Program in Coaching. She also serves on the Independent Review Board (global ethics review board) for the coaching community and is also Past President of the International Coach Federation, Vancouver Island Chapter. In her spare time, Lily is an avid reader, traveller and grandmother, not necessarily in that order! She was the 2016 Recipient of the Prestigious Leadership Victoria Award: Royal Roads Award for Excellence in Coaching and Mentoring. (lilyseto@telus.net)

Dr **Louise Sheppard** has been coaching for over 20 years and has worked with more than 50 organizations globally. As a coaching supervisor, Louise works with internal and external coaches on both an individual and group basis. She is an accredited executive coach and coaching supervisor with APECS (Association for Professional Executive Coaching and Supervision). Louise has a professional doctorate in coaching and mentoring and her research was on the supervisee perspective in coaching supervision. She focuses on encouraging supervisee-led supervision that enables coaches to be the best that they can be. Since carrying out her research, Louise has shared her findings with the coaching community through speaking at conferences and writing articles and chapters on coaching supervision. She can be contacted at louisesheppard1@btinternet.com

Jenny Stacey is an executive coach, coach supervisor and gestalt psychotherapist (UKCP, HCPC) based in Yorkshire, UK. Jenny has extensive experience as an educator and facilitator of adults. Currently she runs the Diploma in Advanced Business and Executive Coaching at Michael Smurfit Graduate Business School, UCD Dublin, a training programme that combines her professional experience in executive coaching and psychological theory. Until 2018 she was tutor on the Postgraduate Diploma in Coaching Supervision at Leeds Beckett University. Jenny and Tsafi Lederman are directors of Creative Expansion, a training organisation with a focus on somatic, embodied coaching and the creative arts. Creative Expansion has a strong track record of devising and delivering successful experiential courses about psychological issues that come up in coaching as part of professional and personal development. Recent course titles include: Body of Awareness, Shame and the Inner Critic, Holding the Mirror Up, Stories We Tell Ourselves (www.creativeexpansion.co.uk).

Benita Treanor is an experienced and qualified coach supervisor, executive coach, facilitator. She has been a supervision assessor for the Association for Coaching and has pioneered supervision for the AC for over ten years. Benita is an AC, CSA and BACP accredited supervisor. Her original background began in the financial sector before setting up her own successful catering business. She founded her own Coaching and Organisational Development business in 1998 and continues to work with private, public, family business and not for profit sectors, locally and globally. Connecting people with their purpose, values and as a catalyst for change is at the core of her practice. Her engaging and inspirational approach maintained by sound integrity and supervision, creates a fertile environment for those who work with her. She works in partnership as an associate with the Oasis School of Human Relations, evolving Whole Person Learning approaches for twenty-first century relationships.

Tammy Turner is the founder of The Centre for Coaching Development and Supervision and CEO of Turner International www.turner.international. As an ICF Master Certified Coach (MCC), Tammy works globally with key industry and government decision makers and has trained, mentored and supervised many hundreds of internal coaches, leaders and HR professionals as well as freelance coaches, mentors and consultants. As a visionary in the international coaching field, she has been a contributing author to articles and books on coaching, mentoring and team coaching including chapters in *Coaching Supervision: A practical guide for Supervisees* (Routledge, 2016) and *Coaching and Mentoring in the Asia Pacific* (Routledge, 2017). She has been instrumental in engaging cross professional body discussions around coaching guidelines and in defining ICF's policy for CPD as an industry standard.

Penny Walker is a coach and facilitator who is also a Chartered Environmentalist and Fellow of the Institute of Environmental Management and Assessment (IEMA). In 1989 she took part in the first UK-wide day of activism on climate change. Swapping placards for post-it notes, she now helps people change their organisations and sectors for the better. Her main focus is facilitating conversations about sustainable development, including low-carbon futures and adapting to a disrupted climate. She's helped people: agree where to let the sea come in; work in their communities to bring in renewables and low-carbon energy; find ways for international bankers and their customers to work towards zero net deforestation in supply chains. She writes extensively on change and collaboration, including two editions of *Change Management for Sustainable Development* (2006, 2017) and *Working Collaboratively: A Practical Guide to Achieving More* (2013). She blogs at www.penny-walker.co.uk/blog.

Carol Whitaker has experience at board level of various NED roles, and an MBA with an early career in HR. The development of potential in the people has always been her passion. She specialises in Executive Coaching, Team/Group Coaching, Coaching Supervision and Mentoring Entrepreneurs in the Middle East and UK. She is a Senior Associate Lecturer with Oxford Brookes University and supervises students doing their MA in Coaching and Mentoring Practice (UK and Hong Kong), ILM7 Executive Coaching PG Cert and their internal coaching programmes. She has co-authored two 5* rated books *Coaching Supervision: A Practical Guide for Supervisees* and *Peer Supervision in Coaching & Mentoring: A Versatile Guide for Reflective Practice*, both published by Routledge. She lives in Oxford, UK, is co-chair of The AC SIG in Coaching Supervision. Her current portfolio is 60% supervision, 30% coaching and 10% mentoring. For more information visit her website www.whitaker-consulting.co.uk

Damion Wonfor is founder of Catalyst 14, a boutique coaching and mindfulness consultancy in London working across the private and public sectors and elite sport. He has been involved in the coaching profession since 1999 and is an experienced coach supervisor, executive coach, facilitator and mindfulness teacher. He has coached and facilitated individuals and groups at all levels within organisations in the UK and globally. He provides supervision to both external and internal coaches using systemic and embodied practises from his London office. In addition to coaching supervision, he specialises in developing coaching, dialogue and group learning and facilitation skills. He is passionate about supporting coaches to develop their presence, resilience and resourcefulness and delivers retreats for coaches in the UK and Internationally. In terms of his corporate experience, he spent 15 years in senior learning and development roles within blue chip organisations in the financial and professional service sectors.

Acknowledgments

Claire Davey: See above.

Christine Mitterbauer is a career and business coach who helps professionals and business owners who feel stuck, confused or unhappy with their career or business. Having launched three businesses, her coaching style is motivational and practical, as she provides insights and advice from her own business experiences. She speaks five languages and takes a broad perspective on life and business. https://christinecoaching.co.uk/

Helen Robson is a coach and coach supervisor. A former book editor, Helen has spent the last ten years in learning and development roles in large organisations, specialising in running bespoke leadership programmes. In 2014, Helen gained a distinction in her Post Graduate Certificate in Business and Executive Coaching (EMCC Senior Practitioner programme), particularly gravitating to the Gestalt/Psychodynamic approaches to the work. Her career as a coach, and the people she meets through her work, continue to inspire her and deepen her beliefs in how coaching can enable, enrich and support people and organisations; alongside her belief that coaches really do benefit from having supervision! Her more recent desire to qualify as a coach supervisor was driven by a genuine passion and curiosity for the work. Having lived and worked in Cambridge, Cardiff, Cape Town and Bristol, Helen has now settled in Somerset.

Foreword

I was in training myself when I first read David Clutterbuck's 2010 article 'The Liberated Coach.' I remember how deeply it resonated with me. An active member of coaching groups, I was constantly exposed to a plethora of different techniques; how easy it would have been to become the 'magpie' that he describes. The lure of a bright and shiny technique, with the potential to unlock things for a client can be difficult to resist. And yet I was always hesitant; two issues were present for me. First, how could I integrate new techniques into my practice such that it felt congruent (to me and to my clients). Second, with psychology in my background I was curious about the origin of the approach not, not just 'Does it work?' but 'Why does it work ... ?' So when Clutterbuck went on to describe 'managed eclecticism,' encouraging us to think about genuine integration and alignment with our practice, I felt empowered. Rather than the 'fear of missing out' if I were not to adopt yet another technique, I recognised the importance of working in a way that had congruence and authenticity at its core. As I have journeyed into coaching supervision this idea has stayed with me. When a supervisee comes to me explore something that did or didn't work, I am curious to know what informed their choice of approach and if they used a technique how they came to know it. With this approach practitioners can come to work with heightened awareness and conscious competence.

The primary readership for this book is designed to be the coaching supervisor, and I hope that the breadth of techniques will appeal to new and experienced supervisors alike. For the new supervisor they may want to focus on a philosophical section that is consistent with their training and broaden the range of techniques and approaches at their disposal. For the more experienced supervisor the book offers a range of alternative approaches to experiment with, and in doing so 'constructively disrupt' their practice keeping it fresh for both themselves and their supervisees. As I have written about elsewhere (Clutterbuck, Whitaker and Lucas,

2016), I fundamentally believe that the supervision relationship is a collaborative one. Therefore, this book intends to share the art of supervision practice in a way which is also accessible to coaches. Indeed, some techniques could be applied with coaching clients too. Whilst most of the techniques offered are intended for use by the supervisor (both professional and peer), some techniques are useful for independent reflective practice, i.e. self-supervision. My experience is that the stronger a supervisee becomes in their independent reflective practice, the more material they discover to bring to professional supervision.

I hope this book appeals to the magpie in all of us and offers inspiration for your own practice. However, I invite you to pause when you find something bright and shiny and new. Please remember where the new trinket has come from and as you return to your nest, don't just take it - truly steal it and make the technique your own.

And finally, if you have favourite techniques that you would like to share with our community - do get in touch ... we can bear this in mind should we update the book in future.

Footnote: Throughout this book both contributors and the editor have done their utmost to honour the origins of the techniques we have come to work with in our current coaching supervision practice. If you discover gaps in our research please do get in touch with michelle@greenfieldsconsultancy.co.uk and we will integrate this into any future editions.

Reference

Clutterbuck, D. (2010) Coaching reflection: The liberated coach. *Coaching: An International Journal of theory, Research and Practice*, 3(1), pp. 73–81.

Introduction

This highly practical book brings together many techniques that are known and used within the coaching supervision community. To orient what follows it may be helpful to offer a working definition of what coaching supervision is.

What do we mean by coaching supervision?

Supervision amongst coaches has evolved from its 'helping profession'" roots. If we look to the literature whether from counselling, social work or coaching there seems to a common pattern of a 'three pronged' explanation for why engaging in this kind of reflective practice might be useful. While each author uses different nomenclature, the content is broadly similar, here the terminology established by Proctor (1991) is used and interpreted for use in the coaching supervision field:

1 Normative - the supervisor and supervisee place the work in its social and organisational context; exploring how the supervisee's work observes professional and ethical guidelines, relevant legislation and organisational norms. The supervision partnership will also consider how the coach articulates their approach to their coaching clients and looks for congruence between their narrative and their practice
2 Formative - the supervisor facilitates the drive for continuous improvement in the practitioner (and indeed in themselves). This developmental perspective will consider the growth of the supervisee's competency, capability and capacity (Broussaine, 1998) as both a coaching practitioner and as a reflective practitioner.
3 Restorative - the supervisor intends to support the well-being of the supervisee. While coaching clients are typically experiencing good mental health (contrary to clients in the therapeutic disciplines) the

> potential for energy in the client system to impact on the energy of the coach remains. This role can be particularly important for the independent coach who may experience a sense of professional isolation. Group supervision can offer a sense of belonging and of community; individual supervision offers a confidential space for surfacing personal issues, doubts and insecurities.

The difference in the context of coaching work compared to its therapeutic origins is often overlooked. However, in 2016 Lucas and Larcombe highlighted that in addition to these three prongs the coaching supervisor needed to be aware of the commercial challenges that face independent (and sometimes internal) coaches. Some coaching supervisors would argue that issues prompted by commercial challenges will simply fall into the existing three categories or conversely that they lie outside the scope of coaching supervision straying into mentoring or consulting territory. Lucas and Larcombe argued that the impact was so significant that it deserved separate attention. Within this book there is an openness to including commercial topics within the scope of supervision, provided that it is contracted for appropriately.

In summary, it is the definition of Clutterbuck, Whitaker and Lucas (2016, pp. 18–19) that shall be observed throughout this book, and is provided below. Where authors take a distinctly different stance to this it will be explicated within the text.

> Coaching supervision is a collaborative process facilitating coaches (and coach supervisors) to grow their reflective practice with a view to continuous improvement and professional development, client safety and the strengthening of professional identity. The process considers the entire system surrounding the supervisee and their client work and seeks to bring value to all those stakeholders connected to that work.

How to use the book

The purpose of the book is to locate techniques into their appropriate context. The working assumption is that to ensure the technique is used 'as intended' the practitioner may need to adopt a particular mindset or attitude that will honour the origin from which it came. Without this it is entirely possible that the technique may become distorted or offered inappropriately.

The book is therefore organised into ten philosophical chapters. To provide the reader with a sense of continuity, each chapter has been structured through posing the following questions to the contributor.

You will notice that some chapters follow this more loosely than others reflecting the particular nuances of the philosophy described.

- How is this philosophy described?
- What are the underpinning principles/beliefs of this philosophy?
- What is the role of the coach supervisor in the context of this philosophy?
- How would you prepare yourself to work congruently with this approach?
- How might this way of working be particularly useful to the supervisee?
- What else might the reader need to consider before using the techniques that follow?

Within each of the philosophical chapters, the techniques are is organised alphabetically according to title (you will find that some contributors offer content across a number of chapters).

At the start of each technique we use icons to illustrate the settings in which the techniques are most suited (see Figure 0.1 below). We consider the type of supervision relationship where it can be used and the range of experience of the supervisee required.

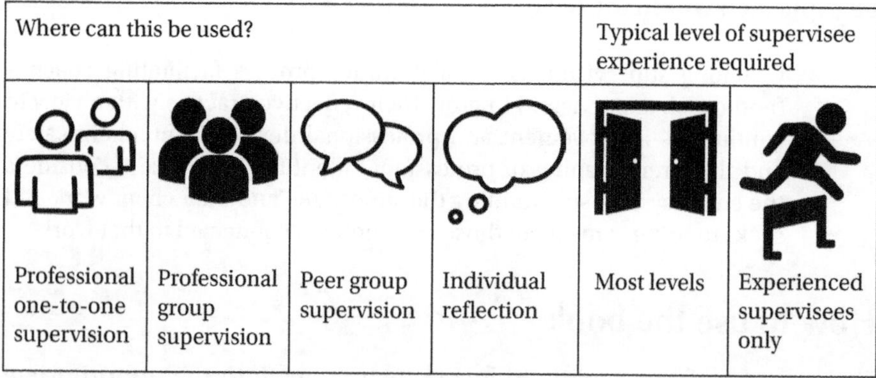

Where can this be used?				Typical level of supervisee experience required	
Professional one-to-one supervision	Professional group supervision	Peer group supervision	Individual reflection	Most levels	Experienced supervisees only

Figure 0.1 Illustration of icons used at the start of each technique

To help provide a sense of alignment across the book, each technique has been structured through posing the following questions to the contributor. You will notice that some techniques follow this more loosely than others reflecting the particular nuances of the technique, approach, enquiry or experiment described.

- Title of 'technique'
- When is this used?
- What is the technique?
- How to work with the technique ...
- What else might need attention?
- A word of caution (i.e. When not to use this technique)
- What other uses are there for this technique? (including coaching clients)
- References; Further reading and Resources

Designed to be read by both coaching supervisors and supervisees alike, the content is highly practical, and could be used to encourage greater transparency and equality in the supervision partnership. The 'how to' section intends to accelerate the reader's understanding of how the 'technique' works in practice. Our contributors generously lift the lid on the art of their supervision practice, condensing their years of experience into careful guidance. Indeed, supervisees may choose to use some of the techniques as a means of self-reflection (see the 'thought bubble' icon in Figure 0.1). This enables supervisees to bring sharper insight into what might lie at the core of their supervision question.

Finally, we often learn how to bring insight to others having had positive learning experiences ourselves. Therefore, for many of the techniques we identify where it could be used with coaching clients even though it may have been developed for supervision work.

How to apply the techniques in your own practice

As you consider experimenting with using a different technique, the following questions could prove useful preparation:

- How does the philosophy behind this technique stand alongside the underpinning beliefs of my own work?
- How would I need to tailor this approach to be congruent (or deliberately incongruent!) with my overarching style?
- What will need to shift in me, in order to embrace this approach fully?
- How might this change how I contract with the supervisee(s)?
- What would I need to share with the supervisee(s) before offering the approach?

After experimenting with the technique, the following questions could prove useful reflection:

- What felt congruent to me as I worked?
- What was the impact of the approach on the supervisee(s)?
- How does this experience stretch my understanding of how my practice is effective?
- What of this approach shall I integrate into my practice?
- Which parts will I discard – and what does that say about how I like to work?
- Does anything in my client 'bio' need adjusting as a result?

And finally ...

With this as the context, the objectives for this book are as follows:

- To provide a compendium of techniques, approaches, enquiries and experiments which can be used with care.
- To place 'techniques' in their original philosophical context, such that practitioners can adapt them to their own style, whilst also respecting the school of thought from which they evolved.
- To share expertise and good practice between coaching supervision and coaching communities.
- To underline that coaching supervision is a shared endeavour.

I hope that you enjoy reading and applying these 101 techniques, approaches, enquiries and experiments as much as I have enjoyed recording them.

References

Broussaine, M. (1998) *The Society of Local Authority Chief Executives and Senior Managers (SOLACE): A scheme for continuous learning for SOLACE members*. Bristol, UK: University of West of England.

Clutterbuck, D., Whitaker, C., and Lucas, M. (2016) *Coaching Supervision: A practical guide for supervisees*. Abingdon: Routledge.

Lucas, M. and Larcombe, A. (2016) Helping independent coaches develop their coaching business: A holistic approach to supervision or an opportunity for supervisors to exploit their position? *International Journal of Mentoring and Coaching*, Professional Section. Volume IX, Special Issue. September 2016, pp. 13–20.

Proctor, B. (1991) Supervision: A co-operative exercise in accountability. In: A. Marken and M. Payne (Eds.) *Enabling and ensuring: supervision in practice*. Leicester National Youth Bureau/Council for Education and Training in Youth and Community Work.

Chapter 1

An eclectic perspective on coaching supervision

David Clutterbuck

How is this philosophy described?

One of the great things about being a coach supervisor is the richness of the issues that coaches bring to explore. Inevitably, these are not the humdrum, predictable topics covered in coach training – they are more typically manifestations of complex, adaptive systems, human dramas and deep uncertainties. The collaborative endeavour that is coaching supervision almost always prompts the supervisor to come away from a session with an experienced coach carrying ideas for their own further development.

When coaches describe themselves as a Transactional Analysis (TA) coach or a Neuro Linguistic Programming (NLP) coach or even a 'life coach,' it generates confusion. What does this really mean? Are they a coach who uses TA as a part of their practice; or a TA practitioner who sometimes does some coaching? Eclectic supervisors take the view that no one toolkit is applicable to all the diversity of issues, circumstances and objectives that clients bring. The eclectic supervisor recognises that *the complexity of the issues brought to supervision requires a portfolio of responses from an eclectic base of multiple disciplines and theoretical approaches.* Just like much of the work of coaches is to help clients view the world through different lenses than their norm.

What are the underpinning principles and beliefs of this philosophy?

A core model of eclectic supervisory practice seems like a contradiction of terms! If it is eclectic, it must draw upon numerous models and precepts. Here we talk of a meta-wisdom approach and describe some of the elements that might underpin this. For example:

- *Valuing a multiplicity of approaches.* In supervision we often spend time deconstructing a coaching session. How do we establish what happened, how and why? What forces were at play that influenced behaviours, thought patterns and outcomes? How did the coach's own fears, insecurities and assumptions affect the coaching conversation? Lancer et al.'s (2016) framework of the seven coaching conversations (the spoken conversation and six silent conversations before, during and after the coaching session); or Hawkins and Smith (2006) seven eyes model can both be a useful starting point for deconstruction. Used on their own, however, these and other models present only one way of looking at a coaching session. An eclectic perspective asks: 'What other model could we apply here, which might give a different story about the events we are discussing?'

In coaching generally, we are constantly reminded of the dangers of taking a single perspective. If a client complains their boss is unreasonable, we would expect to explore the issue from the boss' perspective as well. The same principle holds true for supervision. If we apply one model only, we risk creating a one-dimensional picture of a multi-dimensional situation.

- *The paradox of knowledge.* Intense curiosity, learning by experiment and the humility to be comfortable with the extent of our unknowing – these are a universe away from the stock picture of the supervisor as a coach with a greater store of knowledge. One way to compare a 'normal' supervisor with an eclectic supervisor is that the former may expect to be valued by the supervisee for their expertise; the latter has at least as much expertise, but remembers that an expert is someone whose great knowledge gets in the way of their learning. In short, an eclectic supervisor has so much knowledge that they are able to see the limitations of its value.

What is the role of the coach supervisor in the context of this philosophy?

- *Normative function.* Managing boundaries and other aspects of client safety lie at the core of the normative function, but these tend to be preventative or remedial interventions. To support coaches in becoming more mature, the supervisor has a role in raising the coach's ethical awareness and ethical resilience. Boundary and safety issues are relatively easy to pin down – not least because of the professional bodies' codes of conduct. But ethicality goes to the core of what it means to be human. It's also highly dependent on shifting context – which requires an eclectic knowledge and variable frameworks.
- *Formative function.* Systemic eclectic coaches draw on a wide range of concepts and philosophies but having a lot of models doesn't

in itself make someone a better coach or supervisor. It is how you integrate and apply them that counts. An eclectic approach starts from the assumption that *nothing I know is more than a partial truth.* One team coach with a provocative style contracts with a team that he will share partially formed observations and hypotheses, with the expectation that every now and then he would have to apologise and say: 'I was wrong – but what have we learned as a consequence?'

- *Restorative function.* An eclectic supervisor brings compassion, not just for the coach, but for the entire system and the players within it. Anecdotally, in a recent discussion about sociopaths in the workplace we considered the question 'What must it be like, to be a someone with this personality disorder?' From an eclectic standpoint, even where someone has a malign influence on a system, understanding the systems that drive them may lead to more fluid and imaginative ways of working with them.

How would you prepare yourself to work congruently with this approach?

In 2010 Clutterbuck wrote about 'managed eclecticism' highlighting that an eclectic practitioner does more than offer a 'pick n mix' approach to the work; they have a solid understanding of where different models come from and they blend them seamlessly into a bespoke service for their client.

Leifer and Steinert (2011) suggest that supervision requires higher order reasoning skills that encompass triple loop learning. Similarly, the eclectic supervisor needs to develop an ability to hold and work within apparently or real contradiction, and a multifocal perspective, recognising at least some of the interactions and influences between complex systems.

A supervisor can only develop these foundations by engaging with (reading, discussing, experimenting) many different approaches, reflecting deeply upon them and developing their own mental maps of how they inter-relate. It can also be argued that eclectic supervisors need to possess one of the essential qualities of a mentor – wisdom. If we accept the definition of wisdom as the product of constant reflection on and learning from experience, three further categories can be identified (Clutterbuck, 2020):

- Lean wisdom – context (task) specific.
- Broad wisdom – reflection on life experience (personal and vicarious).
- Meta-wisdom – brings together multiple, shifting perspectives.

From a philosophical, if not empirical, perspective, it is at the third level of wisdom that eclectic supervisors can provide the most valuable support to coaches and enable the greatest change. At a practical level therefore, the eclectic supervisor must prepare themselves to work with the duality of both accepting and rejecting their experience simultaneously. As we seek to understand the supervisee's perspective, we need to park our own insights, labelling them as 'interesting, but premature' (Clutterbuck, 2019). Meta-wisdom recognises that if we prioritise our own sense-making, we will devalue our supervisee's.

How might this way of working be particularly useful to the supervisee?

In Clutterbuck and Megginson's (2011) model of coach maturity (a clumsy phrase, but one we are stuck with for now) there are four distinct mind-frames that coaches go through as they reflect upon and learn from their experiences and gather new knowledge. They map quite closely with Kegan's stages of adult maturity (Kegan, 1992). The first we call 'models-based', because the coach has a single model with a clear structure that they attempt to apply to every client. This is essentially *doing coaching to* someone.

With practice, coaches move on to a 'process-based' mindset, where they have a wider toolkit and can let go of the reins a bit. Instead of trying to control the conversation, the coach shares the responsibility with the client, while knowing they can always take back control, if the conversation starts to flounder. (The idea that coaching is completely non-directive is, of course, nonsense – the coach directs the conversation every time they decide what question to ask.) They are now doing coaching *with* the client.

The third mind-frame, 'philosophy-based', happens over time as the coach learns to *do* less and less. Gradually they integrate who they are as a human being with what they do as a coach – this is about *being* a coach. Finally, a small proportion of these highly reflective coaches go even further in relaxing control. We call them 'systemic eclectics', because they see themselves and the client within multiple complex, adaptive systems. Their role is to 'hold the client, while the client has the conversation that they need to have with themselves'.

When we consider how useful an eclectic supervisor might be to coaches at each of these stages of development, it is possible to identify both benefits and limitations at each stage. See Table 1.1 below:

Table 1.1 Benefits and limitations of an eclectic supervisor working with coaches at different levels of maturity

Stage of development of the coach (Clutterbuck and Megginson, 2011)	Benefits of working with an eclectic supervisor	Limitations of working with an eclectic supervisor
1. Models based	Questions simplistic assumptions about role and practice of coaching	May discourage the novice coach when they become 'unhooked' from certainty, but don't have the toolkit to respond to situations outside their experience
2. Process based	Provides a safe environment to practise letting go of control in the coaching conversation Encourages the coach to build and integrate a wider portfolio of responses to client needs	Conflict between supervisor and coach when the coach is enthusiastic about an approach they have discovered, but lacks the critical ability to put it into perspective as 'just another model'
3. Philosophy based	Makes overt the process of personal and professional integration; helps articulate deeply held values that underpin their practice	At early stages of developing a professional identity, the coach may not be ready to question their own values
4. System eclectics	Joint exploration of complexity enriches the self-awareness and scope of knowledge base	Shared natural curiosity can lead coach and supervisor to go down rabbit holes they find fascinating but may not be what is needed from the perspective of the client

Given that eclectic supervision recognises and embraces complexity in the multiple systems, in which coaching occurs, the supervisee will benefit most when they are at a level of personal and professional maturity that allows them to be comfortable with complexity, unknowing and uncertainty. Within this framework the eclectic supervisor is likely to bring most value to those coaches who have reached levels three and four of development.

Anything else you need to consider before using the techniques that follow?

Our coaching world is still fumbling towards defining what's involved in being a systemic eclectic coach, so it is not surprising that pinning down eclectic supervision is even more challenging. We notice that, in recent years, a significant rise in the number of team coaching articles and in training executive coaches to extend their portfolio to the more complex world of team coaching. The main conclusion from a survey of team coaches (as supervisees) by Hodge and Clutterbuck (2019) is that they require the supervisor to be comfortable with the complexities of multiple-interacting human systems. Supervisors who already have an eclectic approach to the work may therefore be well placed to supervise this burgeoning area of work.

If we borrow from our description of the 'system eclectic' coach – perhaps the purpose of the eclectic supervisor is to 'hold the coach, while the coach has the conversation that they need to have with themselves.' As you consider how you might use the techniques that follow – and indeed any of the techniques within this book, it may be helpful to remember to use them lightly. Rather than consider what technique you could use to help them, perhaps ask 'What does the supervisee need to know so that they can help themselves?'

References

Clutterbuck, D. (2010) Coaching reflection: The liberated coach. *Coaching: an International Journal of Theory, Research and Practice*, 2(1), pp. 73–81.

Clutterbuck, D. and Megginson D. (2011) Coach maturity: An emerging concept. In L. Wildflower and D. Brennan, (Eds.), *The Handbook of Knowledge-based Coaching*. San Francisco, CA: Josey-Bass, pp. 299–314.

Clutterbuck, D. (2019) The moment you think you understand you need to listen twice as hard. www.davidcluttebuckpartnership.com, [blog] 4 March. Available at: www.davidclutterbuckpartnership.com/the-moment-you-think-you-understand-is-when-you-need-to-listen-twice-as-hard/ [Accessed 5 September 2019].

Clutterbuck, D. (2020) *Coaching the Team at Work: The Definitive Guide to Team Coaching*, 2nd ed. Maidenhead: Routledge.

Hawkins, P. and Smith, N. (2006) *Coaching, Mentoring and Organisational Consultancy: Supervision and Development*. Maidenhead: McGraw-Hill.

Hodge, A. and Clutterbuck, D. (2019) Supervising team coaches – Working with complexity at a distance. In D. Clutterbuck, J. Gannon, S. Hayes, I. Iordanou, K. Lowe, and D. McKie (Eds.), *The Practitioner's Handbook of Coaching*. Aldershot: Gower, pp. 331–342.

Kegan, R. (1992) *The Evolving Self.* Boston, MA: Harvard University Press.

Leifer, L.J. and Steinert, M. (2011) Dancing with ambiguity: Causality behaviour, design thinking and triple-loop learning. *Information Knowledge Systems Management*, 10, pp. 151–173.

Further reading

Lancer, N., Clutterbuck, D. and Megginson, D. (2016) *Techniques for Coaching and Mentoring*, 2nd ed. London: Routledge.

Laske, O. (2003) *An Integrated Model of Developmental Coaching: Researching New Ways of Coaching and Coach Education*. [online] Leadershipthatworks.com. Available at: http://leadershipthatworks.com/documentfiles/73.pdf [Accessed 5 September 2019].

~ ~ ~ ~ ~

1. 3-2-1: a reflective writing technique

Liz Ford

Where can this be used?				Typical level of supervisee experience required	

When is this used?

This short, timed reflective writing exercise can be used at several points of the supervision cycle and can be a particularly pragmatic way of introducing reflective writing. Before a session it can help the supervisee prepare their thoughts and decide what to bring. During a session it can enable a supervisee to explore their feelings and thoughts around a particular client, challenge or success. After supervision it can assist the supervisee to gather their learning and identify any actions they want to take as a result of their supervision time.

What is the technique?

This technique encourages freeform reflection for a short, timed period in order to uncover thoughts and feelings surrounding a particular topic or situation.

Step 1: Choose somewhere comfortable to write and gather paper, pens and a timer.

Step 2: Decide what you want to reflect on. This might be a client, a conversation, a feeling or something else about your practice that you'd like to explore.

Step 3: Set a timer for *three* minutes (you could use your phone).

Step 4: Start writing, remember:

- Write quickly.
- Don't worry about spelling, punctuation or grammar.
- Keep your hand moving.
- Write whatever comes into your head.
- Don't sensor what goes on the paper.
- Stop when the timer sounds.

Step 5: Briefly read back through your writing, then write for a further *two* minutes using one of the stems below:

- As I read this:
  - I notice ...
  - I am aware of ...
  - I am curious about ...
  - I feel ...
  - I am surprised by ...

Step 6: Stop writing when the timer sounds.

Step 7: Finally, set the timer for *one* minute and write a list of:

- Items you want to discuss in supervision, or
- Learning you have identified, or
- Actions you want to take, or
- Interventions you could use with that client ...

How to work with the technique ...

Using a short, timed method can introduce reflection in a very practical way to coaches who find reflection difficult or assume it takes up too much time. This technique only needs ten minutes and works particularly well for the first time when incorporated into a supervision session so that the supervisee experiences the power and ease of using it. They are then more likely to adapt and use the technique in their own time.

When used within a session, it is helpful for the supervisor to time the three writing sections and give instructions for each phase. For example: 'Take three minutes to write about whatever comes to mind when you think of that situation.' Then 'As you read what you've written, take two minutes to write what you notice' and, finally, 'Now take one minute to list all the interventions you could potentially use with that client.'

Some supervisees like to use different coloured pens for each of the three writing sections and keep their reflections together in a journal or folder so they can look back on them and reflect further if wished.

Once the technique is understood, supervisees can adapt it to their own needs, doubling or tripling the timings of the writing stages for more in-depth reflection and choosing topics, stem statements and lists that are pertinent to their practice.

A word of caution

The power in this technique relies on completing all three writing stages. Supervisees who err towards spending time on free writing at the expense of stages two and three can sometimes find themselves continuing to feel stuck and lacking any additional insight.

What other uses are there for this technique?

Although an individual reflection technique, this can be used successfully within groups, either to plan the supervision agenda or to personally reflect on learning gained.

It is also an intervention that coaches can use with their clients. It can help clients identify what they'd like to work on in a session or assist them to see what they've gained or learned. It has also been particularly beneficial for clients who feel overwhelmed because of its ability to get thoughts down on paper, explore feelings and identify actions or strategies within a short space of time.

Further reading

Adams, K. (2011) The journal ladder: A developmental continuum of journal therapy. [pdf] Available at: https://journaltherapy.com/wp-content/uploads/2011/01/CJT_Journal_Ladder-FINAL.pdf [Accessed 4 September 2019].

Hay, J. (2007) *Reflective Practice and Supervision for Coaches*. Maidenhead: McGraw Hill.

Holder, J. (2014) Notes to self. *Coaching at Work*, 9(2), pp. 38–41.

~ ~ ~ ~ ~

2. Affirmations and alternatives

Michelle Lucas and Carol Whitaker

Where can this be used?				Typical level of supervisee experience required	

When is this used?

This technique offers a balance of feedback, so it can be useful for supervisees with a tendency to be either self-critical or overly optimistic. It could also be useful when the supervisee is overwhelmed by a client session and needs to work out 'what contributed to what'.

What is the technique?

This technique is sometimes referred to as 'Angels & Devils' (Whitaker and Calleja, 2018). We have re-named here it to have less emotive language.

Step 1: The group is briefed along with following lines:

> *Listen to the supervisee and notice what you think they did well with this client and what you notice a concern about, for which you would offer an alternative suggestion. It is helpful to notice both significant things and little things, and, to be as specific as possible. Remember to link your feedback to the supervisee's reason for bringing the client scenario.*

Step 2: The supervisee talks through the client scenario. Before contributions are given, the supervisor asks the supervisee how they would invite the group to focus their feedback.

Step 3(a): Invite each group member to share something they noticed that they would like to affirm, as well as offering some developmental feedback (for example, an alternative suggestion or challenge). Reassure the group that it is OK if some people say similar things. Multiple endorsements or critiques can be particularly powerful for the supervisee. Further, each member's contribution will come with its particular nuanced observations.

Step 3(b): The supervisee is invited to say a simple 'thank you' when each person gives their contributions. This provides additional reflection time and helps minimise any defensiveness. Encourage the supervisee to make a note of the feedback for future reference.

Step 4: Once everyone has contributed, the supervisor returns to the supervisee. Pause before asking questions like:

- So, hearing the feedback, what's been the impact on you?
- What action(s) do you feel would be helpful now?

How to work with the technique ...

Depending on the size of the group and the time available, you may need to limit contributions to one affirmation and one alternative. Where time allows, ensure that both positive and developmental feedback are offered in equal measure.

Despite choosing a technique that offers balance, the supervisee may take on board only the negative or only the positive feedback. As the supervisor it can be helpful to reflect back your observation to bring this imbalance into the supervisee's awareness.

What else might need attention?

On occasions the feedback offered by a group member may affirm something that would not be regarded as best practice. It can be helpful to clarify the thinking of this group member before moving on. Where the supervisor still has a concern, this is best explored once the current supervisee has finished their presentation, otherwise it could divert attention.

A word of caution

There are many different ways of organising the feedback in a group. For example, the supervisee can receive all the positive feedback first or developmental feedback first. Alternatively, they might want each person to give both affirmation and alternative feedback together. It can be helpful to put the supervisee in control of the sequencing. This can get complicated to facilitate and so it can be a useful discipline to go 'around the circle' for this technique.

What other uses are there for this technique?

When engaged in a more free-flowing supervision dialogue the group may get into a groove of feedback that only provides reassurance or conversely that is predominantly focused on generating different options. This technique can be a useful way of re-balancing the conversation to bring a wider range of perspectives into the supervision discussion and these principles could equally be applied by coaches with their clients.

Reference

Whitaker, C. and Calleja, A. (2018) *Group Supervision Approaches for Coaching Supervision.* [pdf] Available at: www.whitaker-consulting.co.uk/resources-and-papers [Accessed 2 August 2019].

Further reading

Turner, T., Lucas, M. and Whitaker, C. (2018) *Peer Supervision in Coaching and Mentoring: A Versatile Guide for Reflective Practice.* Abingdon: Routledge, pp. 125–160.

~ ~ ~ ~ ~

3. Arrivals and departures with picture cards

Michelle Lucas and Charlotte Housden

Where can this be used?				Typical level of supervisee experience required	

When is this used?

Typically, the cards are used at the beginning of a session as an ice-breaker or arrivals exercise. Alternatively, they can be used the end to help close a session.

What is the technique?

The pack contains ten double sided picture cards, which are offered as a 'muse' to help develop a response to a question. Typically, referring to an image invites a more reflective and richer contribution than simply speaking to the group.

Step 1: Spread the cards out on a flat surface (a table top or floor) so that they are easy to view.

Step 2: Pose a question as appropriate to the situation.

- For arrivals:
  - What's happened since we last met that feels important to share?
  - What are your hopes for this session?
  - What do you need to say to help you become truly present today?
  - How are you arriving today?
- For departures:
  - What are you noticing about how you/we have worked today?
  - What learning are you taking away?
  - What will you reflect further upon when you leave?
  - How are you leaving today?

Step 3: Encourage the supervisee(s) to peruse the cards noticing which images appeal to them. Remind them not to overthink it, but to use a more instinctive approach - they may not know yet why they are drawn to an image and that is fine too.

Step 4: Invite the group to describe the image they selected and, as far as they can, what the image means to them in the context of the question posed.

Step 5: When everyone has spoken, suggest they might like to take a photograph of their image to act as an aide-memoire. Where the question posed relates to a group dynamic it may be appropriate to arrange all the chosen cards into a collage before taking a picture.

Step 6: Collect all the cards and ensure the pack is intact.

How to work with the technique ...

As the supervisor it can be informative to watch how individuals choose their cards. The manner in which they select an image may hold some information about the clarity, thoughtfulness and difficulty experienced by each person in making their selection. Where this is a group exercise, you may invite those who chose their card swiftly to lead the group exchange. Occasionally, one of the group will need significantly more time to select their card - in which case remind them not to overthink things and suggest that they have another 'moment' in order to decide. To give them some space, it may be helpful to turn to the remainder of the group and invite them to see what more they are now noticing about their image.

When working in a group, should there be time constraints, Step 4 could be done as a pairs or triads exercise. Alternatively, where time is particularly tight, the group could simply be invited to reveal their chosen card without offering an explanation.

A word of caution

Some individuals can become very attached to their chosen image and want to take the card with them. If it is important to keep a full set of cards then you will need to be vigilant about the number of cards returned.

Conversely, some people will struggle to connect with imagery; covering off this possibility in Step 3 is likely to reduce their sense of 'difference' within the group. An alternative is to suggest they think of a song title or theme tune; or perhaps to create a metaphor that means something to them; or indeed just to share their answer in a more conversational style without using any prompts.

What other uses are there for this technique?

This tool is hugely flexible and can be used in many individual, group and workshop settings in support of any avenue of enquiry. The only limit is your own imagination!

Resources

Picture cards can be purchased from www.charlottehousden.com/cards.

~ ~ ~ ~ ~

4. Building confidence: authority, presence and impact

Julia Menaul

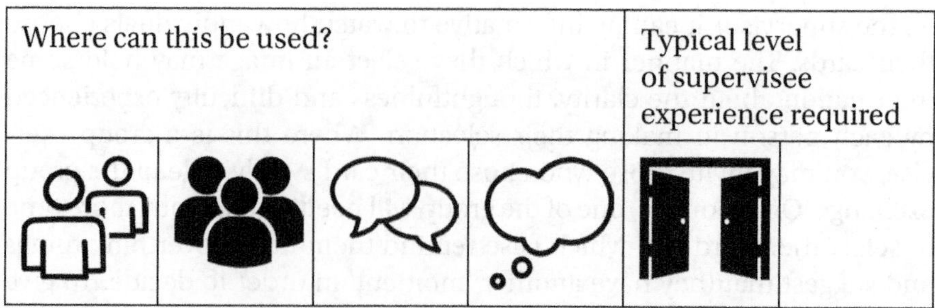

Where can this be used?				Typical level of supervisee experience required	

When is this used?

This technique is useful when the supervisee specifically asks to work on their own confidence, perhaps following a client session where their 'imposter syndrome' drew their energy away from their client.

Confidence is central to the model and helps supervisees reflect on where they are strong and where they might need development. Balancing all three positions equally is the key.

What is the enquiry?

The model is based on the work of Hawkins and Smith (2006) and uses physical placement and somatic information to help generate increased confidence.

Step 1: Contract appropriately for sharing a framework to guide the work.

Step 2: Offer a brief description of what Authority, Presence and Impact might mean within a coaching context. Check in with the supervisee to shape and craft a description that has meaning for them.

Authority – This often comes from what you know; what you have achieved in the past – typically qualifications, accreditations, experience, knowledge, job title, status. Using authority can be advantageous but on its own it's not enough to create lasting change or build a deep relationship. Overusing authority can look like showing off and people may wonder why you are promoting yourself so hard. Others may see this as a compensation for deficiency in the other two areas.

Presence – This is the ability to build rapport with people quickly and to command attention easily. People with presence have an immediacy to them plus poise and grace. They are aware of many things at the same time, i.e. thoughts and feelings of self, but also what is happening for others.

Impact – With impact comes the ability to create shifts and change mindsets; influencing the emotional climate in a session. They use interventions that shift emotional energy like a focussed challenge or encouraging unexpressed feelings. They generate more candour and directness by expressing often what others may be feeling but fear to express.

Step 3: Create a triangle on the floor using four labelled Post-it notes, See Figure 1.1.

Step 4: Invite the client to step into one corner that feels like a strength for them.

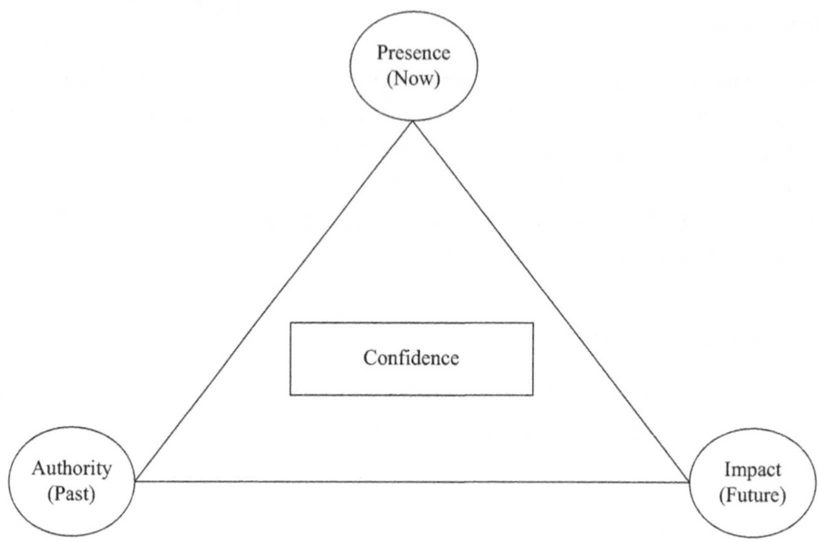

Figure 1.1 The API model

Step 5: Ask them 'What is your reason for starting there?' 'What are you doing from that position that makes it a strength for you compared, to the other areas?' 'What do you notice about yourself as you stand there?'

Step 6: Invite them to move to one of the other corners and ask, 'What are your reasons for picking that corner next?' 'What do you notice as you stand in that corner?' and 'How do you feel right now?'

Step 7: Invite them to move to the final corner 'What do you notice about yourself here?'

Step 8: Finally, ask them to step into the centre (Confidence) and reflect on what they have become aware of in each corner. A useful question may be 'What's been important to you from all this?'

How to work with the enquiry ...

The best way of working is for the supervisee to explore the model somatically and for experiential learning to emerge from moving physically around the triangle.

Often the supervisor may have to encourage the supervisee to slow down in each position and notice what is happening in their body as well as what they might be thinking or feeling. For more cognitive practitioners, they may need more specific prompts for example 'Tell me about a time when you created a felt shift in a client and how you did that?' or 'When have you underplayed/overplayed your credentials as a coach?'

What else might need attention?

This technique may prompt a great deal of reflection with no obvious and immediate actions. It can be helpful to enquire in future supervision sessions if it would be helpful to re-contract for working on any development areas.

A word of caution

Novice coaches may have a focus on building their Authority through gaining additional knowledge, more qualifications, more tools. Encourage the supervisee to step into the other areas of Presence and Impact and help them embrace the uncomfortableness of growing these more subjective and personal qualities.

What other uses are there for this enquiry?

This can be used with managerial coaching clients, as this model is equally applicable for professional confidence.

Reference

Hawkins, P. and Smith, N. (2006) *Coaching, Mentoring and Organisational Consultancy: Supervision and Development.* Maidenhead: McGraw-Hill. p. 32.

Further reading

Estacio, E.V. (2018) *The Imposter Syndrome Remedy; A 30 Day Action Plan to Stop Feeling Like a Fraud.* South Carolina: CreateSpace Independent Publishing Platform.

~ ~ ~ ~ ~

5. Capturing journeys on a big scale

Michelle Lucas and Andy King

Where can this be used?				Typical level of supervisee experience required	

When is this used?

The technique can be at the end of a programme of supervision to capture the learning gained along the way.

What is the technique?

Working on a large scale, the creativity and physicality of this approach helps to embed the learning more fully than story telling alone.

Step 1: Pre-prepare the paper drawing out an undulating path or river – see Figure 1.2. Ensure the supervisee has some Post-it notes and a pen.

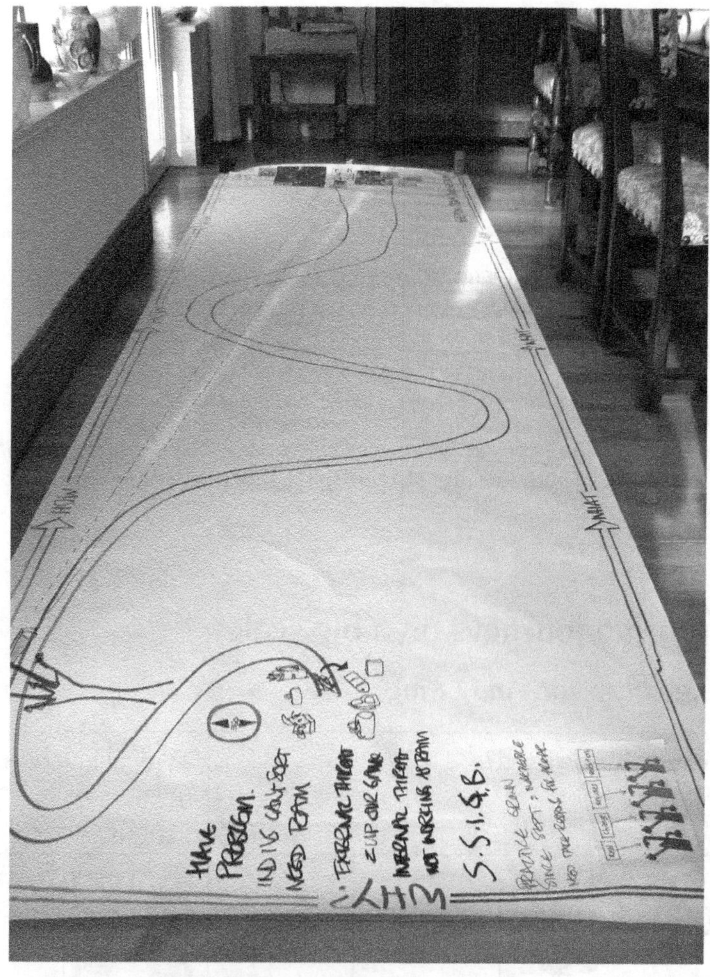

Figure 1.2 The start of a journey map

Step 2: Invite the supervisee to find a place near the start of the drawing that feels like a representation of them at their beginning.

Step 3: Ask 'What did you learn here?' plus follow-up questions like 'What else do you remember about being here?' and 'What do you notice now about being here?'; you can move to deeper exploration through metaphor for example 'And when you were XXX that was like what?' (See Using metaphor to explore 'At my best', pp. 210–212).

Step 4: Ask 'What would you like to capture about this part of your journey?' Answers are put on Post-it notes and placed onto the paper.

Step 5: Encourage the supervisee to move forward on the path to a place where additional learning occurred. Repeat Steps 3 and 4.

Step 6: Continue the process until the supervisee has reached a point that represents where they are today.

Step 7: To draw the session to a close, pose a meta question like 'What have you learned today about how you learn best?'

Step 8: Take a photo of the completed journey.

How to work with the technique ...

The exercise works because of its large scale, which necessitates access to a large space and a long enough stretch of paper (joining together flip chart paper works equally well). Preparing the paper saves time; however, it can be more powerful to invite the supervisee(s) to create their own picture. There are many metaphors that can be used; rivers, paths, stepping stones, roads ... allow the creativity of the individuals to shine. To encourage creativity the supervisor might inject some playful challenge – for example, inviting supervisees to consider any moments where they 'fell off the path' or 'went backwards rather than forwards' or 'wished they were on a different path.' Additionally, encourage supervisees to respond with drawings rather than words – it can help to have magazines available so that people can cut out images to accompany their own words and pictures.

This could be done as a group exercise, travelling down the path together. Participants can either put their Post-it notes on the paper (themes could be explored as a follow-on activity) or simply put them in their own journals.

What else might need attention?

As with any group work there may be differences in engagement amongst the supervisees. Depending on the maturity of the group and the supervisor's facilitation skills this could be covered off in a group process review, or may need separate individual discussions.

A word of caution

Occasionally, supervisees struggle to answer directly the questions about their learning. If so, then in Step 4, simply invite them to move forward in time on their journey map. Then ask some more exploratory questions like, 'What do you remember about being here?' and 'What might have been different about you, or your work then, compared to now?' and then, finally, 'What learning is occurring to you now?'.

If a sense of competition emerges during the exercise, you could invite supervisees to respond silently and to keep their notes private.

What other uses are there for this technique?

Used at the start of a programme of supervision, this would help supervisees define their goals and ambitions for their learning. The places along the way might consider how they will gather evidence for progress, or the different ingredients that are necessary for goal attainment, or it could include the obstacles that they anticipate they will need to overcome. The approach could equally be applied to individual coaching clients.

This technique stemmed from work with teams helping them plan or problem solve or to reconnect with their past successes when facing an apparent impasse. Whatever the content, this approach can help to create a STAR moment, i.e. Something They will Always Remember.

Further reading

Sibbet, D. (2010) *Visual Meetings*. Hoboken, NJ: John Wiley & Sons.
Sibbet, D. (2011) *Visual Teams*. Hoboken, NJ: John Wiley & Sons.

Resources

Purchase the roll of paper here. Available at: www.plot-it.co.uk/p/canon_group_oce_ijm123_matt_premium_coated_130g_m_42_1067mm_x_30m_inkjet_plotter_paper_roll_ [Accessed 6 September 2019].

~ ~ ~ ~ ~

6. Deepening reflection

Michelle Lucas and Tammy Turner

Where can this be used?				Typical level of supervisee experience required	

When is this used?

Where a supervisee has already engaged in independent reflection or peer supervision and yet resolution is elusive. This technique generates a greater diversity of insights to raise and deepen the supervisee's self-awareness and explore the wider client system.

What is the approach?

Similar to some action learning methodology, the group combines their thinking to first help generate clarity and then to generate a range of reflexive prompts.

Step 1: Invite the supervisee to present their client scenario in three stages:

a General overview and factual elements of the scenario.

b A summary of the reflections they have had so far and asking them about their self-awareness, blind spots and understanding of personal reactions.

c What they think they need in terms of feedback/observations or ideas/questions from the group.

Step 2: Brief the group to take a few minutes to pose any questions for clarification purposes to fill in gaps of information. Remind them that the first round of clarifying questions is intended to:

- Extend the group's understanding of the client scenario.
- Check accuracy of information already offered.
- Check understanding of the supervisee's supervision goals.

Step 3: Facilitate the group's clarification questions and remind the supervisee to respond factually, rather than defending their work.

Step 4: In the second round, alert the group that they will have a few moments to craft their probing questions, the intention of which should be to extend the supervisee's current perspective.

Step 5: Facilitate the group's probing questions, ensuring the supervisee has sufficient time to consider each question before receiving the next.

Step 6: Give the group a moment to consider all of the new perspectives in view of their own practice. Invite the group to offer any final thoughts for the supervisee and to declare what the discussion has caused them to reflect upon personally. If there is time, explore session themes to highlight future reflective practice for all group members.

Step 7: Bring the work to a close by returning to the supervisee and checking what the impact of the session has had on them in the moment. If appropriate enquire what has resonated with them most that they will continue to reflect upon.

How to work with the approach ...

Having the supervisee prepare or read from their journal may help to keep Step 1 succinct. In Step 3 where questions illustrate 'What if...' thinking or hint at judgements being made, the supervisor may need to help supervisees refocus their questions.

Step 5 may unfold differently depending on the supervisor's facilitation style and the supervisee's learning style. It may be helpful to explain that there is no correct way for the supervisee to respond to a question. Perhaps they respond immediately – typically this happens when they have thought about it (or something similar) already. Perhaps they don't respond because they need time to process it. Not responding may also mean that they have discounted the question as they cannot understand its relevance right now. The supervisee does not need to defend or explain how they respond (or not) to a question, although it may inform further reflection.

What else might need attention?

This approach provides a rich array of new perspectives for the supervisee to consider. It works best when the group's input provides a comparison rather than a substitute for independent reflection.

If the supervisee cannot offer quality responses to Step 1 (b) and (c) it may be better to use a different approach that will require their active participation.

A word of caution

Probing questions from group members that start with 'Why ...?' are likely to provoke a level of defensiveness. Support group members to start their question more gently ... for example, starting questions with 'How ...?' or 'What ...?' can be used to create a more respectful but still powerful *enquiry.*

What other uses are there for this approach?

When used in peer group supervision, it can ease the facilitation task if in Step 5 the supervisee is briefed to reflect upon rather than to respond to each question in turn. An additional step allows the supervisee to choose one question to delve deeper and explore the entire system. See Line of Enquiry, pp. 57–59.

The skills required to ask good clarification and probing questions are essential ingredients for any client conversations.

Further reading

Turner, T., Lucas, M., and Whitaker, C. (2018) *Peer Supervision in Coaching and Mentoring: A Versatile Guide for Reflective Practice.* Maidenhead: Routledge, pp. 100–102.

~ ~ ~ ~ ~

7. Developing behavioural flexibility

Anne Calleja

Where can this be used?				Typical level of supervisee experience required	

When is this used?

Useful when the supervisee recognises a need to be more flexible in their approach or they want to change a behaviour.

What is the technique?

Developed from an NLP strategy, referred to as the 'New Behaviour Generator'. The supervisor systematically guides the supervisee to use all of their senses to create a confident base line state of mind. Partnering with the supervisee, the process helps to create new behaviours by mentally rehearsing and 'acting out' future behaviour.

Step 1: The supervisee reflects on a client situation and identifies the behavioural change they wish to make.

Step 2: Together articulate a well-formed outcome or goal; which will typically clarify:

- How you will look, sound and feel with this new behaviour.
- The effect on others – the client, the system, the organisation.
- What you will have achieved in service of your client.

Step 3: Sitting side by side, the supervisor guides the supervisee as follows:

1 Look down left [to access thinking – see Figure 1.3] and talk to yourself. Ask yourself, 'What do I want to do differently?' Allow your thoughts to flow freely without criticism.

2(a) Then say to yourself, 'If I could do that, would it look like?'

2(b) Look up right [to access imagination – see Figure 1.3]. Watch yourself as in a video doing that new behaviour. Notice what happens to your state, how you are behaving and the effect upon any other people involved.

3 Look down right [to access somatic awareness – see Figure 1.3]. Step into the experience and feel how it is. Feel what you feel, embody the experience, walk through the new behaviour experiencing how you feel.

Repeat the process at least three times, using the three steps systematically. The supervisee may make any necessary adjustments, modifications or embellishments as they work.

Step 4: Invite the supervisee to think of a time in the future, when they want to have this behaviour. Instruct them as follows:

'Imagine yourself in that context, run through the new behaviour. As you watch yourself, notice what happens, and then fully

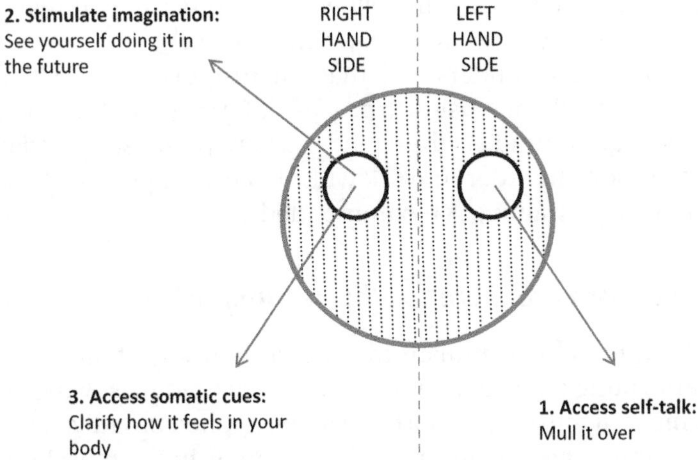
2. Stimulate imagination:
See yourself doing it in the future
RIGHT HAND SIDE
LEFT HAND SIDE
3. Access somatic cues:
Clarify how it feels in your body
1. Access self-talk:
Mull it over

Figure 1.3 Typical eye accessing cues

embody the experience in the situation with your client in that future.'

Step 5: Encourage the supervisee to set up the room appropriately in order to act out the situation to embed the learning.

Step 6: Draw the work to a conclusion. Review the initial desired outcome. Then ask - and what is your next step, now?

How to work with the technique ...

Ensure you are a witness to the process, follow the process systematically without offering any observations. Watch how the supervisee responds to your guidance - check that they are moving their eyes and body such that they locate the three senses, so that they see, hear and feel.

In Step 3 it is critical that they connect with their state - as this forms their evidence procedure. It enables them to evaluate the new behaviour and make any necessary adjustments. You are the guide to enable the supervisee to access all senses and fully embody the desired state.

What else might need attention?

If the supervisee does not obtain any new insight or behaviour, then personal work may be required to unlock what may be limiting them.

A word of caution

Where there is genuine rapport between supervisor and supervisee, the matching of response will happen naturally. However, as you learn the approach and are distracted by following the process, you may need to monitor and adjust your own presence more closely.

NLP practitioners understand that micro-movements will indicate which sense their client is using to process information. Where the supervisor's language contradicts the client's current processing modality, this can dent rapport. In order to work with this technique effectively some foundational NLP training is recommended.

What other uses are there for this technique?

This technique helps stimulate the neural pathways that are involved when performing an actual behaviour. The technique is widely used for improvement in music and sport, so can be applied broadly. It makes the new skill familiar and creates micro movements in the muscles that you will need in reality. The process helps an individual organise information in such a manner that they can develop these new skills rapidly.

Further reading

Dilts, R. and Epstein, T. (1991) *Tools for Dreamers*. Capitola, CA: Meta Publications.

To understand more about New Behaviour Generator Strategy: www.nlpu.com/Patterns/patt16.htm [Accessed 3 September19].

To understand more about eye movements: www.nlpu.com/Articles/artic14.htm [Accessed 5 September 2019].

Resources

See website NPL University: www.nlpu.com [Accessed 5 September 2019].

~ ~ ~ ~ ~

8. Developing coach maturity

David Clutterbuck

Where can this be used?				Typical level of supervisee experience required	

When is this used?

This approach is useful as part of an ongoing developmental supervisory relationship. While recognising that an individual's development will have its own pace, an awareness of our current stage of development can prompt an exploration of what might move us to the next.

What is the approach?

Developing coach maturity is informed by the four-stage model of coach maturity articulated by Megginson and Clutterbuck (2009) – see Table 1.2. Working over time the intention is to help the supervisee identify where most of the questions that they bring to supervision sit within this model. With permission the supervisor can pose questions that deliberately stretch the supervisee.

Step 1: Build the supervision relationship and contract for developmental work.

Step 2: Find a mechanism for capturing what is brought to supervision and for reflecting on that data either independently or jointly.

Table 1.2 Megginson and Clutterbuck (2009) Four stages of coach maturity

Stage	Style of working	Typical supervision questions
1. Models based	*Doing* coaching *to* the client	Why didn't 'X' work? What did I do wrong?
2. Process based	*Doing* coaching *with* the client	What could I do that would be most helpful for this client?
3. Philosophy based	*Being* a coach	What am I experiencing that might be of use to my client?
4. System eclectics	*Being part of the system* in which coaching occurs	What's really going on here?

Step 3: Dedicate time to evaluating the content of both sessions and reflections to hypothesise on which stage captures the supervisee's typical enquiry. For example, is their focus on whether they are doing it 'right' or on understanding the situational dynamics?

Explore how ready the supervisee is to be stretched. Remember that it can be helpful to actively consolidate our understanding of operating at one level of maturity before rushing to achieve the next.

Step 4: At the end of a session, consider what evidence would corroborate both parties' sense of the supervisee's stage of development. Where different perspectives are held, consider what might have caused the supervisee to have worked more or less maturely on this occasion.

Step 5: Once both supervisor and supervisee have established a way of working that allows developmental exploration, the supervisor might experiment in the moment with questions aimed at prompting exploration towards the next level of maturity.

How to work with the approach …

The model is intended for reference over time such that both supervisor and supervisee have a sense of their centre of developmental gravity. Once this is understood, any variations from this centre offers data for another level of enquiry (see Step 4) It is important to remember that our professional maturity is not a constant. In certain contexts, with particular clients, or even on a specific day, even the most experienced practitioner can be catapulted back to a place where they feel like a novice and start to question 'How am I doing?'

What else might need attention?

Where it emerges that a particular set of conditions routinely push the supervisee to an earlier stage of development this could hint at the need for some personal work.

A word of caution

We occasionally find that ego-driven supervisees attempt to 'act up,' taking on the mantle of a maturity stage they have not yet reached. It has been described as 'like a five-year-old putting on lipstick.' It can be challenging for the supervisor to work with such lack of self-awareness. A helpful analogy, achieving mastery in a sport, could be shared. At key periods the sportsperson is taken right back to basics, because it is at this level that the foundations for fine adjustments typically lie.

What other uses are there for this approach?

Typically, it is easier to take this approach in individual supervision. It may also be possible in groups with experienced supervisors already masterful at managing group dynamics and who can therefore manage this developmental exploration in parallel.

Once a supervisee experiences and understands how to work with this model, they could equally apply it with their own clients.

References

Megginson, D. and Clutterbuck, D. (2009) *Further Techniques for Coaching and Mentoring*. Oxford: Butterworth Heinemann.

Further reading

Bachkirova, T. and Cox, E. (2007) A cognitive-developmental approach for coach development. In S. Palmer and A. Whybrow (Eds.), *Handbook of Coaching Psychology: A Guide for Practitioners*. East Sussex: Routledge, Ch. 17, pp. 325–350.

Clutterbuck, D. (2010) Coaching reflection: The liberated coach. *Coaching: An International Journal of Theory, Research and Practice*, 3(1), pp. 73–81.

Hawkins, P. and Smith, N. (2006) *Coaching, Mentoring and Organisational Consultancy: Supervision and Development*. Maidenhead: McGraw-Hill, pp. 136–159.

~ ~ ~ ~ ~

9. Developing courage: naming elephants and speaking truth to power

Marie Faire

Where can this be used?				Typical level of supervisee experience required	

When is this used?

When the supervisee is aware that something 'in the room' was not named and wishes to explore further. Alternatively, when it occurs to the supervisor that something may not have been named and has permission to challenge their supervisee.

What is the technique?

A series of questions that help the supervisee to gain an evolving sense of their own courage, to knowing its limitations and to decide what action is possible.

Step 1: Ensure that there is an appropriate level of safety.

Step 2: Within the session explore with the supervisee these questions in order:

1. If you had been guaranteed that it would have 'landed well,' what would you have liked to say to your client that you didn't?
2. How come you didn't say it?
3. If an appropriate opportunity were to arise, or be created, how could you say what you wanted to say, and minimise the risks you identified in 2?

Step 3: Once familiar with how the questions unfold, the coach may be able to reflect upon these questions immediately after a client session. They would ask themselves:

1. If I had been guaranteed that it would have 'landed well,' what would I have liked to say to my client that I didn't?
2. How come I didn't say it?
3. If an appropriate opportunity were to arise, or be created, how could I say what I wanted to say, and minimise the risks I identified in 2?

How to work with the technique ...

Explore each question in turn. Question 1 helps to articulate the 'elephant.' Question 2 is the challenging and big question, and it will typically require the supervisor to explore some deep issues such as fears, self-limiting beliefs, conflict management styles. It almost always results in the supervisee exposing their own patterns in relation to speaking truth to power, which are usually as a result of limiting beliefs that have been established in early childhood. Examples of what emerges are fear of:

- upsetting someone,
- speaking out
- being 'seen'
- risking conflict
- loss of rapport
- not being liked
- losing business
- and so on ....

Most of the time, when a supervisor helps their supervisee name the elephant and to consider what blocked them, a more liberated awareness and energy emerges within the session. The supervisee is able to determine what they will do (or indeed what they deliberately choose not to do) in future with their client. Occasionally, the supervisee is only able to 'begin' the work within the session, and further independent reflection may be required. The supervisee may reflect upon the questions in Step 3 post-supervision, or once familiar with the approach, directly after a client session.

What else might need attention?

When insight and alternative actions are elusive, this may indicate that the supervisee needs additional and alternative support to deal with the realisation that a deep-rooted issue exists.

A word of caution

Although this is written with the supervisee in mind, a supervisor may use the same process for how they managed the supervision session. This is especially useful because parallel process may abound. These questions are usually challenging to ask and be asked, the questions will likely provoke in the supervisee, what they fear may be evoked in their client, and for the supervisor likewise.

What other uses are there for this technique?

With experience, this framework becomes useful for a coach to develop their own 'internal supervisor' (Casement, 1985) by using it for an immediate post session reflection.

Because of the nature of the challenge it may need to be used with discernment within group supervision with a professional supervisor.

Subject to appropriate contracting and sufficient rapport, this approach could equally be used by coaches with their clients.

Reference

Casement, P. (1985) *On Learning from the Patient.* London: Tavistock Publications.

~ ~ ~ ~ ~

10. Dilemma cards

Michelle Lucas and Carol Whitaker

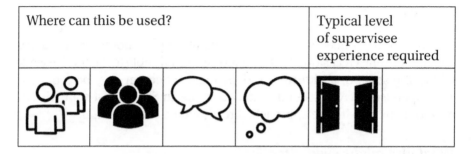

Where can this be used?				Typical level of supervisee experience required	

When is this used?

These cards offer real scenarios of tricky situations indicating the kind of topics that could be brought to supervision. They are particularly useful for novice coaches or newly formed supervision groups. The cards were created as a bridge between CPD and supervision; the hypothetical examples provide a launch pad for people to share their own experiences.

What is the technique?

The Coaching Dilemma Cards are copyrighted by Collaborative Coaching Supervision. Some examples are in the public domain (see Turner et al., 2018). Currently, the cards reflect four different coaching contexts (Coaches; Internal Coaches; Mentors; Line Managers). Each set is organised into four categories: Confidentiality; Conflicts of Interest; Boundaries; Dual Relationships.

Step 1: Share a number of the cards with the supervisee(s), inviting them to select a dilemma that resonates for them.

Step 2: Each Coaching Dilemma Card© ends with the question 'What could you do?' – so the first round of dialogue draws out all the different approaches that come to mind. The challenge is not to agree a single, preferred way forward, rather to flush out the multiple options the supervisee could have.

Step 3: The cards work best when they draw out actual experience. While the discussion might start hypothetically, the supervision task is to help supervisees connect with their own stories and build awareness of how that informs their actions. Helpful questions could be 'So has something similar happened for you?' or 'What does this scenario remind you of in your own experience?'.

Step 4: Each Coaching Dilemma Card© is designed to highlight complexity. Therefore, draw attention to what in the scenario makes the situation 'grey' rather than black and white. This is an opportunity to look at the dilemma from different stakeholder perspectives.

Step 5: To wrap up the discussion enquire what impact reviewing this scenario will have on their practice. Ask 'What's your learning?' or 'How will you be more mindful in the future?'

How to work with the technique ...

The philosophy behind these cards is to encourage a diversity of ideas and yet often supervisees want to know the 'right answer'. As the supervisor keep the discussion broad and explore the nuance of each situation or context to understand what influences subtle differences in approach. It can be helpful to deliberately showcase alternative strategies, for example if A was true, it might be useful to do X; but if B was also true then it might be more helpful to do Y.

What else might need attention?

Occasionally, a supervisee becomes very attached to their instinctive response, and despite hearing a variety of alternatives, stays fixed in their thinking. Reflect this back to the individual concerned and invite them to play with what might need to change in the scenario in order to trigger in them a different response. This may be a useful opportunity to raise awareness of the potential for confirmation bias.

In order to encourage mental flexibility, invite the group to take an opposite stance. For example, when a particular way forward seems to be 'obvious' or preferred, ask 'And when wouldn't that approach be appropriate?'.

A word of caution

It is important that the supervisor maintains a flexible and open stance rather than 'supervisor knows best'. Should an unethical approach be suggested, before correcting the supervisee, help them explore what's informing their choices. Enquire when they would take an opposite view – they may already have a sense of when this would not be appropriate.

What other uses are there for this technique?

Typically, the supervisee(s) choose which card to work with. Where an individual has a blind spot, the supervisor may suggest a particular card that because of its hypothetical nature can encourage them to stand back, prompting a fresh perspective.

By focusing on one category at a time, it is possible to create a theme for a session or perhaps give inspiration/practical application for a CPD session.

The cards can be used in many ways, which CCS share in their Train the Trainer workshop.

Reference

Turner, T., Lucas, M. and Whitaker, C. (2018) *Peer Supervision in Coaching and Mentoring: A Versatile Guide for Reflective Practice.* Abingdon: Routledge, pp. 125–160.

Resources

Purchase a sample set of Coaching Dilemma Cards© Available at: www.greenfieldsconsultancy.co.uk/latest-thinking/resources/ [Accessed 19 August 2019].

~ ~ ~ ~ ~

11. Exploring boundaries

Angela Dunbar

Where can this be used?				Typical level of supervisee experience required	

When is this used?

To help the supervisee mentally step outside the coach–client relationship and explore wider perspectives. It invites consideration of contexts and boundaries beyond the immediate 'in the room' information. Rather like exploring through the lenses of the seven-eyed model (Hawkins and Shohet, 2012), this process reframes the situation/relationship within a continually widening frame.

This can be particularly useful where the coach notices boundary issues, or if they tend to be rather introspective or narrowly focused. It is especially useful when all appears to be OK, yet something outside of the immediate system seems to be getting in the way.

What is the technique?

Clean Boundaries* was developed by the late David Grove and adapted for use in supervision. The questions are clean, enabling supervisees to think for themselves and encourages insightful breakthroughs. This could be a follow-up to the Exploring Relationships with Clean Networks technique (see pp. 40–43).

Step 1: Begin by inviting your supervisee to share the client situation they would like to explore and the question they have for supervision.

Step 2: Ask the supervisee to draw a representation of their client and also themselves (as they are when they are coaching this client).

Step 3: Explore what the supervisee puts on their paper with a series of Clean Language questions (up to six):

- What kind of client/coach is that?
- Is there anything else about that x?

Invite the supervisee to put anything else they want to on their paper.

Step 4: Explore the space around the supervisee and the client:

- What kind of space is the space around you both?
- What are the qualities of that space? And how far could that space go?
- And what kind of boundary or edge does that space have? Show that on your paper (the supervisee may at times need to re-draw and rescale their picture to be able to place the boundary on the paper).

Step 5: Ask questions of the boundary:

- What kind of boundary is that boundary?
- Is there anything else about that XXX boundary?

Step 6: Expand awareness still further by asking;

- And what's beyond that boundary?
- What kind of space is that? etc. (same questions as before).

You can continue to explore the spaces and boundaries until the supervisee has reached a space of infinity.

Step 7: At each boundary, invite the supervisee to re-draw/rescale their picture to fit the boundary of their paper.

Step 8: Invite the supervisee to understand more about the client and their situation from the position of each space and boundary. Ask:

- From this boundary/space, what do you know about your client/you?
- And what does this space know about your client/you?

Step 9: Continue to ask about each boundary and space coming back from the outermost place right back to the centre representations of the client/coach again. At the end ask, 'And what do you know now?' to conclude with key learnings.

Step 10: Complete by re-grounding the exploration into the supervision space. For example, ask 'And how does what you know now make a difference to your clients/coaching work?'

How to work with the technique ...

Those unfamiliar with the technique may be fearful that the repetitive questioning is experienced as irritating. In fact, supervisees typically report experiencing the question differently each time - probably because their thinking has moved on and so they place different meaning to the same words.

When posing questions within a clean language context, we need to be particularly conscious of intonation, pace and inflection of our voice. As far as possible keep your voice neutral, and deliver the questions slowly, emphasising each word clearly and with a slight pause between each word.

A word of caution

The technique encourages expansiveness, so you may need to find a way of helping *you* stay on track without placing your own interpretation to your supervisee's work.

What other uses are there for this technique?

With group supervision, as the questions require no content, you could pose the questions, then invite everyone to explore their client silently, before sharing final reflections (and their drawing). The technique can also be applied with coaching clients, especially exploring the wider picture around any relationship.

References

Hawkins, P. and Shohet, R. (2012) *Supervision in the Helping Professions*, 4th ed. Maidenhead: Open University Press.

Resources

* Clean Boundaries is covered in-depth on the Clean Coaching training programme, as part of Module Three. For general information see our website: www.clean-coaching.com [Accessed 6 September 2019].

~ ~ ~ ~ ~

12. Exploring relationships with clean language

Angela Dunbar

Where can this be used?				Typical level of supervisee experience required	

When is this used?

Useful as a 'next step' when a supervisee has already explored a client scenario study, and this generates a curiosity about the coaching relationship itself. It can be used as a follow-up to the 'At your best' exercise on pp. 210–212.

What is the technique?

This uses Clean Language questions that help expand attention and widen perspectives. Coupled with an understanding of the seven-eyed model and other supervision frameworks that focus on parallel process and patterns across multiple relationships, this technique provides a way of exploring without influencing (and potentially biasing) the supervisee to take on your view.

The questions are clean as they are non-directive and stripped of the supervisor's own assumptions, bias and metaphors of their own. The questions are used to focus attention on the metaphorical element of the supervisee's narrative.

Step 1: Explore the supervisee's client scenario as you would normally (or you could use Clean Language questions to do this).

Step 2: Once the supervisee's client feels 'alive in the room' and the supervisee has spent some time exploring aspects of their work and their relationship with this client, ask 'And your relationship with this client is like what?'.

Step 3: Follow the process described on pp. 210–212 for exploring 'at your best' from Step 3 onwards. This time you are focusing on the metaphor that the supervisee uses to describe this relationship.

Step 4: Keep exploring until there are a number of different components to the metaphor, (for example, 'This relationship is like a sheep dog trying to herd a flock of sheep that are in no hurry'). Each of the symbols 'sheep dog,' 'sheep' and 'flock' could be further explored, as well as the state 'in no hurry' and the activity 'trying to herd' This is likely to uncover more symbols and sensations, for example possibly 'feeling frustrated'; 'the farmer is not looking'; 'Sheep just want to eat grass.'

Step 5: Once you feel there is a whole 'landscape' or map of this metaphor for the relationship, help the supervisee consider the relationship patterns and connections by asking Clean Language questions that invite comparison. Choose two aspects of the supervisee's narrative to question further:

- And is there a relationship between the sheep dog and the farmer?
- And when sheep just want to eat grass, what happens to the sheep dog?

Step 6: With the seven-eyed supervision model in mind, you can also cleanly invite the supervisee to reflect beyond the immediate relationship:

- And what is *around* the flock of sheep? (reply – a field)
- And what's *beyond* the field?
- And what's happening *now*?
- And where could XXX have come from?
- And is there a relationship between that and your coaching relationship?

Step 7: You could move into another supervision approach when this feels done. Or you could wrap up learnings with the following the Clean Language question sequence:

- And now you know your relationship is like XXX, what difference does knowing that make?
- And what needs to happen next?
- How will you do that?
- When will you do that?

How to work with the technique …

As a facilitator of this Clean approach, you may at times feel excluded from the exploration. The supervisee is likely to be making connections and understanding the meaning behind each metaphor, without verbalising an explanation to you.

This can be beneficial as it allows the supervisee to uncover deeply personal and significant connections with no obligation to disclose it all to you. This makes the process incredibly respectful, and keeps the ownership completely with the supervisee.

It may not be necessary for you to ever understand the meaning of a supervisee's metaphor. In Step 7 the follow up questions are likely to bring any insight out into the open and helps the supervisee translate insight into behavioural change or to take action.

A word of caution

See points raised for the 'At your best' technique on pp. 210–212.

What other uses are there for this technique?

It is useful to explore any relationship – with practice supervisees could use it with their own clients.

Further reading

Dunbar, A. (2018) *Using Metaphors in Coaching.* [pdf] Available at: https://cleancoaching.com/files/2018/04/Using%20Metaphors%20with%20Coaching%20April%20'11.pdf [Accessed 1 September 2019].

Wilson, C. (2004) *Metaphor and Symbolic Modelling for Coaches.* [pdf] Available at: https://cleancoaching.com/files/2018/04/Metaphor-Symbolic-Modelling.pdf [Accessed 1 September 2019].

Smith, K. (2012) *A Clean Corner of Coaching Supervision.* [online] Available at: www.cleanlanguage.co.uk/articles/articles/318/1/A-Clean-Corner-of-Coaching-Supervision/Page1.html [Accessed 1 September 2019].

~ ~ ~ ~ ~

13. Exploring the supervisee's client with clean networks

Angela Dunbar

Where can this be used?				Typical level of supervisee experience required	

When is this used?

Useful in many situations, this can help the supervisee consider multiple perspectives while keeping supervisor input to a minimum. It may be a good way of starting an exploration before deciding what in particular to focus on.

What is the technique?

The technique involves representing the client on a piece of paper then exploring that from a number of different spaces and directions. It capitalises on the principle that where you stand affects what you know, and visually exploring the paper from different directions often reveals patterns unnoticed at the start. The process is facilitated using Clean Language, which helps guide but not contaminate the supervisor's own lens.

Step 1: Ask the supervisee to represent their client on a piece of paper, using words, symbols and/or drawings.

Step 2: Ask a series of simple Clean Language questions to explore further:

- What kind of client is this?
- Is there anything else about this client?
- What would this client like to have happen?
- And what would you call this client?

Invite the supervisee to add anything else that needs to be on the paper

Step 3: Ask them to place the paper in a space somewhere around them that represents where their client is. Encourage experimentation.

Step 4: Invite the supervisee to place themselves in a space that seems right in relation to where they have placed their client

Step 5: Ask a series of positional questions that help fine tune a spatial metaphor of how the supervisee sees their client and their relationship with them:

- Are you/the client in the right space?
- Are you/the client at the right height?
- Are you/the client facing the right direction?
- Are you/the client at the right angle?

Step 6: Conclude by checking for new understandings: 'And what do you know, now?' Invite the supervisee to put that down on their paper too.

Step 7: Now, invite the supervisee to move around with the question 'Is there another space that you could go to from that space, there?' then ask 'And what do you know from that space there?' Continue to invite the supervisee to move to more spaces, until the supervisee says there are no more spaces, or they have moved to a total of six spaces.

Step 8: Invite the supervisee to return to the space where they first started and ask 'And what do you know, now?' You can continue to prompt with further clean questions 'Is there anything else you know now?'

How to work with the technique ...

Due to the intentional 'vagueness' of the questions, you may need to give some explanation at the start on what the process will involve, for instance the repetitive nature of the questions. It is not unusual for the supervisee to reach an impasse after moving to three or four spaces. Continuing with the process beyond this point helps the supervisee push past the obvious and reach an insight/new understanding.

What else might need attention?

You may also choose to explore the space between the supervisee and their client using a similar set of questions. Should the supervisee seem drawn to notice something particular, you may also ask the occasional 'extra' clean question within any of the spaces, for example, 'What kind of x is that x?'

Keep this exploration brief (no more than two further questions) so the whole 'network' of information stays active.

A word of caution

While there are some similarities between this technique and those in the Systemic section they are distinctly different. This technique is informed by David Grove's work on Emergent Knowledge (Wilson, 2017). It is based around the theory of emergence, which is defined as 'the arising of novel and coherent structures, patterns and properties during the process of self-organization in complex systems.'

What other uses are there for this technique?

Although most appropriate for one-to-one work, it could be adapted for group supervision, for instance by inviting supervisees to work through the questions silently.

For a coaching client, you could invite them to put on the paper a representation of their goal, or a significant other they wish to understand more about.

References

Wilson, C. (2017) *The Work and Life of David Grove: Clean Language and Emergent Knowledge*. Matador: Leicestershire.

Further reading

See www.cleancoaching.com. (2018) *Emergent Knowledge – An Introduction to the Process*. Available at: https://cleancoaching.com/files/2018/04/Emergent%20Knowledge%20-%20An%20Introduction%20to%20the%20Process.pdf [Accessed 24 February 2020].

~ ~ ~ ~ ~

14. Feeling stuck

Anne Calleja

Where can this be used?				Typical level of supervisee experience required	

When is this used?

When a supervisee feels 'stuck' or frustrated or overwhelmed when with a particular client or they notice unhelpful patterns as they work with a number of clients.

What is the technique?

It is based on the work of Dilts and Bateson who identified a hierarchy of Neuro Logical Levels. Working systematically, the technique helps to identify the 'level' where the 'stuckness' is experienced, before creating alignment and next steps.

Step 1: Ask the supervisee to find a space within the room, then guide the supervisee to bring the client they feel 'stuck with' into that space, and to connect with how they are in this client's presence. Suggest that the supervisee do a body scan; perhaps encourage them to notice what they notice, feel what they feel and hear what they say. The intention is to re-live the stuckness.

Step 2: Ask the supervisee to step out of the space, to share any insight and then physically 'shake off' the sensations.

Step 3(a): The supervisee writes on six pieces of paper and then places them on the floor in 'hierarchy' order, i.e. Environment; Behaviour; Capability; Values; Identity; Purpose. See Figure 1.4.

Step 3(b): The supervisee steps into the space represented by each piece of paper and connects with the experience of being there. Use this specific order and the following tailored prompts, beginning each prompt with 'And when with your client ....'

i Environment: ... where are you? Notice what you notice, feel what you feel and hear what you hear.

ii Behaviour: ... what were you saying and doing?

iii Capability: ... what skills were you using?

iv Values: ... what were you believing or valuing?

v Identity: ... what role were you playing, who were you?

vi Purpose: ... what was your purpose or aim?

Pause in each space for the supervisee to process their sensations and thoughts.

Step 4: The supervisee steps off the pieces of paper and reflects on what they noticed, felt or heard.

Step 5: The supervisee now finds an 'observational space' where they can be an observer to themselves. From there ask them to re-live walking through each 'level', encouraging them to notice the place where there may have experienced the 'stuckness' or any insight.

Step 6 (a): The supervisee now finds a different space, which represents where they have been able to achieve a resolution. Identify this space as a 'positive resource space'. Allow the supervisee to access that state.

Step 6 (b): Ask them to use their positive resource state, and to walk through the levels E-B-C-V-I-P again.

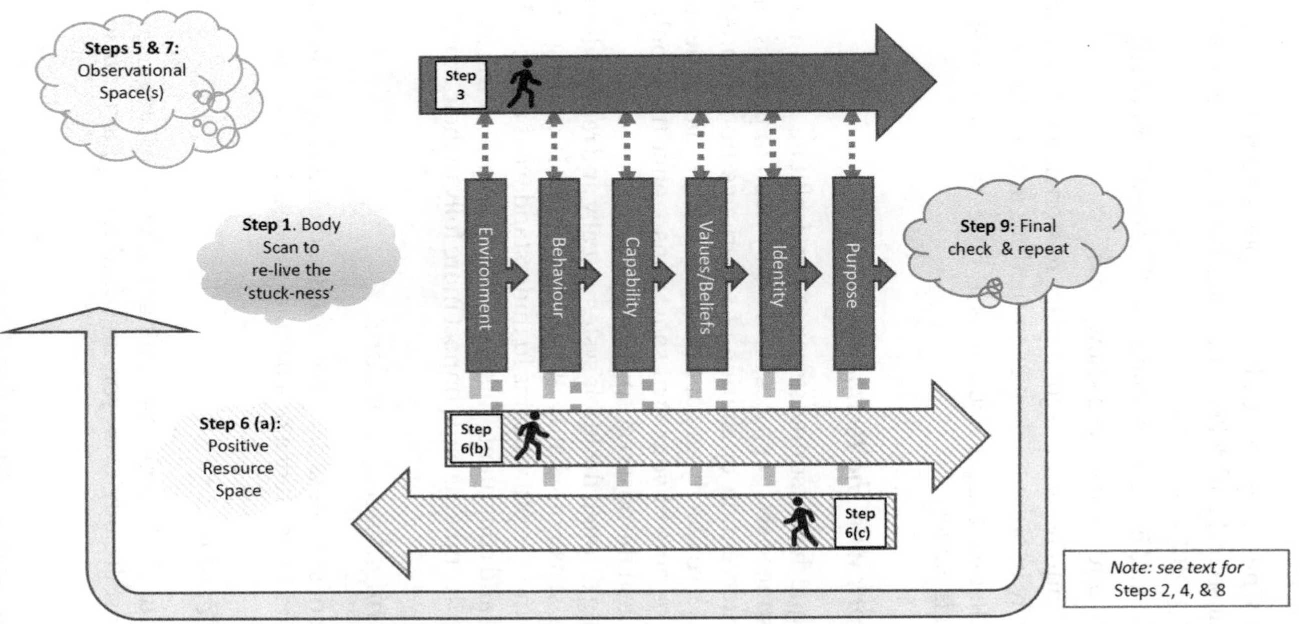

Figure 1.4 'Feeling stuck' the alignment exercise

Step 6 (c): After a pause, maintaining their positive resource state, invite them to walk through the levels in reverse order, i.e. P-I-V-C-B-E.

Step 7: When they are ready, the supervisee moves to an 'observational space' and reflects on their learning. The supervisor might offer prompts such as:

- '... and is there anything else?' (repeat as needed)
- '... and what do you know now?'

Step 8: Enquire 'Is this a good place to stop now?' responding appropriately in order to identify any actions and to close out the work.

Step 9: Repeat the previous steps as necessary until a sense of alignment is achieved.

How to work with the technique ...

The technique has a strong structure, so facilitate the process lightly. Guide the supervisee to process what they need to process without any cognitive intervention or sharing of experience from you. As the work unfolds, observe quietly and at a distance. Gently match the supervisee's posture. Take note of your own sensations - offer these only when the supervisee is in the observer space.

By walking through the levels systematically and repeatedly, the supervisee gets a sense of what is out of 'sync' (and is causing the sense of stuckness) and therefore begins to understand what needs to be done to feel aligned and congruent. This repetition is helpful. It will allow them to consolidate the process and connect more fully to their experience.

What else might need attention?

If the sense of stuckness does not resolve, then it may be helpful to consider whether transference or a parallel process is occurring.

A word of caution

If you are not NLP trained or familiar with Clean Language and Clean Space, or gestalt body work you may find it helpful to do some further reading.

What other uses are there for this technique?

With deeper understanding of Dilt's logical levels, coaches could facilitate something similar with their clients.

Further reading

Bateson, G. (1979) *Mind and Nature*. London: Fontana/Collins.
Dilts, R. (1990) *Changing Belief Systems With NLP*. Santa Cruz, CA: Meta Publications.
Dilts, R., Hallbom, T. and Smith, S. (2012) *Beliefs: Pathways to Health and Well-Being*, 2nd ed. Camarthen: Crown House Pub Ltd.
Dilts, R. (2017) *From Coach to Awakener*. Santa Cruz, CA: Meta Publications. (See Appendix A), pp. 299–324.

~ ~ ~ ~ ~

15. Fishbowl supervision

Michelle Lucas and Tammy Turner

Where can this be used?				Typical level of supervisee experience required	

When is this used?

It is most useful when the supervisee feels they are 'too close' to their work, perhaps recognising that a parallel has occurred with their wider life and/or they are being drawn to colluding with their client.

What is the technique?

This technique helps widen perspective and gain additional information. Group members deliberately take a more observational stance by being physically placed outside of the circle in order to 'look in' on the work.

Step 1: Set up the room to create a 'fishbowl'. Place yourself and the supervisee in the middle of the room and the remainder of the group form an outer circle, looking in.

Step 2: Brief the group members to listen actively when the supervisee outlines their client scenario – remind them to listen for content, emotion and intent. Ask them also to observe both the supervisee's energetic responses and their own.

Step 3: Invite the supervisee to outline the current situation with their client, articulating their current level of awareness. What can they see clearly? What might they be missing?

Step 4: Check in with the supervisee what outcomes they are hoping for.

Step 5: Allow the group a round of targeted clarifying questions – facilitate this to focus on facts – e.g. How many sessions have you had? Rather than exploratory or hypothetical – e.g. 'What do you think will happen if the client doesn't progress?' The supervisee may respond to fill in gaps, rather than to defend their choices.

Step 6: Invite the supervisee to find a place in the room where they can observe the discussion in Step 7.

Step 7: The supervisor re-joins the outer circle to facilitate the discussion inviting the group to talk about the supervisee as though they were not present.

Step 8: At an appropriate point, the supervisor draws the discussion to a close and invites the supervisee to re-join the group.

Step 9: Check in with the supervisee to understand their experience of 'being talked about' before enquiring what impact the supervision has made to their thinking about their client.

Step 10: Ask the whole group to reflect on the experience, and to make a few notes regarding what implications for their own practice.

How to work with the technique ...

Sometimes the group members forget that the supervisee is still in the room and they lose sensitivity and empathy as they discuss the client scenario. The supervisor's role is to help keep the discussion in a space of curiosity. For example, re-framing input from opinion based 'I think the XYZ technique would have worked better' to something more tentative and constructive 'I wonder if they considered using the XYZ technique.'

The point of this technique is to widen the range of options the supervisee might consider. It can be useful to hold a particular supervision framework in mind and to check which elements are naturally being offered and then prompt for elements that have yet been considered.

What else might need attention?

This technique places the supervisee in a relatively 'passive' role. Steps 3, 4 and 9 are the opportunities for the supervisee to do some quality self-reflection and need ample time. Where an individual routinely prefers to work with this approach, consider whether the supervisee is genuinely engaged or using it as an easier option.

A word of caution

Step 5 can be a time stealer and if not managed carefully can draw the group towards a discussion with the supervisee, which causes the discussion to stay more subjective. Until the group (and the supervisor) appreciates the difference between clarification and exploratory questions, it may be helpful to omit this Step. Any questions that people do have could be integrated into Step 7.

What other uses are there for this technique?

One variation is for supervisor and supervisee to engage in individual supervision, witnessed by the group. In this case both supervisee and supervisor would remove themselves from the middle of the circle to a place of observation while the rest of the group embarks on the discussion. Potentially, this could be translated into client work where there is a team, indeed some action learning sets might use this approach. In either case, it will require a high level of facilitation skills.

Further reading

Shohet, R. (2001) *Supervision as Transformation: A Passion for Learning.* London: Jessica Kingsley Publishers.

~~~~~

16. I am part of a system

Tammy Turner

Where can this be used?				Typical level of supervisee experience required	

~~~~~

When is this used?

This technique is used when a group has extensive reflective practice and/or to understand group dynamics. This enquiry works well with established groups to enhance systems awareness and/or for an annual process.

What is the enquiry?

Prior to the session, alert members that you will be using this enquiry. To prepare, ask them to think about where they've been triggered in the supervision group, or the patterns they've noticed about themselves in their reflective practice which also arise in the group. Advise them that each individual will share their observations during the next session. An example might be 'I notice I defer to Ann because she is the most experienced person in the group. I do the same with my clients who have positional power'. Repeat this instruction at the session and remind supervisees that whatever is in the room is also outside of the room.

Step 1: Taking an active role to ensure supervisees don't step into teaching or points of view, invite each supervisee to concisely share:

a *One* of their summary reflections they have had of their experience both inside the group and with others, including their reactions, triggers and/or what's become easier over time for them.

b The supervisor either says thank you or may draw out a few themes that may be emerging about the entire group system as the process unfolds. Avoid processing until Step 3.

Step 2: Allow group a few minutes to consider what they've heard and assemble their observations about how the group is operating together. Prompt them around the *collective*:

- Themes or triggers.
- Blind spots, scapegoating, deference, transference, politeness and/or over-responsibility.
- And their individual contributions to these.

If the group is familiar with the Seven-Eyed Model (see pp. 292–295), other modes can be examined.

Step 3: Facilitate the group's observations as a reflection of how they work *collectively*, reminding supervisees to remain observers, rather than personalising the information. Useful questions may include:

- What patterns has the group developed as a result of this pattern?
- How do you as an individual interpret the group dynamic impacting on you?
- What have you noticed contributed to this group dynamic?
- What options does the group have to break this?

Step 4: Bring the work to a close by each member sharing what has been most useful for them and what they will practice in the upcoming sessions as a result.

How to work with the enquiry …

In Step 1, encourage supervisees to be vulnerable and succinct. It is unhelpful to recount complete reflections, share commentary or offer sugary acknowledgments, e.g. 'It's been great working with the group, thank you all so much ….' Use probing follow-up questions to get underneath the surface of genuine but safe responses. For example: What particularly was great for you? And what impact did you notice that having on you? And on the group as a whole?

Where there seems to be a reluctance to speak openly, gently remind supervisees that all observations are valid, group process may mean that they are noticing dynamics on behalf of the group rather than the supervisee's reflection in isolation.

What else might need attention?

In Step 3, exploring group blind spots can be powerful learning.

A word of caution

Throughout the process, be on alert to parallel process as the tendency to personalise, transfer and/or avoid can arise. If the group is advanced enough, you can bring any instances of these to the group's awareness to help them to work through. If inappropriate, simply direct the group to take a moment to reflect and redirect them back to the most useful collective observation to resume the process.

What other uses are there for this enquiry?

The focus of this enquiry is around individual contributions to a system. It is useful on an annual or bi-annual basis and/or when an individual supervisee notices a particular habit, which also shows up in the group. Content from Step 4 can be used in future group sessions to form group agreements for the contract.

Further reading

Turner, T., Lucas, M. and Whitaker, C. (2018) *Peer Supervision in Coaching and Mentoring: A Versatile Guide for Reflective Practice.* Maidenhead: Routledge, pp. 104–105.

~ ~ ~ ~ ~

17. Issues, insights, ideas and intentions

David Clutterbuck

Where can this be used?	Typical level of supervisee experience required

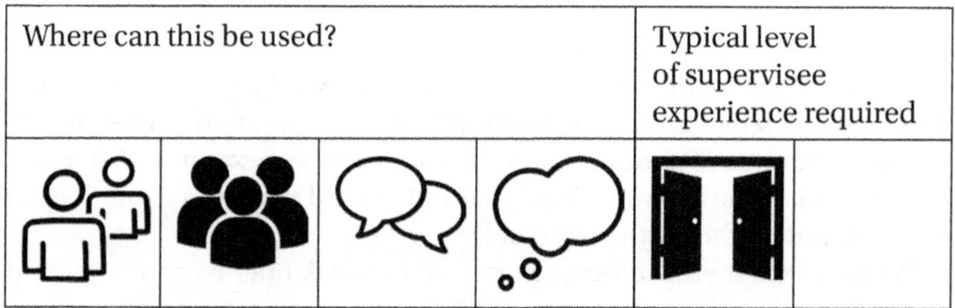

When is this used?

It is typically used to help close a session or summarise progress part way through. It offers a useful counterbalance for a session that has meandered and/or which did not have a clear focus at the start.

What is the technique?

This technique is a simple set of four questions that are used to help draw out learning or close a session in a meaningful way.

Step 1: Pause the session at an appropriate juncture. Perhaps when the supervisee (or supervisor) has lost the thread of the conversation, or when there is say 10 minutes before time expires and it is not otherwise clear how to draw the discussion together.

Step 2: Check out with the supervisee how they might like to close the session and include the questions in the next step as an option.

Step 3: When invited, offer the following questions:

- What are the issues we have talked about?
- What are your insights?
- What ideas have emerged?
- What are your intentions?

Step 4: The supervisee responds to those questions either through dialogue or journaling their responses.

Step 5: Where appropriate build in a meta-reflection.

- What are you learning about how you use our session time?
- What of that works well for you?
- What is working less well?
- What might you like to differently in future?

How to work with the technique ...

This approach can help bring structure to a fluid session. Alternatively, if there is insufficient time within the session, the four questions offer a useful framework for further individual reflection. The supervisor may well hold their own answers to the four questions. It is important not to offer the supervisee your thoughts before they have shared their own. To do so would take responsibility from the supervisee. Moreover, it can be illuminating to hear the supervisee's sense of their learning – often it is markedly different from the story we are holding of them. Where that difference seems to hint at a blind spot of the supervisee; then it can be useful to compare and contrast each of your perspectives to prompt further awareness. However, often this brings into the supervisor's awareness what it is that *they* are hoping for in their supervisee – and could indicate material for supervision of their own.

Depending on the supervision contract and your supervisor style, the output from this exercise could be used as a start point for the next session. Not only does this offer a place of accountability, it also signals an openness to whatever additional reflection, insight and action happens between sessions.

3D coaching (Pedrick, 2019) have suggested adding a fifth 'I' for 'Instead.' Often, we uncover that an intention has not been executed. Asking 'What did you do instead?' helps the supervisor stay away from a judging frame. Additionally, it is useful to capture what was possible when other things were not, it offers material for further exploration.

What else might need attention?

Where a supervisee seems to lack focus in the sessions, consider how well they understand the supervision process. It may be necessary to go back to basics. Ensure the supervisee knows how to be an equal party in the conversation and how to gain maximum value from the supervision.

A word of caution

While the technique offers a neat way of closing a session - not all sessions need a neat close. Use your judgement about the genuine purpose of closing this way. If it is for your reassurance that you have 'tied up the session with a bow,' then perhaps this is the time to just allow it to 'be.' Why not sit with your supervisee with the messiness of things as yet unfinished?

What other uses are there for this technique?

In addition to using the four questions as a reflective exercise, they could be used for pair work within a group session.

The questions can also be used by coaches with their individual and team clients. Within teams it highlights to individuals what colleagues are taking from the dialogue, bringing diversity and challenge to their own perspective.

Many clients bring this approach into their business meetings, where there is discursive dialogue.

Reference

Pedrick, C. (2019) 3D ideas 838: Insteads. [blog]. Available at: www.3dcoaching.com/blog/3d-ideas-838-insteads/ [Accessed 16 August 2019].

~ ~ ~ ~ ~

18. Keeping it real

Michelle Lucas and Carol Whitaker

Where can this be used?				Typical level of supervisee experience required	

When is this used?

The benefit of this technique is to generate a diversity of ideas for the supervisee to bring more variety into their practice. It is useful when the supervisee feels particularly stuck or when they realise their practice is becoming habituated.

What is the technique?

Step 1: Brief the group along the following lines:

> *'Listen to the supervisee and notice what in their story resonates for you as you will be invited to share your similar experiences. Remember similarity may be through:*
>
> *Experiencing an almost identical scenario*
> *Experiencing a similar response from the client although in a different scenario*
> *Connecting with the emotions evoked in the supervisee (or the client)*
> *Something resonates for no apparent reason*
> *When sharing your experience, share the true reality of the situation, i.e. What worked? What didn't? How did it feel at the time? How do you feel about it now? What has your learning been?'*

Step 2: Invite the supervisee to talk through their client scenario, then enquire what outcome they want from hearing the others experience.

Step 3(a): Each group member is invited to share something.

Step 3(b): Depending on time the supervisee may have some follow-up questions, or they simply say 'thank you' after each contribution.

Step 4: Once everyone has contributed and after a pause, the supervisor returns to the supervisee. Some useful questions follow that can be tailored to link back to the supervisee's expressed intention:

- Which experiences resonated for you? Why do you think that was?
- Which experiences didn't connect for you? Could this indicate a blind spot or bias?
- What new insight do you have about your situation?
- How has this helped you think about what you could do in future?
- What else has occurred for you during this process?

How to work with the technique ...

Occasionally a peer does not feel they have anything to offer. It can be helpful to remind them of how similarities can occur and to consider their wider life experience not just their coaching experience.

Use the technique to generate lots of different experiences and to allow them to stand together, rather than looking for the 'best' solution. This helps avoid the 'Why don't you ...' form of sharing experiences – where there can be a subtle suggestion that a better result could have been achieved if they had done what the contributor would have done. The supervision task is to help each group member articulate and locate their experience in their unique context. The supervisee is then at liberty to draw what is meaningful to them given their preferences and specific situation.

In Step 2 it can be informative to hear why they have chosen this particular technique. Coaching can be an isolating profession, sometimes practitioners need to know that they are not alone in their struggles. As long as the supervisee can make this need explicit, the technique will be of use. Without expressing this, group members may feel they are giving too much without knowing why?

What else might need attention?

On occasions a group member shares an experience that would not be regarded as best practice. Ask for some clarity from them before moving on. Where the supervisor still has a concern, this is best explored once the current supervisee has finished their presentation, otherwise it could divert attention.

A word of caution

Without good facilitation this technique could allow the supervisee to 'hide', by asking for other people's experiences they avoid having to analyse their own. For this reason, Step 4 needs to be appropriately robust so that the technique is not seen as a soft option.

What other uses are there for this technique?

This technique is unlikely to be useful with individual coaching clients as it encourages the practitioner to share their own experiences, which could shift the coach towards a more directive stance. The approach could, however, be adapted for group coaching, Action Learning Set or Communities of Practice discussions, e.g. focus on a specific topic and generate a range of ideas to 'top up' people's tool boxes.

Further reading

Turner, T., Lucas, M. and Whitaker, C. (2018) *Peer Supervision in Coaching and Mentoring: A Versatile Guide for Reflective Practice*. Maidenhead: Routledge, pp. 68–69.

Whitaker, C. and Calleja, A. (2018) *Group Supervision Approaches for Coaching Supervision*. [pdf] Available at: www.whitaker-consulting.co.uk/resources-and-papers [Accessed 2 August 2019].

~ ~ ~ ~ ~

19. Line of enquiry

Michelle Lucas and Carol Whitaker

Where can this be used?				Typical level of supervisee experience required	

When is this used?

This technique can be useful when a supervisee can't make sense of a situation, or doesn't know where to start their exploration.

What is the technique?

Step 1: The group is briefed along the following lines:

> *Listen to the supervisee and notice what questions arise in you. It is helpful to notice both significant things and little things. The best questions are those where you are truly curious with no idea how they might respond. You will have time to write down your question before you ask it. Make this as succinct as possible. The supervisee will make a note of all your questions although typically there will only be time to explore one of them fully.*

Step 2: The supervisee is invited to talk through the client scenario. Given this technique is often used when they feel lost, it can be helpful to encourage them to share more about how they are feeling as they hear themselves speak.

Step 3: The group pauses for each peer to develop a short question before offering it to the supervisee. Guide the supervisee to make a note of each question, without responding to it.

Step 4: The supervisee selects one question to explore further with the group. Clarify that here is no need to explain or defend their choice.

Step 5: The peer whose question was selected for further discussion, now poses this question directly to the supervisee, and the discussion begins.

Step 6: When the discussion slows or when getting close to time the supervisor offers the supervisee a wrap up question, e.g. 'What have you learned from that discussion?'

Step 7: Before closing, pose the supervisee a question for reflection. For example, 'So what drew you to choose that particular question?' or 'Why do you think that question chose you?!' Typically, this is taken away for some independent reflection.

How to work with the technique ...

Depending on the size of the group and time available, you may only be able to discuss thoroughly one of the questions raised. It is important therefore to manage the expectations of both the supervisee and the group in this regard.

Sometimes the supervisee will struggle to capture the questions as they are busy reflecting in the moment. The supervisor could act as scribe, or each peer could jot their question on a Post-it; this provides a record of all the questions which the supervisee can take away to reflect upon after the session.

What else might need attention?

The purpose of this technique is to facilitate the discussion towards a depth rather than a breadth of exploration, so encourage members to navigate away from their own frame of reference and to more fully pursue the chosen 'line of enquiry'.

This technique also offers the opportunity for group members to practice their succinct questioning skills. However, unless this is contracted for with the group, the supervisor should only encourage group members to re-state their question where the supervisee wants greater clarity. Sometimes the messy questions are the useful ones!

A word of caution

Some groups experience a sense of competition with this exercise – assuming that the question chosen must be the 'best' question. So, the supervisor may need to explain that there may be many reasons why a question is chosen or not. The question may be too risky to explore in a group, it might be pertinent but not of interest at the moment, on a different day the supervisee may have chosen a different question.

Depending on the group, the supervisor may consider offering a question too. This is most helpful, when an ethical issue is present and has not yet been noticed.

What other uses are there for this technique?

A variation of this is the 'tag coaching supervision'. In this version there is no offering of different questions at the start. The supervisor starts the discussion and then passes the baton. This is a great exercise to use in group or team coaching as it encourages people to truly listen to their colleagues so that the conversation builds.

Further reading

Turner, T., Lucas, M. and Whitaker, C. (2018) *Peer Supervision in Coaching and Mentoring: A Versatile Guide for Reflective Practice.* Maidenhead: Routledge, pp. 100–102.

Whitaker, C. and Calleja, A. (2018) *Group Supervision Approaches for Coaching Supervision.* [pdf] Available at: www.whitaker-consulting.co.uk/resources-and-papers [Accessed 2 August 2019].

~ ~ ~ ~ ~

20. Making friends with our inner critic

Clare Norman

Where can this be used?				Typical level of supervisee experience required	

When is this used?

This can be useful at the start of a supervisory relationship, to help the individual to notice what might be holding them back from being fully vulnerable in the supervision.

In group supervision and group mentor coaching, individuals often feel worried about their capabilities in comparison to others in the group. They build up an often-false impression that others in the group are better than them, more experienced, more prepared. This creates an apprehension about exposing themselves, despite the fact that most people will be in the same boat. This exercise normalises the feelings as they see that others have concerns and inner critics of their own.

What is the technique?

The individual identifies the little voice in their head that creates an unwanted inner state; and rather than pushing the voice aside, embraces what it has to offer. As a result, the voice doesn't need to shout so loud to be heard and is easier to put on mute.

Step 1: The supervisor asks the supervisee(s) to watch this 13-minute video by Steve Chapman as part of their preparation for their first session:

https://www.youtube.com/watch?v=lnf-Ka3ZmOM or to read Rick Carsons' book *Taming Your Gremlin.*

Step 2: The supervisor asks for the supervisee(s) insights. For example: 'Don't fight it: The practice of bearing witness is potent – a deeper awareness of what is, without judgement. Take care of it.'

Step 3: Invite the supervisee(s) to draw their own inner critic. They should make it as vivid as possible, but their drawing skills are not being tested here – this is for their own use, to really get up close and personal with their inner critic. If they say, 'I can't draw,' say to them 'Brilliant, that's it, draw the part of you that is telling you right now that you can't draw.' The supervisor may share a picture of their own inner critic to demonstrate that the picture really could be anything and to model vulnerability.

Step 4: The supervisor offers questions for reflection:

- What is its name?
- What does it believe? What does it say to me?
- Who does it hang out with? Tiredness, hunger, loneliness ...?
- When are you vulnerable to it?

- What is the positive intention that it has to share with you? Listen to it with curiosity, not fear.
- What relationship do you want to have with your inner critic?

Step 5: The supervisor asks:

- What have you learned by getting intimate with your inner critic?
- What positive intention does it have for you today?
- How does this help you to bring your whole self to supervision today?

How to work with the technique ...

Group members may wish to keep private their picture and what their inner critic says to them. This will still be a useful exercise. The final questions in Step 5 allow them to share learning, revealing only what they choose to.

A word of caution

Not everyone feels comfortable drawing, so it is important to assure them that you are not expecting masterpieces and that stick-personas are fine. If they really resist, you could use magazines from which they can create a collage. Picture cards could be an alternative but may not capture the exact essence of their inner voice.

What other uses are there for this technique?

You might come back to it when you notice people holding back from saying what's on their minds, you can then enquire what their inner critic is saying right now that's getting in the way of being fully present/unmasked.

It can also be used to have a discussion about coaching presence: How will you harness your inner critic to help you to be more present in your coaching work?

This can also prove a useful tool for coaching clients especially where the coach senses that the client is getting in their own way, or is making unhelpful comparisons with their peers.

References

Carson, R. (1984) *Taming Your Gremlin*. Glasgow: Harper Collins.

Chapman, S. (2017) TedX Royal Tunbridge Wells. This Talk isn't very good. Dancing with my inner critic. [video online] Available at: www.youtube.com/watch?v=lnf-Ka3ZmOM [Accessed 6 September 2019].

Resources

See Steve Chapman's website. Available at: https://canscorpionssmoke.com/about/ [Accessed 6 September 2019].

~ ~ ~ ~ ~

21. Mentor Coaching

Clare Norman

Where can this be used?				Typical level of supervisee experience required	

When is this used?

Mentor Coaching is useful when you want to re-sharpen your coaching edge or step up to use more advanced coaching skills.

It is a mandatory part of the International Coach Federation credentialing process.

What is the approach?

Mentor Coaching is a form of supervision where a mentor coach observes a supervisee at work and gives feedback. This can either be live or a recording. It works best when the feedback is benchmarked against a competency framework (see further reading), providing structure to identify strengths and development areas.

Step 1: The supervisee coaches someone in the (virtual or physical) room while the mentor coach observes. Alternatively, they record a session to review later. The live session would likely be 25 minutes; a recording could be longer.

Step 2: The supervisee highlights one competency that they used well and one competency that they could improve. The mentor coach works with the supervisee to be specific about the exact behaviours and language displayed.

Step 3: When in a group, each group member offers an observation about one competency they saw the supervisee using well, and one competency they might improve upon.

Step 4: The mentor coach gives feedback; once more focusing on one thing the supervisee did well in service of the client, and one thing they could do differently. Take care to precisely reference the competency framework and role model giving good feedback.

Step 5: The mentor coach asks the supervisee to summarise what he/she is taking away, and what he/she will work on in future coaching sessions.

Step 6: When in a group, the mentor coach asks what each person has learned from this session that they are going to apply to their own coaching practice

Step 7: The coach(es) practices what they committed to in between mentor coaching sessions

Step 8: The process is repeated so that new habits are built over time

How to work with the approach …

When using a recording, stop and start throughout the session to reflect together in the moment. You can also fast-forward to sections that the supervisee would like to reflect most on. Ideally, listen to both the contract and the ending as these are such vital parts of the session.

With a live session, the client may also provide feedback. Typically, they will need some time to process this, as the supervisee's performance was not their focus of their attention. Additionally, you could call a 'time out', so that the supervisee can adjust their approach there and then. The mentor coach might ask the supervisee, 'What is happening right now?' and then elicit ideas for how to switch gear to meet the needs of the client. Clearly this must be contracted for at the start as part of the learning process.

When working in a group, practitioners who are new to this approach may offer generic feedback. Encourage people to give supportive *and* challenging feedback; succinct and useful. You may need to manage the feedback offered towards the supervisee's requested competency focus.

What else might need attention?

Mentor coaching can be behaviourally oriented, offering feedback that links directly to competency frameworks. It can be interesting to consider *why* a particular competency is under-developed. For example, what might be contributing to a lack of challenge? How come there is a reluctance to contract more clearly? These are the kind of explorations that could then inform a more traditional supervision exploration.

A word of caution

Individuals could self-assess using recordings of their coaching. This is not always as beneficial as they often have blind spots, but the more practiced they become, the more they can see.

Occasionally, ethical issues arise. This might require a switch into formal supervision, so it is useful if the mentor coach is also a trained supervisor.

What other uses are there for this approach?

While this is mandatory for those going for an ICF credential, mentor coaching offers high impact, individualised continuous professional development and can be used at any time to sharpen your edge. Individuals can benchmark themselves against any set of competencies from their chosen professional body.

If they are competent at competency-based feedback, coaches can also do this with peers in a triad, for example.

This could also be used for clients – especially where organisations work to competency frameworks and there is opportunity to observe the client at work.

Resources

International Coach Federation competencies: Available at: https://coachfederation.org/core-competencies [Accessed 19 July 2019].

Association for Coaching Competencies: Available at: cdn.ymaws.com/www.associationforcoaching.com/resource/resmgr/Accreditation/Accred_General/Coaching_Competency_Framewor.pdf [Accessed 19 July 2019].

European Mentoring and Coaching Council competencies: Available at: https://emcc1.app.box.com/s/4aj8x6tmbt75ndn13sg3dauk8n6wxfxq [Accessed 19 July 2019].

~ ~ ~ ~ ~

22. Metaphor magic box

Lily Seto

Where can this be used?				Typical level of supervisee experience required	

When is this used?

This creative tool is especially useful when a supervisee gets stuck or needs to identify patterns or is interested in accessing what lies outside of current awareness. The choice of symbols encourages the use of metaphors that act as a conduit for different kinds of knowing.

What is the technique?

The work is carried out using a small box of approximately 21–30 mixed charms and can be used alongside other supervision tools.

Step 1: Start by asking 'What question or client scenario would you like to examine today?'

Step 2: Encourage the supervisee to handle the charms in the magic box in an unhurried fashion, noticing their weight and texture.

Step 3: Brief the supervisee along the following lines:

> *'I invite you to choose an item/s that best represents your client and place it/them on the mat.'*
>
> *'Choose an item/s that represent you in the scenario and place it/them on the mat.'*
>
> - *'If there is anyone else who needs to be represented; choose items to represent them and place them on the mat.'*

Step 4: Encourage description for example:

> *'Please describe the item(s) that you chose to represent each of the elements (your client; yourself; other representative) and how it or they represent that element.*
>
> *What else?*

What else?

What else?'

Repeat these questions for each of the remaining elements.

Step 5: Encourage the supervisee to take a meta-position, being guided by their sense of flow.

- *'If you stand and look at the system that you created, what do you notice? There is no need to try to interpret the system yet, perhaps consider ...*
- *... Patterns that you might notice, what colours you are drawn to, how you laid the items out, e.g. What came easily, what order felt right.*
- *... Where you laid the items out, i.e. their relationship to each other, e.g. How near or far are they from each other.'*

Step 6: Build awareness through unpacking the metaphoric landscape they have depicted and by making connections to other models and modalities:

1 Referencing the Seven-Eyed Model:
- (Eye 3) Describe the relationship between client and coach/other relationships in the system.
- (Parallel process) What might be happening now between you (coach) and myself (supervisor) that is mirrored in your creation?

2 Referencing alternative modalities:
- (Emotions) What feelings are you present to in the moment?
- (Kinesthetics) What sensations are you noticing now?

3 Alternative lines of enquiry:
- What do you think the client would want to discuss about the system that you have depicted?

Step 7: Check in on learning. Ask:

- What is emerging for you and what are you present to right now?
- What are your learnings?

How to work with the technique ...

Respect the supervisee's ownership of their creation, so refrain from naming the item(s) until the supervisee has done so and do not touch items until supervisee has deconstructed the field.

In Step 3, repeating 'What else?' invites deeper exploration. Initially, the supervisee goes to a place they already know. After three or four repetitions, they will likely come to new discoveries. Pay attention to your pace and tone, allowing for lots of silence and notice when the supervisee is ready for another question.

What else might need attention?

Strong emotions may emerge, so allow sufficient time for processing this heightened awareness. Occasionally, some unfinished business is evoked and so referral to an alternative helping professional may be appropriate.

A word of caution

Avoid offering what may be intended as subtle prompts, they have the potential for contaminating the process. Simply holding the space and asking succinct, curiosity questions allows the supervisee to do the work they need to do in the moment.

What other uses are there for this technique?

When using this tool in group supervision, pose a common question, e.g. How do I best resource myself? This allows everyone in the group to work independently, answering the questions by journaling their responses. Alternatively, have the group ask questions or make observations about the system that the supervisee has built. The supervisee listens to all the questions or observations and choses which questions or observations resonate and create emergent thoughts and learnings. It has also been adapted to other settings including professional coaches, leaders and counsellors.

Further reading

Seto, L. and Geithner, T. (2018) Metaphor magic in coaching and coaching supervision. *International Journal of Evidence Based Coaching and Mentoring*, 16(2), pp. 99–111.

Resources

For more information or to purchase or be trained in using the Metaphor Magic Box, please contact Lily directly. Available at: www.lilyseto.com/ [Accessed 6 September 2019].

Acknowledgements

Thank you to Edna Murdoch and the Coaching Supervision Academy for introducing me to the power of metaphors in supervision.

~ ~ ~ ~ ~

23. Misfits

Michelle Lucas

Where can this be used?				Typical level of supervisee experience required	

When is this used?

This is useful when a coach wants to explore how they show up to clients, or in life generally. Perhaps because many supervisees assume they should have a coaching identity grounded in theory, they become stuck. This exercise takes a playful and creative approach to help generate additional insight.

What is the technique?

This technique uses the children's game of 'Misfits' – it contains 12 characters printed on card, each divided into five pieces – a hat, a face, a body with arms and two legs. The aim is to create a character that works as a metaphor for your particular coaching style.

Step 1: Ensure each supervisee has access to a box of 'Misfit' characters to work with. Give some time to explore the pieces.

Step 2: Invite the supervisee to create a character that says something about how they work. Encourage them not to overthink it, but to simply choose five pieces that hold some appeal. For example, a popular piece is a mermaid's fishtail; some say it symbolises an ability to be fluid and change direction quickly.

Step 3: Ask the supervisee to tell the story of their creation. There is no particular order to do this in, in fact the order they choose is interesting in itself.

Step 4: Depending on the focus of the supervision enquiry, you may then follow up with some additional questions.

For example, if they had recently had a tough client session, it might be interesting to ask which parts of their Misfit were working well and which parts weren't on that occasion. Or perhaps explore how the session would have been if a different misfit piece was present and active.

When you are doing this with a group, then it can be useful to invite comment from the other members. Ask open questions like 'What resonated for you?' or 'What did you notice as XXX told their story?' The intention is to generate more food for thought rather than get into a discussion about how they interpreted a particular piece.

Step 5: Take a picture of the Misfit created as an 'aide-memoire' for the session (see Figure 1.5).

How to work with the technique ...

This apparently simply exercise is deceptively powerful so ensure you give it the space it deserves. Sharing the Misfit without a narrative could confuse rather than inform - people often interpret the pieces differently. For example, the mermaid tail may be seen as 'slippery' rather than 'fluid'.

Observe how the supervisee(s) approach the task - there are often parallels with their signature style.

Figure 1.5 An example of a supervisee's Misfit

What else might need attention?

This exercise works as a catalyst, generating a positive energy for individual(s) to articulate their sense of their coaching presence. A more conventional dialogue might then be required to develop their insights into a more formal expression of how they work.

A word of caution

You may notice what of their narrative seems congruent with how you experience them in supervision. Where something doesn't feel quite congruent – that in itself might be something to explore (although this may be less possible in a group). It is important to work tentatively because the incongruence may well lie outside of their awareness. Alternatively, the exercise is often experienced as 'just a bit of fun' and the dissonance may simply be a quirk holding no particular significance.

What other uses are there for this technique?

This technique is a useful ice-breaker when bringing a group to work together for the first time. It's relatively non-threatening as there can be no 'right or wrong' answer – it also highly memorable. You could revisit the technique with an ongoing group; 'What is constant?' and 'What is evolving?' are interesting questions to explore.

There are many different slants with which to position this exercise:

- How do you see yourself as a coach – when you do your best work?
- How might your clients experience you as a coach?
- What kind of coach would you like to become?
- Which parts of you are core and which parts are more peripheral?
- What happens to your coaching presence when you are not working at your best?

This exercise could also be translated for work with coaching clients who want to explore their leadership style.

Resources

The game Misfits can be purchased from Rocket Games. Available at: www.amazon.co.uk/Rocket-Games-ROC032-Misfits/dp/B0006D393Q/ref=cm_cr_arp_d_product_top?ie=UTF8 [Accessed on 21 October 2019].

~ ~ ~ ~ ~

24. Quiet

Michelle Lucas

Where can this be used?				Typical level of supervisee experience required	

When is this used?

This technique is useful as part of an arrivals phase, especially where supervisees have had a busy or demanding day prior to the session. It provides a segue into a more reflective space.

What is the technique?

Step 1: Physical set-up.

- Remind people to sit in a relaxed but grounded manner:
  - Feet planted on the floor.
  - Back supported by the chair.
  - Shoulders relaxed.
  - Hands placed in lap.
- Invite people to wriggle away any tension.
- Suggest to people that they may be becoming aware of the heaviness of their limbs, for example the weight of their hands as they rest in their laps ...

Step 2: Putting attention to the breath.

- Direct people's attention to their breathing, invite them to notice how air comes into their body and how it leaves.
- Reassure them that there is no need to alter the pace of their breathing, just become increasingly aware of the sensations as they breathe in and out.

Step 3: Mental set-up.

- Explain that it is quite natural to have competing thoughts during the exercise.
- Invite them to imagine that in their mind's eye there is a window frame and that their thoughts are clouds. It's OK to notice their thoughts as they move into their field of view and encourage them to trust that in their own time they will move out of view too. There is no need to hurry the thought along – should they become distracted simply gently move attention back to their breathing.

Step 4: Final set-up 'script'.

- So, in a moment I'm going to stop talking and put the timer on for XX minutes.
- Focus on your breathing – notice how the air comes in to your body and how it goes out of your body.
- If your mind wanders that's OK. Just let those thoughts pass by like clouds through a window frame and gently return your attention to your breathing.
- Some people like to close their eyes, some prefer not to – do what feels comfortable for you.
- Notice how the air comes into your body and how it goes out of your body ...

Step 5: Timer is set and goes off.

Step 6: Close out 'script'.

- OK, so that was XX minutes.
- When you are ready give yourself a little wriggle and bring your attention back into the room.
- Give people time to re-orient before asking ... so how was that for you?

How to work with the technique ...

While initially you might want to read this like a script – or create your own version, in time it can be helpful to ad lib so that you can take into account any situational information occurring in the moment. For example, if there is an open window, you could remind them that should they become distracted by the breeze, that this is OK, and encourage them to gently, without rushing, return to a focus on their breath.

Where you have an established supervision relationship, especially as a group, it can help create a sense of partnership if members of the group take turns to lead the mindfulness exercise. This also allows the supervisor to fully engage in mindfulness.

A word of caution

When working with organisations, mindfulness may be seen as incongruence with a business environment. It can be helpful to refer to some of the neuropsychology to offer them evidence that by quietening the amygdala, people are more able to make good decisions.

What other uses are there for this technique?

There may be many opportunities for using mindfulness within supervision work. For example, it can be helpful as a precursor to doing more emotional, somatic or creative work. The technique tends to help people move out of cognitive intelligence into different ways of being. This is useful when supervisees are distracted and indeed it's helpful should you need some time to centre yourself!

Further reading

Brown, P. and Hayes, B. (2011) *Neuroscience. New Science for New Leadership*. Developing Leaders, Issue 5, pp. 36–42.

~ ~ ~ ~ ~

25. Reflecting through action inquiry

Christine Champion

Where can this be used?				Typical level of supervisee experience required	

When is this used?

This developmental technique can be applied by experienced supervisors for reflective practice during supervision through inquiry on self as supervisee and to explore the impact of one's practice. Through the lens of the self as an instrument (Bachkirova, 2016) of coaching, the process can guide an exploration to expand our capacity and awareness. It can help guide and identify the development 'Growth Edge' for the supervisee.

What is the approach?

The approach is informed by Kegan's work on Adult Development Theory and Torbert's Action Inquiry and is introduced here in a supervision context through the individual's Four Territories of Experience – see Table 1.3.

Table 1.3 The individual Four Territories of Experience as applied in coaching supervision (Torbert, Fisher and Rooke, 2004).

Territory	Description	Examples of inquiry
1. Outside world	Objective description of events, consequences and environmental effects	What happened? What did you see/ hear/observe? What were the consequences?
2. Sensed performance	Own sense of performance, behaviours, skills actions, as experienced in the moment	What did you do? How did you behave? What did you sense/ experience?
3. Action logic	Realm of thought and how we interpret our behaviours and make sense of the world	What did this mean to you? Where are you focusing your thinking? Do you notice any patterns?
4. Intentional attention	Building on the above three territories, our presencing, awareness, vision and intuition	What are/were you aware of? How are you feeling? What are you noticing in your body?

The supervisor may use the framework explicitly by broadly following the steps outlined below or it may simply provide an underpinning frame to guide a reflective exploration. The sample questions provided are by no means exhaustive and depending on the responses there may be an opportunity to inquire more deeply into the fourth territory.

Step 1: Invite the supervisee to outline what they would like to explore.

Step 2: From your prior knowledge of the supervisee, or your current understanding of what is being presented, commence an exploration using questions from the Territory that best reflects the supervisee's current level of processing (see Table 1.3 above).

Step 3: Taking a sensitive and compassionate approach, work through questions of increasing levels of complexity, being mindful of the supervisee's developmental readiness to continue to deepen the inquiry.

Step 4: To conclude the learning it will be helpful to explore the experience of the supervisee in this session by encouraging reflection and feedback. The supervisor could readily loop back into the Four Territories Framework to switch the lens of enquiry to focus on the present experience.

How to work with the approach ...

It will be important that supervisors choosing to engage with this approach, have a good understanding of Adult Development Theory and how this can be usefully applied in a coaching and supervision context.

The supervisor needs to work without implying judgement of those supervisees who may be centred in earlier Territories and Action Logics.

It is important to start at the supervisee's indicated current development stage of Action Logic rather than imposing or rushing to a later stage approach until the readiness has been developed in the supervisee.

What else might need attention?

Depending on what is emerging for the supervisee, there may be an opportunity to explore any parallel process in relation to the coaching client. For example, if their coaching client is stuck in a transactional mode of operation, you may witness that the supervisee's focus and attention resides mostly in Territories 1 and 2.

Word of caution

Given its potential for complexity, supervisees may be more open to working with this approach in a one to one setting, or in mature groups of very experienced supervisees.

What other uses are there for this approach?

As an individual reflective practice, typically through journaling, the Four Territories Framework is used as a basis for inquiry.

In a coaching context this approach can also be usefully applied, especially with Expert, High Achieving Leaders whose developmental focus is on moving toward more transforming leadership approaches that are needed for effectiveness in the volatile, complex, uncertain and ambiguous environments of today.

References

Bachkirova, T. (2016) The self as coach: Conceptualisation, issues, and opportunities for practitioner development. *Coaching Psychology Journal: Practice & Research*, 68(2), pp. 145–156.

Torbert, B., Fisher, D. and Rooke, D. (2004) *Action Inquiry: The Secret of Timely and Transforming Leadership*. Oakland, CA: Berrett-Koehler Publishers Inc.

Further reading

Berger, J.G. (2012) *Changing on the Job*. Stanford, CA: Stanford University Press.

Kegan, R. (1982) *The Evolving Self*. Cambridge, MA: Harvard University Press.

~ ~ ~ ~ ~

26. Reflective writing

Michelle Lucas and Christine Champion

Where can this be used?				Typical level of supervisee experience required	

When is this used?

This process of capturing systematic, tangible written reflections will deepen insights into the coaching practice of supervisees and can also help access relational dynamics. For this reason it is helpful in preparation for Accreditation.

It can be used between supervision sessions to prepare written reflections in advance, and equally during one-to-one and group supervision sessions. Encouraging supervisees to engage with this regularly and systematically helps them create a robust and professional coaching practice.

What is the approach?

Based on Gibbs' (1988) model of reflection the supervisee revisits a written reflection through three increasingly complex lenses of description, analysis and reflexivity.

Step 1: Invite the supervisee to consider a moment or a theme in their client work – this could be something that was perplexing, or equally something that had a positive outcome for the client.

Step 2: Using Gibbs' model of reflection as a guide (see Figure 1.6), invite them to write about the moment or theme. There are no particular time boundaries for this. It is important, that they can fully engage with the approach.

Step 3: Pause and ask the supervisee to consider how they felt about the writing activity; making notes to capture this.

Step 4: Individuals naturally write at different levels of complexity. Typically, in the first iteration the writing is broadly descriptive and factual. For example, 'I did X and upon reflection I realise that Y might have been more useful.'

Step 5: Invite the supervisee to review the written reflection with the aim of becoming more analytical. For example, consider:

- Which coaching competencies can be identified in the reflection? Are any missing?
- Consider a framework, e.g. seven-eyed model ... which eyes do you tend to focus on? Which seem to be absent? Why might that be?
- Which of your reflections are subjective, i.e. About how you are experiencing the moment? Which of your reflections are objective, i.e. Have a detached, observational quality reviewing the client and their wider context?

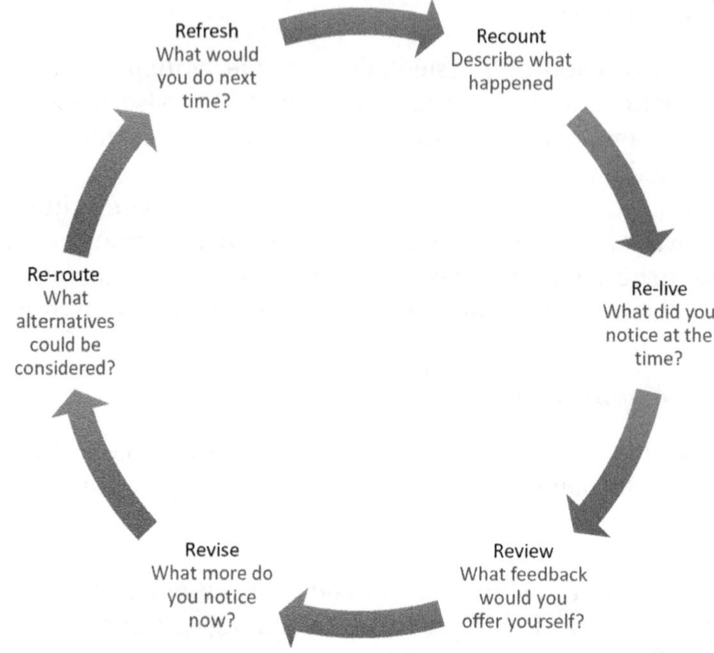

Figure 1.6 The Reflective Cycle, based on Gibbs (1988) and adapted by Lucas and Champion

Step 6: Pause for a moment and capture any feelings emerging from the writing activity - make a few notes.

Step 7: Revisit the written piece with the intention of being more reflexive. For example, consider:

- What senses were evoked in you by reflecting on the moment?
- How does your practice align with your coaching philosophy/model? What level of intentionality was in evidence?
- What can you learn about yourself from this work?

Step 8: Pause and consider how you felt about the reflective writing activity - make a few notes.

Step 9: Over time gather a collection of reflections and see what you notice. This meta-reflection may highlight a journey into greater maturity of writing and coaching approach. It can reveal strengths and also new opportunities for exploration and growth.

How to work with the approach …

Reflective writing can feel challenging for some. For those who are reluctant it can help to be experimental and to write in shorter, focused bursts. Typically, the act of reflective writing is a developmental experience, bringing greater depth and breadth of insights thereby raising consciousness. It can be helpful for supervisees to share their reflections with their supervisor and this can deepen levels of reflexivity still further.

A word of caution

The writing process may surface fears of uncertainty and ineptitude. Therefore, it will be important for the supervisor to blend encouragement and creative challenge such that the process leaves the supervisee feeling 'whole.' Similarly, it is important to create a constructive experience and to celebrate developmental success for novice supervisees engaging in written reflection on practice for the first time.

What other uses are there for this approach?

When working with a supervision group, peers can work in pairs to review examples of reflective writing and offer observations and feedback to help deepen each other's reflection. The approach is equally useful with coaching clients - perhaps using leadership competencies as an analytical frame.

References

Gibbs, G. (1988) *Learning by Doing: A Guide to Teaching and Learning Methods.* Oxford: Further Education Unit. Oxford Polytechnic.

~ ~ ~ ~ ~

27. Rehearse, review, repeat …

Michelle Lucas, Tammy Turner and Carol Whitaker

Where can this be used?				Typical level of supervisee experience required	

When is this used?

This technique is useful for experiential learners. It often appeals to those who want to try out new interventions and get valuable feedback in a safe environment. It is particularly useful where the supervisee faces a number of different options and wants real-time feedback on how each option might impact upon their client.

What is the technique?

The supervisor facilitates a role play involving the supervisee and other members of the group focusing on a particular 'moment' in a client session.

Step 1: Invite the supervisee to give a succinct account of the client context and/or story, clarifying what particularly would be useful to rehearse and what kind of input they want to receive from the group.

Step 2: Elicit specific information about the client; including what they have noticed about how they respond when they are fully engaged and when they are more resistant.

Step 3: Ask the supervisee to set up the room to replicate how they imagine working with their client. Invite them to select who they would like to take the role of client and ensure they determine where the other group members will be positioned.

Step 4: Once everyone is in place, check with the supervisee precisely what they want to practise. Help them refine this until they feel ready to start.

Step 5: Brief the group to observe in detail language, non-verbal responses, energy and intent, how the supervisee intervenes and how the role play client responds. If appropriate to the outcome (Step 1) the group might suggest alternative interventions.

Step 6: Invite the supervisee and role play client to start rehearsal.

Step 7: Intervene and stop the role play at an appropriate point – which could be pre-agreed or which could rely on the supervisor making a judgement call about how the learning is unfolding.

Step 8: Invite the supervisee to reflect on what 'felt good' and what 'felt clunky' and then seek similar feedback from the role play client.

Step 9: Co-create what happens next, perhaps another rehearsal of the same thing, or perhaps try a different approach. After each rehearsal repeat Step 8.

Step 10: By way of conclusion, invite feedback from each of the group members, ensuring their observations focus on the noticeable impact on the role play client, rather than commenting on what worked well (or not) for them personally.

Step 11: Before closing the supervision help both the supervisee and the group member role playing the client to de-role, for example, move chairs, or shake off the role play persona.

Step 12: Allow some time for everyone in the room to reflect on what they will apply to their own practice.

How to work with the technique ...

This tends to be most impactful when the rehearsal focuses on a specific moment in a session. For example, practising – how do I share my frustration with a client who keeps cancelling? What do I do when I ask a question and they look at me blankly? There are many different ways of rehearsing and it is best to co-create this with the supervisee. Trying things out with their peers takes courage and designing what happens gives them greater sense of control. Depending on the size of the group and the time available, Step 10 could be integrated more fully by consulting with the group after each rehearsal.

A word of caution

Although similar to teaching techniques, it is not intended that the supervisor correct how the supervisee works. The supervisor only offers observations on cause and effect as outlined in Step 10.

What other uses are there for this technique?

Where the supervisee wants to practise a particular technique, or they want to see how something unfolds in a more extended dialogue, it can be helpful to use 'stop – start'. When the supervisee gets stuck, they 'stop' and invite group members (including the supervisor) to suggest specific alternatives. Once satisfied, the supervisee 'starts' the role play with this new perspective.

This is easily adapted to use with clients, although probably best on an individual basis, in which case the practitioner needs to be both facilitator and role player.

Further reading

Turner, T., Lucas, M. and Whitaker, C. (2018) *Peer Supervision in Coaching and Mentoring: A Versatile Guide for Reflective Practice.* Maidenhead: Routledge, pp. 103–104.

Whitaker, C. and Calleja, A. (2018) *Group Supervision Approaches for Coaching Supervision.* [pdf] Available at: www.whitaker-consulting.co.uk/resources-and-papers [Accessed 2 August 2019].

~ ~ ~ ~ ~

28. Rush writing

Clare Norman

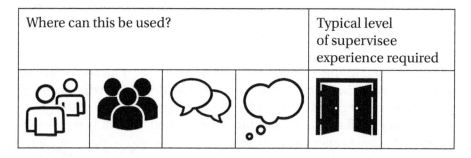

Where can this be used?				Typical level of supervisee experience required	

When is this used?

This technique is used at the end of a supervision session, as a means of reflecting on what they are learning.

What is the technique?

Rush writing requires a person to write continuously for a short period of time, perhaps three minutes, without stopping and without editing. A question or series of questions are posed at the start for the person to write about. The idea is to access the non-editing part of their brain, to access thoughts and ideas that may be underneath the surface.

Step 1: Ask supervisees to write for three minutes on a question or questions that you pose to them such as:

- What stands out most in your mind about the session?
- What really worked well and added value?
- Looking back, what would you have done differently?
- How might you be of greater service to your peers?

- In this moment of reflecting, what are you noticing that you may not have noticed before?
- How do you feel about the session now?
- What creative or intuitive thoughts are you having about how you might work in future in this group?

Write the question(s) on a flip-chart so that they can refer to them as a reminder while they are writing.

Step 2: Brief them to continue writing, no matter what comes into their mind. They can edit later. If their mind goes blank, instruct them to doodle until a new thought comes to mind. Explain that the pen must keep moving at all times to access their sub-conscious thoughts. Reassure them that the rush writing is for their personal use, they will not be asked to reveal their writing to the supervisor or to the group.

Step 3: Time them and stop at three minutes.

Step 4: Ask supervisees what they notice as a result of writing in this way. Encourage them to add a few notes to the end of their written piece.

Step 5: Ask them what learning they wish to share with the group.

How to work with the technique ...

Occasionally, people freeze at the start of this exercise, so encourage them to doodle until a thought pops into their head. You may decide to do the exercise yourself at the same time to role model how to focus.

Encourage them to do this after each session and to keep their notes over time so that they have the opportunity to collate their work and carry out a meta-reflection

What else might need attention?

It is entirely possible that new thoughts might come up at the end of the supervision that need attention. In that case, encourage supervisees either to self-supervise to continue the learning or to reach out for additional support.

A word of caution

The prompt need only be a single question. If you offer many questions at once, the brain will simply work through the questions rather than going deeper on any one. It can be helpful to repeat the question a couple of times before starting the clock to ensure it has been heard.

What other uses are there for this technique?

This can be used any time an individual wants to reflect or get to deeper thoughts about an issue or opportunity. It can be useful for coaching clients and could act as a more meaningful 'aide-memoire' than generating a list of actions.

~ ~ ~ ~ ~

29. Seven conversations

David Clutterbuck

Where can this be used?				Typical level of supervisee experience required	

When is this used?

This approach can be useful where either the supervisee or the supervisor has a sense that they are 'missing something'. Additionally, it is useful when the client's engagement seems good and yet the coach is questioning the client's progress.

What is the approach?

Here the notion is that there are many more conversations to explore than the coaching dialogue itself. Further, each conversation may hold useful information about the coaching dynamic.

According to Lancer et al. (2016) the seven conversations are:

1 The client's conversation with themselves as they prepare.
2 The coach's conversation with themselves as they prepare.

3 The unspoken conversation that takes place in the client's head during the session.
4 The actual conversation between the client and the coach.
5 The unspoken conversation that takes place in the coach's head during the session.
6 The client's conversation with themselves as they reflect.
7 The coach's conversation with themselves as they reflect.

Step 1: Enquire whether exploring what was happening beyond the coaching session itself would be of interest.

Step 2: With consent, the supervisor then evaluates which of the other six conversations might be a useful start point. Note: Steps 3–6 could be done in any order.

Step 3: Consider what the supervisee was thinking but not saying as they worked with their client. Enquire what might have been preventing that expression.

Step 4: Invite the supervisee to use their 'best guess' as to what their client might have been thinking but was not yet prepared to voice and why.

Step 5: Consider what the supervisee knows about how their client prepares and/or reflects on their session. The supervisor probes to clarify what is truly known and what is an assumption.

Step 6: Explore how the supervisee prepares for and reflects on work with this particular client, drawing attention to how similar or different this is to other clients.

Step 7: Pause for the supervisee to reflect on how this exploration is moving their understanding of their initial supervision question.

Step 8: As appropriate the supervisor may offer observation on any of the conversations where information is missing. This could be an opportunity for a line of enquiry at the next coaching session.

How to work with the approach ...

A supervisor is unlikely to use this approach from the start, rather use it as a reference point when noticing that there is an absence of 'grit' in the supervision. The exploration could be done explicitly, sharing the model with the supervisee. Alternatively, the supervisor may hold the seven conversations as a mental map to inform their exploration.

What else might need attention?

This approach often highlights that the supervisee has overlooked what is expected of the client outside of the session. This is an opportunity for stronger contracting on what responsibilities each party has in order to make the coaching a success. Sometimes it highlights an expectation that change needs to happen 'in the room.' They may need reassurance and a reality check that often great insight for clients comes when the coach is not present. If this notion is bothersome for a supervisee it may be helpful for them to do some personal work on their desire for influence and control.

A word of caution

The supervisee may not have explored with their client what happens before and after a session. This could lead to the supervisee maybe answering 'I don't know' to many questions. For the less experienced or less confident supervisee this could easily lead to a sense of incompetence. The tone of the supervisor's voice will determine whether the enquiry is experienced as one of curiosity or of judgement.

What other uses are there for this approach?

Provided that the model is understood by participants it can be used with a group. However, given its emergent nature, this can be awkward to facilitate. Often, when a line of enquiry emerges a deep dive is needed, and the danger is that while one person becomes deeply engaged the remainder disengage.

The model can be useful for coaching clients – the principle of drawing attention to what is being thought about beyond an interaction itself has application to many leadership issues. The same words of caution are as relevant for coaching clients as for supervisees.

Reference

Lancer, N., Clutterbuck, D. and Megginson, D. (2016) *Techniques for Coaching and Mentoring*, 2nd ed. London: Routledge.

~ ~ ~ ~ ~

30. Situation-thoughts-consequences

Carmelina Lawton Smith

Where can this be used?				Typical level of supervisee experience required	

When is this used?

This technique highlights for the supervisee how their own thoughts might be affecting or influencing their relationship and activities with a client. They may feel that the relationship is not quite right, or that the client does not like or respect them. It is probably most effective when working with a supervisee who has very negative thoughts about a client, or their own performance. This technique requires a good level of trust and supervisee awareness.

What is the technique?

Step 1: Situation.

Ask the supervisee to explain the scenario/situation/feeling or relationship they wish to explore.

- Tell me a bit about this situation ...
- What prompted you to bring this to supervision?
- What makes this important?
- What is your concern?
- What feelings are you aware of?

Step 2: Thoughts.

- What are you thinking, when you work with this client/situation?
- What is the voice in your head saying?

- What are you stopping yourself saying to the client?
- What thoughts would you prefer not to discuss here?

Step 3: Consequences.

- What are the consequences of these thoughts? (start with a very open question but if an area is not being explored you may want to prompt for focus, e.g. for your behaviour, for your choices, etc.).
- What tends to happen and how might that impact on the coaching?

Step 4: Reframing.

- Which thoughts would help you perform at your best?
- What could be the consequences of thinking in this way?

How to work with the technique ...

At a simple level, the technique can be offered as a structure for the supervision enquiry. More often though, it is useful when following a general exploration, the supervisor hypothesises that the supervisee's concerns or frustrations might be influencing the coaching dialogue. The supervisor's style is important, investigating the thoughts that the supervisee is holding in an honest and non-judgemental way. This is followed by reflection on the possible consequences of those thoughts. In Step 3 and Step 4, the supervisor then encourages even deeper consideration, investigating each thought in more detail. Once thoughts are expressed, there is often a shift in energy and alternative perceptions and thoughts that may be more fruitful for the coaching work can be articulated.

What else might need attention?

If the supervisee is struggling to identify alternative thoughts you may need to suggest hypotheses, e.g. 'Might you be concerned about their opinion of you as a coach?', 'What pressures might your client be under that could be relevant?'.

Another aspect you may want to discuss is the potential for transference (Sandler, 2011). This happens when the supervisee picks up feelings that actually reside in the client. For example, a client who is very frustrated about their lack of promotion may 'transfer' that frustration to the coach. Explain that this can happen and probe with something like: 'Could your feelings be a result of how the client is actually feeling?'

A word of caution

Recognise that the supervisee may not be ready to alter their perception. If no other options are forthcoming after questioning and hypothesising, move on. There may be times where the issue is very sensitive or genuinely bad, under which circumstances there needs to be an acceptance to learn and let go.

What other uses are there for this technique?

An evaluation of thought patterns can be valuable to supervisees as they may not appreciate how much it can affect their coaching practice. They may be anxious about their own performance or be concerned about what a coach 'should do' and such thoughts might, for example, lead to the consequence that they appear unengaged to the client. They may have thoughts about how their client should deal with a situation that they are withholding, but that leads to certain choices in questioning and lines of enquiry.

The supervisee may also find this technique helpful in their own coaching practice when clients demonstrate rigid thought patterns. For example, if the client finds it hard to address difficult conversations that they need to have it can be helpful to investigate what thoughts are associated with this. They may expect conflict or have a fear of being disliked. This thought pattern could then have the consequence that they are seen as lacking assertiveness.

Reference

Sandler, C. (2011) The use of psychodynamic theory in coaching supervision. In T. Bachkirova, P. Jackson, and D. Clutterbuck (Eds.), 2010. *Coaching and Mentoring Supervision*. Maidenhead: McGraw-Hill, Ch. 8, pp. 107–120.

Further reading

Rao, S. (2010) *Happiness at Work*. London: Mc Graw-Hill.

~~~~~
~~~~~

31. Supervising with developmental Action Logics

Claire Davey

Where can this be used?				Typical level of supervisee experience required	

When is this used?

Used to explore a success or challenge brought to supervision, the coach's development and the supervision process.

What are Action Logics?

Action Logics can be described as orientations that inform our experience and shape action in the moment. There are seven Action Logics (see Table 1.4) below, which emerge from deepening levels of self-awareness.

Table 1.4 Torbert and Associates (Torbert, 2004) Seven Action Logics

Action Logics	
1. Opportunist	Wins for self in any way possible
2. Diplomat	Wants to belong and fit in
3. Expert	Focuses on logic and expertise
4. Achiever	Driven by personal and team achievement
5. Redefining	Reframes in unique ways
6. Transforming	Generates organisational and personal transformations
7. Alchemical	Integrates material, spiritual and societal transformations

Source: Copyright © 2019 Global Leadership Associates & Center for Creative Leadership

What is the technique?

Torbert's (2004) work suggests that until the later Action Logics we may be unaware of what drives our actions. Only by observing and witnessing how we orientate ourselves in any given moment does our awareness increase and our potential to self-transform occur.

The intention of the cards is therefore to bring an individual's preferred Action Logic 'states' into awareness and to highlight what other 'states' might be accessible (both in themselves and others). This heightened understanding can reduce unintentional conflict and misunderstanding. In so doing, we can 'help ourselves and others transform beyond the limits of our present assumptions' (Torbert, 2004, p.66).

Step 1: Context and card sort

Invite the supervisee to share their supervision topic, seek clarification as appropriate.

Place all the transformation cards face up on the table/floor and ask the supervisee to select three to five cards that best describe each of the questions below:

- How is your client showing up?
- How are you showing up?

Step 2: Looking though the Action Logics lens

Offer an overview of Action Logics and then invite the supervisee to make visible their two collections of cards. See Figures 1.7 and 1.8.

a Invite the supervisee to look at the first collection of cards and to consider what patterns or themes they notice, e.g. is one Action Logic represented more than any other?

b Experiment with what kind of enquiry the coach would explore with their client when using the Action Logics chosen.

c Using the second card collection, explore with the supervisee what their chosen Action Logics prompt in their awareness.

Step 3: Reflection section

Allow enough time for the supervisee to capture their personal reflections. Once complete invite any closing comments from an individual or process perspective.

Figure 1.7 Collection One (client)

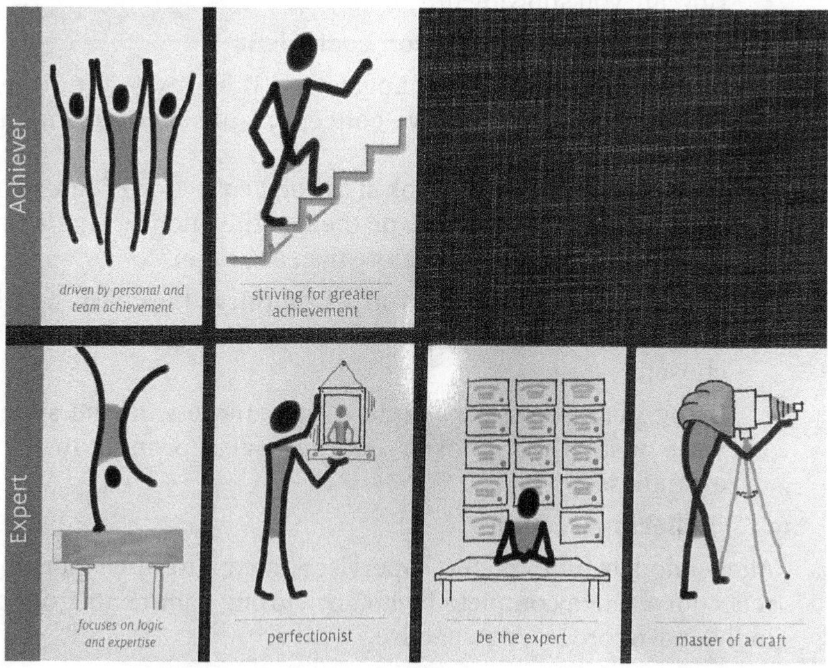

Figure 1.8 Collection Two (supervisee)

How to work with the technique ...

When using the cards for the first time, ensure you provide enough opportunity for the supervisee(s) to become familiar with the pack before selecting cards. It can be helpful to hand the supervisee a few at a time or to arrange them in small random clusters (do not organise them into the Action Logic categories). Note there is a letter on the back of each card that indicates which Action Logic the card represents.

What else might need attention?

Ensure you are well versed in Action Logics and Inquiry in order to get the depth and breadth of dialogue required in the exploration.

If the supervisee wants to explore with more accuracy which Action Logic might be their Centre of Gravity, they could undertake the Global Leadership Profile (GLP) with a certified practitioner.

A word of caution

It is common for individuals to see the Action Logics as hierarchical and therefore a safe environment needs to be created. Further, in a group of mixed maturity the cards may cause individuals to perceive themselves as 'better than/worse than' so referring to a 'state' rather than a 'stage' or 'level' is most effective. The supervisor's role is to hold the group in a grounded state.

What other uses are there for this technique?

This is a really effective exercise for a coach to review their practise, particularly when embarking on accreditation or an organisational coach validation process. In this instance ask the supervisee to review their coaching practise based on the Past, Present and Future by selecting four to five cards for each, working with them to identify patterns and create a narrative to their coaching journey, future focus and development plan.

The cards can also be used in a group setting with appropriate adjustments. Similarly, it could be used with Coaching Clients.

References

Torbert, B. (2004) *Action Inquiry – The Secret of Timely and Transforming Leadership* San Francisco, CA: Berrett-Koehler Publishers.

Global Leadership Associates (2019) Global Leadership Profile (GLP) [online] Available at: www.gla.global/the-glp-overview/ [Accessed 17 October 2019].

Rooke, D. and Torbert, B. (2005) Seven transformations of leadership, *Harvard Business Review*, April 2005, [online] Available at: https://hbr.org/2005/04/seven-transformations-of-leadership [Accessed 17 October 2019].

Further reading

Kegan, R. and Lahey, L.L. (2009) *Immunity to Change: How to overcome it and Unlock the Potential in Yourself and Your Organisation (Leadership for the common good).* Boston, MA: Harvard Business Review Press.

Petrie, N. (2015) *White Paper: The How-To of Vertical Leadership Development Part 2–30 Experts, 3 Conditions and 15 Approaches.* [pdf], Colorado Springs: Center for Creative Leadership. Available at: www.ccl.org/wp-content/uploads/2015/04/verticalLeadersPart2.pdf [Accessed 17 October 2019].

Herdman Barker, E. (2017) *Images in Leadership Development.* [pdf] Available at: www.gla.global/wp-content/uploads/2017/07/Images-of-Leadership-Development.pdf [Accessed 28 October 2019].

Herdman-Barker, E. and Wallis, N.C. (2016) *Imperfect Beauty, Heirarchy and Fluidity in Leadership Development* [pdf] Available at: www.gla.global/wp-content/uploads/2017/02/Imperfect-Beauty-Herdman-Barker-and-Wallis-2016.pdf [Accessed 28 October 2019].

Tobert, W.R. (2017) *The pragmatic impact on leaders and organisations of interventions based on the collaborative developmental action inquiry approach.* Integral Leadership Review, November 2017, pp. 1–16.

Resources

Bill Torbert's resources via his website. Available at: www.williamrtorbert.com/resources/ [Accessed 28 October 2019].

A pack of Transformation Cards is available at: www.gla.global/the-glp/transformations-deck/ [Accessed on 17 October 2019].

~ ~ ~ ~ ~

32. Supervision with LEGO

By Dr. Damian Goldvarg

Where can this be used?				Typical level of supervisee experience required	

When is this used?

For supervisees who have difficulties expressing verbally, LEGO provides an opportunity to explore issues in a creative space.

What is the technique?

LEGO Serious Play enables three modes of communication: verbal, auditory and kinesthetic, providing opportunities for enhanced expression, and deeper listening (Blair and Rillo, 2016). LEGO Serious Play is a systematic method to help solve problems, explore ideas and achieve objectives. It is a structured process where participants proceed through a series of steps to think, build, tell a story, reflect and refine to develop a shared understanding of the issues at hand.

Step 1: The warm up.
Help the supervisee become familiar with the LEGO pieces. For example, ask the supervisee to quickly build a tower (allow just two or three minutes). Once built, invite the supervisee to share a brief story about the tower. Playing background music can help mask the silence while the build progresses, it also provides a creative environment.

Step 2: Develop the supervision question.
LEGO Serious Play can be used in different ways to explore issues such as, the world of the client, the relationship with the client, the desired outcome of the relationship with the client, the supervisee's reactions to the work with the client. Use your judgment to suggest a focus for the supervision LEGO play. For example: 'What if you built a model that represents your inner world, i.e. what was in your mind as you worked with this client?'

Step 3: The build.
Allow the supervisee a short amount of time (probably no longer than 5 minutes) to build a model.

Step 4: The story.
Invite the supervisee to share their story about the model. The story is very important because it generates the material that will be discussed in the session.

Step 5: Embellish the story.
Help the supervisee explore their creation – for example:

- Tell me more about the pieces you chose ...
- What significance are the colours you have used?

- What did you notice about the tactile process of building your model?
- How satisfied are you with what you have created?

Step 6: Developing a desired future (optional).

Offer the opportunity to make changes to the model based on the learning or discussion. For example, the supervisor may ask 'If you could change anything in the model, what would that be?'The process of Steps 3 and 4 are repeated.

Step 7: Close out the work.

Invite the supervisee to take a picture as an aide memoire of the session.

How to work with the technique ...

LEGO offers many different products. For supervision work, the Windows Exploration Bag that contains 48 pieces is recommended. This technique can be used in person or virtually. However, when working virtually regular LEGO might be more accessible and can also be used to good effect. Ideally, virtual work will include video – so that the supervisee can visually share their models. However, it's not essential for the supervisor to see the model; questions can be posed from a place of genuine curiosity instead, e.g. 'What does it look like? Describe what you have created for me? How colourful is your model?'

The steps above are modelled on an individual supervision. With group supervision the supervisee and the group members work simultaneously to build a model that is connected to the supervision question. Everyone shares a story about what they have built, generating alternative insights for the supervisee about the work with their client.

What else might need attention?

Working with LEGO is often a catalyst for a discussion. There may come a point where the LEGO has served its purpose and a different approach to the supervision discussion feels more appropriate.

A word of caution

Some people may initially find working with LEGO naive or childlike and become resistant. The supervisor may need to create a more logical argument to explain the usefulness of creative and kinesthetic learning. Remember, just because you enjoy experimenting with LEGO you need to use the technique judiciously, it may not suit everyone.

What other uses are there for this technique?

LEGO serious play offer a range of toolkits and training for facilitators. See www.lego.com.

Reference

Blair, S. and Rillo, M. (2016) *Serious Work. How to Facilitate Meeting and Workshops Using the LEGO® Serious Play® Method.* London: ProMeet.

Resources

Lego Serious play starter kit. Available at: www.lego.com/en-gb/product/starter-kit-2000414 [Accessed 18 August 2019].

~~~~~

33. Tapping into the client perspective

Lesley Matile

Where can this be used?				Typical level of supervisee experience required	

When is this used?

A supervisee may find this approach helpful should they be curious about their impact on a client. This could relate to an existing or a new client. The supervisor could select this approach if they believe that 'hearing from the client' might provoke useful fresh thinking for the supervisee.

What is the approach?

With the supervisee listening with curiosity, each group member speaks directly to the supervisee sharing how they are experiencing the client: coach relationship through personally crafted impact statements. This 'one step removed' feedback often enables powerful messages to be
~~~~~

offered. The supervisee, equipped with new insights, can then decide on their next steps.

Step 1 (a): Invite the supervisee to introduce the coach/client relationship they wish to discuss.
Engaging with the group, the supervisor encourages questions that focus on Mode 1 (bringing the client into the room) and 3 (the relationship between coach and client) in Hawkins and Smith's (2006) Seven-Eyed Model. For example:

- How did the coaching come about?
- Describe the client and what you notice about them
- How do you feel about this client?
- What do you notice about the nature of this relationship?
- What do you think is going on which is not being said?
- What do you think may be getting in the way of a really productive relationship?

Step 1(b): Meanwhile, the supervisor encourages group members to listen carefully to the language and body language used by the supervisee; and to notice how they are reacting themselves.

Step 2: The supervisor agrees with the supervisee the exact wording of the question(s) for the group members. For example:

1 What is it like being coached by me?
2 What opinions have you formed about me personally?

Step 3: The supervisor advises the group to respond as though they were the client regarding how they are experiencing the coach and the coaching relationship. Each group member answers the specified question with only 'I' statements looking directly at the supervisee as they do. They can share what they imagine they would think and feel or if this would duplicate an earlier response, they can offer a different but equally plausible reaction to help add to the variety of perspectives.

Step 3(b): The supervisee listens without responding and notes what resonates for them.

Step 4: After each group member has spoken, the supervisor encourages the supervisee to reflect, while others remain silent. When appropriate, the supervisor poses a question such as 'What new helpful insights have you had?' or 'What in particular resonates for you?'

Step 5: To conclude, the supervisor then asks:

'With these fresh thoughts about what may be going on from the client's perspective, what might you do in subsequent sessions?'

How to work with this approach ...

From the perspective of flow, it is most useful if the approach is introduced at the outset of the supervision process. The supervisee can then give their informed consent to this approach without significant explanation at the point of it being suggested.

When crafting their impact statements, the supervisor should remind group members that the supervisee is not seeking advice, or comments about the wider system, rather to understand what possible impact their approach may have on the client (in so far as they understand them).

The supervisee need not respond to each comment in turn, rather process out loud only what resonates as most valuable.

What else might need attention?

One might expect a mixture of positive and less positive comments, a bias in any one direction might hold information about the current group dynamics. This could provide useful material for a group process review.

A word of caution

As always, the supervisor needs to gauge the level of trust in the group and manage the level of candour according to the resilience of the supervisee. The supervisor needs to invite the group members to speak boldly but with sensitivity, holding the tension of stimulating helpful new thinking and appreciating that recognising potentially negative impacts can be difficult to hear. Group members may feel they are being judgmental, and that is what is being asked for!

What other uses are there for this approach?

With appropriate contracting this could be used between coaches and their clients where feedback is expressly requested.

Reference

Hawkins, P. and Smith, N. (2006) *Coaching, Mentoring and Organisational Consultancy Supervision and Development*. Maidenhead: Open University Press.

~ ~ ~ ~ ~

34. The supervisor in 'tutor' mode

David Clutterbuck

Where can this be used?				Typical level of supervisee experience required	

When is this used?

The 'tutor' role can be seen as separate and parallel to good supervisory practice. Within our 'normative' role, sharing information may be ethically appropriate in order to improve the coach's practice and/or prevent harm to them, their client or other stakeholders.

What is the approach?

Supervisors often have a wealth of experience as coaches both in their own right and vicariously through their supervisees, it's inevitable therefore that the supervision conversation evokes numerous associations in the supervisor's mind. Deciding whether, and how, to use those associations can determine whether the intervention is a distraction or an invaluable source of insight.

Some courses teach us to boundary such thoughts. Yet those thoughts continue to exist, making it possible they will exert an influence outside our awareness. Gestalt teaches us to recognise and use our own physical and emotional reactions. Tutoring goes one step further and obliges us to consider the relevance and utility of our own experiences and expertise.

Step 1: The supervisor takes a grounded and adult mind set to consider 'How do I help the coach become wiser?' They will weigh up honestly whether their sharing of information is done with the client's benefit in mind or their own desire to appear knowledgeable.

Step 2: This is followed by some in-the-moment reflexivity 'What context does the supervisee appear to lack, that I have, and which would help them become wiser about the issue they have brought?'Note: Context may take many forms.

- *Formative* examples: evidence from research about good coaching practice, an alternative tool or technique, an approach tried by another coach in similar circumstances, a model from leadership theory or behavioural science, or a similar dilemma that you have encountered.
- *Normative* examples reference to ethical standards or to consequences of accepting an assignment that has the potential to harm a client or their organisation.
- *Restorative* examples might open up the patterns of self-doubt that commonly affect coaches at transition points in their competence (and which everyone assumes to be an experience unique to them).

Step 3: Check in with the supervisee about the potential usefulness of your mentoring role. For example:

- Would it be helpful right now to look at how other coaches have tackled this, or better to stick with our current line of exploration?
- In our contract we agreed it might be helpful on occasion to share my own perspective, my sense is that now could be one of those occasions ... what's your sense?
- I notice a level of concern arising in me, would it be OK if I shared my perspective to explore how it affects your thinking?

Step 4: Consider, 'What would be the best way to gift them that contextual understanding?' Each situation will be unique, however, perhaps draw attention to the apparent 'gap' you have noticed; be empathic about why their experience might be missing; own your reactions within the supervision dialogue (see the parallel with conversation 5 of the Seven Conversations pp. 84–86); and demonstrate humility that you may have misread their perception.

Step 5: Once the information has been shared, check in with how the supervisee's perspective is changing and/or invite them to engage in further reflection before the next session.

How to work with the approach ...

While the supervisor may offer tutoring' within a supervision session, it should not be seen as a substitute for it. The core of this approach is to gift 'just enough' information to be helpful (and responsible) without undermining or overwhelming the supervisee. This requires a cautious and iterative approach, not a monologue; check-in with both oneself and the supervisee about the timeliness of the intervention.

A word of caution

The supervisee, who feels stuck, may default to asking for advice. Advice differs from context-giving in that it implies a judgement on the other person and their circumstances. It also implies a directive exertion of power-of-expertise. It can therefore help to draw attention to the parallel of what the supervisee would do, if asked for advice by one of their clients. This leads naturally to greater awareness and clarity about the contextual information needed to move forward.

What other uses are there for this approach?

The effect of this approach is to make both parties aware of gaps in their perceptions and to share information in service of the supervisee. Provided that the supervisee can routinely work from a secure base, the approach could be applied similarly with their clients.

Further reading

Clutterbuck, D., Kochan, F., Lunsford, L., Dominguez, N. and Haddock-Millar, J. (2017) *The Sage Handbook of Mentoring*. London: Sage.

~ ~ ~ ~ ~

35. The threes Cs: contract, competence and client's best interest

Marie Faire

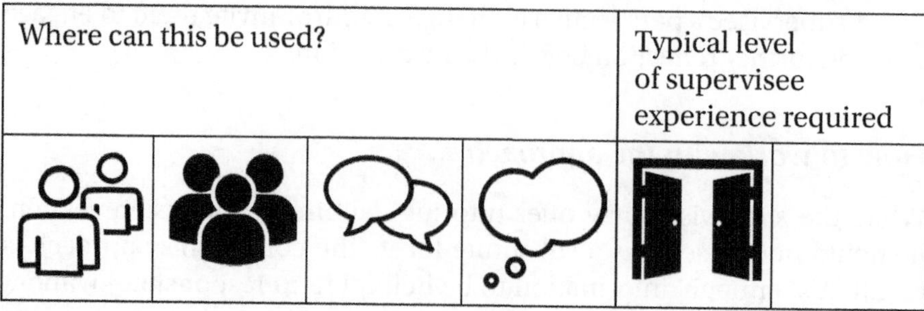

Where can this be used?	Typical level of supervisee experience required

When is this used?

This technique is used when the supervisee expresses concern (or the supervisor is concerned) about whether they are overstepping their role as a 'coach' into a different helping practitioner role (counselling, therapy, mentoring, consultant). They might be seeking reassurance from the supervisor asking 'Is what am I doing/want to do coaching?'

What is the enquiry?

While there are some situations that would be better suited to a particular helping strategy, the search for precise definition of what any given practitioner does, presupposes that we could produce definitions that would be isolated and separate. This technique offers three questions to help generate a more fruitful discussion concerning *how* we determine professional practice rather that *what* it is called.

Step 1: Questions relating to the contract.

- Is what you are doing within the contract between you and your client?
- Is what you are working on what you agreed you both would work on?
- If not, is it appropriate and in your gift to re-negotiate the contract?

Step 2: Questions about competence (capability and capacity).

- Do you have the competence and capability to work in this way?
- Do you have the capacity to address this issue appropriately?

Step 3: Questions about the client's best interest.

Is it in the client's best interest?

- Is it appropriate for this client to work on this issue with you?
- Is it appropriate for this client to work on this issue in this context?

Step 4: Close out.

- Explore what actions will be taken and the learning that can inform future situations.

How to work with the enquiry …

Explore the supervisee's answer to each question in turn, as well as holistically.

Much has been written about the importance of getting the contract right and then delivering what has been agreed. (Block, 1981; Fielder and Starr, 2008). So, while the supervisee may have answered Questions 2 and 3 positively if the work is not contracted (or re-contracted) for, then the supervisee has no business going there.

The question about competency is more than what we are 'qualified' to do. It is about asking the supervisee as a professional to use their 'internal supervisor' (Casement, 1985) to check their own competency and capacity for doing the work. The work may be in the contract yet if the coach is not competent (skill) or not capable (i.e. without the resources, time, or energy) then they need to refer.

Finally, every client is part of a system and we need to ensure that what the supervisee does attends to the client's best interest in the ecology of that system. So, the work may be contracted for and the coach may be competent, but it may not be right to proceed. For example, this may occur when both parties work for the same organisation and the issue is of a deeper or personal nature. In other words – just because we can, doesn't mean we should.

The metaphor of a three-legged stool works well – if one leg is missing, the stool falls over.

Likewise, the answer to all three questions needs to be 'Yes.' If not, then it may be necessary to support your supervisee to consider how they will refer their client elsewhere or to boundary the work that they do with their client.

What else might need attention?

You may want to discuss issues arising about re-contracting and what development issues might be helpful to work on.

A word of caution

If the answer to Question 2 is 'No' and the answer to Question 3 is 'Yes,' it would be necessary for the coach to refer. This can happen where the practitioner does not have the required expertise, but the client is insistent that they want to work with them on it 'regardless.'

What other uses are there for this enquiry?

This enquiry is specifically oriented to the coach:client relationship; it could in certain circumstance also apply to the supervisee: supervisor relationship. It does not easily have wider application.

References

Block, P. (1981) *Flawless Consulting*, New York: Jossey-Bass.

Casement, P. (1985) *On Learning from the Patient*. London: Tavistock Publications.

Fielder, J.H. and Starr, L.M. (2008) What's the big deal about coaching contracts? *International Journal of Coaching in Organisations* 6(4), pp. 15–27.

Further reading

Faire, M. (2013) The three Cs of professional practice. *AICTP Journal*, November 2013, Issue 6, pp. 13–15.

~ ~ ~ ~ ~

36. Tree perspectives: growing your practice through creative reflective writing

Jackee Holder

Where can this be used?				Typical level of supervisee experience required	

When is this used?

The reflective nature of the exercise is explorative, intuitive and reflective. It can be applied to almost any theme or issue. In the example below the questions are focused on a developmental exploration of the supervisee's coaching or supervision practice.

What is the technique?

This technique is inspired by the quote from St. Bernard of Clairvaux:

'Trees and stones will teach you that which you can never learn from Masters.'

Taking time to stand back and reflect is a positive practice to embrace. Trees, nature images and metaphors provide particularly stimulating writing prompts. Trees remind us of the natural elements of growth and are associated with generative metaphors including balance, alignment, rhythms and cycles, loss and resilience. They serve to ignite right brain thinking allowing exploration of issues and themes from a more organic and intuitive perspective.

Step 1: Collect ten or more varied images of trees (see Figure 1.9), and create picture cards. Lay out the images so that all are in view.

Step 2: Invite the supervisee to select an image that appeals to them. Help them move into a reflective space. For example; 'Consider what parallels, connections, similarities or differences the tree stimulates in relation to your practice ....'

Step 3: As you notice the supervisee moving into a more creative space, move the discussion towards the focus for supervision. Typically, the supervisee may need only one or two prompts; here are some examples:

- What aspect of your practice does this tree remind you of and why?
- Metaphorically, how is this tree a reflection of how you currently feel about your practice? How would you like to be feeling? What specific aspect of where you want to be is reflected in your tree?

Figure 1.9 An example image of tree for use as a picture card

- What is the tree reflecting back to you about the issue you have chosen to focus on?
- Imagine your tree sharing its wisdom with you. What ideas does it have of how to grow your practice and how to nourish your well-being?
- If your inner wise self was next to you on a branch of this tree, what would they be saying to you right now that would be encouraging and motivating about your progress and growth?
- How could this tree be a resource to you in the future?

Step 4: Encourage the supervisee to free write in an unhurried fashion, allow their thoughts and ideas to unravel. Note: once in flow one's sense of time evaporates. Set an alarm if a time boundary is important.

Step 5: Make some additional time and space to reflect afterwards on the writing along with any thoughts and ideas that are sparked by the tree image. Make a note of these.

How to work with this technique?

The approach is organic and fluid, intentionally connecting supervisees to their personal power and resourcefulness and strengthening the internal supervisor. You may need to remind the supervisee to suspend the need for 'right' answers.

This exercise could be done be as pre-work, post-work or an activity with an individual or group session. When working virtually share the images on screen. You can adapt the exercise for example the image could be chosen at random or consciously. Have some fun with it! Perhaps place a random tree image in an envelope and stick it under each chair?

What else might need attention?

A short free writing exercise can help people to warm up. Be explicit about not worrying about grammar or punctuation. The prompts help provide focus and direction but also freedom to go with whatever emerges.

A word of caution

Set-up is important. Before offering this to a supervisee, be sure to try it out yourself to get a feel for how it works and to notice any resistance. A break away from logical thinking can create anxiety for some people so introduce the exercise with a light touch.

What other uses are there for this technique?

This technique can be used as a prompt with almost any supervision discussion. It is a way of mining for different insights and perspectives on an issue using language, imagery and visualisation. It stimulates the imagination and encourages thinking outside of the box. The technique can be adapted for use with individual and team coaching clients.

Further reading

Holder, J. (2013) *49 Ways to Write Yourself Well: The Science and Wisdom of Reflective Writing and Journaling*. Brighton: Stepbeach Press.

Holder, J. (2014) Imagine a world without trees. [online article] 28 August. Available at: https://welldoing.org/article/imagine-world-without-trees [Accessed 6 September 2019].

Holder, J. (2014) The write stuff. *Coaching Today*, January 2014, pp. 28–33.

Holder, J. (2014) Notes to self. *Coaching at Work*, 9(2), pp. 38–41.

Holder, J. (2014) *Slow Hand*. London: MSLEXIA, pp. 18–19.

Holder, J. (2015) The wisdom of trees. [online article] 29 July. Available at: https://welldoing.org/article/wisdom-trees [Accessed 6 September 2019].

Holder, J. and Levin, S. (2016) *Writing with Fabulous Trees: A Writing Map for Parks, Gardens and Other Green Spaces*. London: Writing Maps.

Holder, J. (2019) Creative forms of reflective and expressive writing in coaching supervision. In E. Turner and S. Palmer (Eds.), *The Heart of Coaching Supervision: Working with Reflection and Self Care*. Abingdon: Routledge. Ch. 7.

Turner, T., Lucas, M., and Whitaker, C. (2018) *Peer Supervision in Coaching and Mentoring: A versatile Guide for Reflective Practice*. Abingdon: Routledge, pp. 34–35 & 46.

~ ~ ~ ~ ~

37. Trial triumph trivia

Clare Norman

Where can this be used?				Typical level of supervisee experience required	

When is this used?

This technique is used at the beginning of a group supervision session, to get everyone's voice in the room so that they are present to do the work. This also helps to build trust as by sharing what's been difficult, what's been successful and something fun, it shows the gamut of our experiences and creates a more level playing field.

What is the technique?

Step 1: Set up the technique by placing it into context. For example, reminding them much may have happened since the group was last connected in the supervision session; reminding them that all sorts of experiences are welcome and can provide learning in the supervision space.

Step 2: Brief the group to share one trial (something that has been difficult or not gone well), one triumph (something they feel was successful) and one piece of trivia (something fun).

Step 3: Give them a minute or so to reflect.

Step 4: Invite them to talk about their trial, their triumph and their trivia; this could be done in turn around the circle, or group members can contribute when they feel ready. Depending on time, you can keep this brief - purely as an exercise to get everyone's voice in the room - or you can go deeper into the learning for each of them.

Step 5: Where you decide to go deeper, you might ask:

- What have you learned about yourself as a result of the trial? And the triumph? The trivia?
- What do you need to let go of from the trial? What do you need in order to move on? How might we support you in that today?
- What of your strengths contributed to your triumph? How will you celebrate the triumph? Who needs to know about the triumph?
- What parallels are there between your trivia and your coaching practice? What do you notice about that?

How to work with the technique ...

For the supervisor this can be a helpful way of getting a 'heads-up' about what each supervisee might bring as a supervision question. Certainly, the information gained here could be used as a prompt should the supervisee be uncertain what to bring. It is also an opportunity to spot developmental themes amongst the group, which could be used as a line of enquiry later in the session.

Supervisees get worried about saying something that is interesting enough. Perhaps their trial doesn't feel 'difficult enough' compared to others, or perhaps it feels difficult to share it because it felt 'harder' than the other examples. The same goes for the triumph: they may not feel that it is worthy of being called a triumph. The trivia may not feel interesting enough. They often compare themselves with others in the group, which can be detrimental to group dynamics. It can be helpful therefore to 'call' this possibility as you set the exercise up.

Interestingly, these comparisons could be used as a point of reflection as it is often a parallel process with what happens when they are working with groups themselves. You could ask:

- How does it feel to expose your trials, triumphs and trivia in this group?
- What does your feeling of XXX suggest that we need to be aware of when working with groups?
- How do we enable individuals in groups to claim their full power rather than to minimise themselves and their experiences?

A word of caution

If supervisees repeatedly minimise themselves in front of the group, you may challenge them to centre themselves, claiming their potency, and start the sentence again, this time without minimising.

If supervisees repeatedly show-boat, you could ask them and the group to reflect on the impact that has on the group.

What other uses are there for this technique?

This can be used in any group work, including team coaching.

38. Use of attachment theory in supervision

Henry Campion

Where can this be used?				Typical level of supervisee experience required	

When is this used?

Relationship is core to a coach's work. Attachment theory provides a framework for the supervisee to understand both their own and their clients' patterns of relating to those around them. It is for all supervisees who wish to deepen their understanding of themselves, their relationships with clients, and their clients' behaviour in the workplace.

What is the approach?

Our 'attachment pattern' develops in early childhood. It is internalised as a lifelong working model for relationship which, while it cannot be fundamentally changed, may be shaped by subsequent experience. Secure attachment is associated with self-confidence and trust in others. With the more insecure, wary attachment patterns (known as self-reliant, anxious and (rarely) fearful – see Figure 1.10), there are respectively reduced levels of trust in others, or increased levels of anxiety, or both.

A secure attachment figure gives people a strong and pervasive feeling of security and so encourages them to value and continue the relationship. So, as supervisors it is worth exploring with the supervisee what it takes to be a secure attachment figure. This is useful for establishing a productive supervision relationship and in turn helps the supervisee do the same for their clients.

Step 1: Setting up an appropriate contract.
Due to the potential depth of discussion and discovery, any use of attachment theory should be properly explained and covered by the initial supervision contract. While the supervisee will gain insights into their general patterns of relating (see Step 2) the

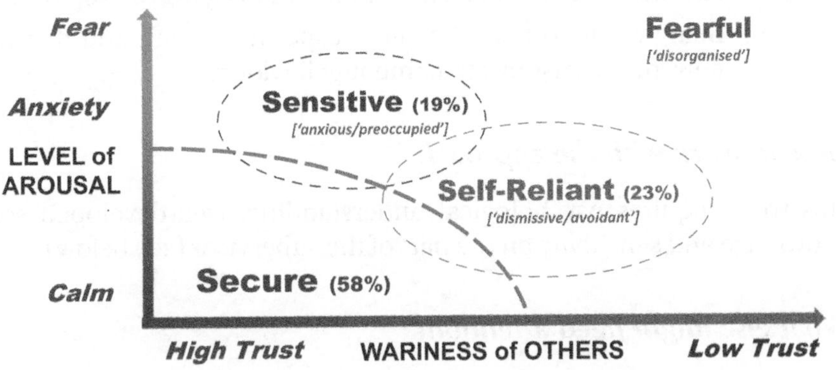

Figure 1.10 Attachment patterns in adults

purpose is to apply these insights specifically to their professional work as a coach. Set boundaries to reflect that.

Step 2: Understanding the supervisee's own pattern of relating.

At the outset of the supervision, invite the supervisee to fill in a family history form briefly outlining their relationships with grandparents, parents, siblings, significant others and themselves. Reflect together on the patterns of relationship within the family system, how these have evolved over the three generations, and how this might have affected their own patterns of relating.

Step 3: Deepen the supervisee's awareness of how their attachment pattern impacts their clients.

Help the supervisee understand more about attachment theory and the different patterns of secure and insecure attachment (Brown et al. (2019). For an explanation available online, see Drake (2009) pp 49–54). Then prompt them to consider how their own attachment pattern might be reflected in their behaviour towards their clients.

Step 4: Explore client behaviours through the lens of attachment.

A coach modelling a secure attachment figure can provide a safe haven and a secure base for the client, enabling them to explore potentially difficult issues with greater trust and confidence. Depending on their background and experience, and on the nature and purpose of the coaching engagement, the supervisee may also be able to work directly with attachment issues by:

- Reflecting on, making sense of and working with the attachment behaviours of themselves and their clients.
- Understanding and managing the behaviour of an insecurely attached client, for example responding to 'resistance' by being curious about the need for it rather than trying to overcome it.
- Being ready to help the client experiment with and develop new, more trusting attachment behaviours.

How to work with the approach

This work requires psychological understanding, well-developed self-knowledge and sensitivity on the part of the supervisor (see below).

What else might need attention?

This approach relies on the supervisee's ability to interpret the feelings and sensations they experience in the course of a coaching session, and to distinguish between those and the ones they are picking up from the client. It can therefore be useful to encourage them to develop their mindful awareness practice.

A word of caution

- Attachment theory and its application is a huge subject. Yet even a basic understanding of attachment theory can be useful, as long as we remember it is not about labelling people.
- The supervisor's own attachment pattern can have a profound effect on the supervisory relationship. (Beinhart and Clohessy, 2017, p. 38.) Supervisors need to be familiar with any insecurity of attachment in themselves and be able to take account of it in their supervision relationships.

What other uses are there for this approach?

This description applies to individual work. For group work, ideally it would be used where all members understand Attachment theory.

References

Beinhart, H. and Clohessy, S. (2017) *Effective Supervisory Relationships: Best Evidence and Practice*. Hoboken, NJ: Wiley-Blackwell.

Brown, P., Hasanie, S., and Campion, H. (2019) Neurobehavioural supervision: applied neuroscience in the context of coaching supervision. In J. Birch and P. Welch (Eds.) *Coaching Supervision: Advancing Practice, Changing Landscapes*. Abingdon: Routledge, Ch. 3, pp. 35–52.

Drake, D.B. (2009) Using attachment theory in coaching leaders: The search for a coherent narrative. *International Coaching Psychology Review*, 4(1), pp. 49–58. Available at: http://study.sagepub.com/sites/default/files/using_attachment_theory_in_coaching_leaders.pdf [Accessed 20 August, 2019].

Further reading

Bowlby, J. (2005) *A Secure Base*. Abingdon: Routledge Classics.

Brown, P. and Brown, V. (2012) *Neuropsychology for Coaches: Understanding the Basics*. Maidenhead: Open University Press.

Cozolino, L. (2014). *The Neuroscience of Human Relationships: Attachment and the Developing Social Brain*. New York: W.W Norton & company.

Mikulincer, M. and Shaver, P. (2016). *Attachment in Adulthood: Structure, Dynamics and Change*, 2nd ed. New York: The Guilford Press.

~ ~ ~ ~ ~

39. Using AI in supervision

David Clutterbuck

Where can this be used?				Typical level of supervisee experience required	

What is AI?

AI or Artificial Intelligence is a rapidly developing technology that supports, and in some cases may supplant, humans in carrying out a wide variety of tasks. Unlike coachbots, which simply employ algorithms to carry out routine, predictable tasks, AI learns from each interaction, constantly adapting to its environment.

AI is also different from virtual tools such as ProReal, which uses the medium of virtual reality to facilitate the supervision discussion. Thinking is done by the human beings, not the technology.

When is this used?

AI generally still has many challenges to overcome before it can replace coaches or supervisors generally, but advances are happening rapidly. This is an emerging concept in both coaching and supervision, so what follows is extrapolation from current developments in the application and development of Artificial Intelligence.

What is the approach?

At more complex levels of interaction, like the coaching supervision partnership, practitioners will have to create working partnerships with AI systems – as if they had a shadow consultant in the room.

There are two main scenarios, where AI is used as an aide for the supervisee and the supervisor:

1 The coach brings his or her issue to the supervision session. The AI provides support by:
   - Monitoring and sensing patterns in body language, conversational tone and repeated use of similar significant words or phrases.

- Linking back to previous supervision sessions to identify patterns of issues.
- Responding to references to literature or theoretical models by searching the internet and/or the supervisor's files to have them ready, should the supervisor choose to share them.
- At the end of the supervision session, suggest themes for summarising (which can also be helpful for the supervisor's subsequent reflections).

2 The coach also has an AI assistant, which has been present at his or her coaching sessions. The two AIs may interrogate and support each other during the supervision conversation. One of the benefits of this arrangement is that the supervisee and supervisor can call up and replay at will the exact words a client has used. The two AIs may also look together for signs of parallel process, for example, body language of the coach in supervision emulating that of the client in the coaching session.

How to work with the approach ...

Once both supervisor and supervisee genuinely see the AI as a welcome resource it should be possible for both human intelligences and artificial intelligences to work in harmony. Just as satnavs have become an accepted and welcome part of our driving experience, so too will we find a way of integrating additional input from AI into a supervision session.

Among the challenges of working with AI are:

- Being overwhelmed by information – having a 'voice in the ear' can be a major distraction, making it harder to be client-centred and fully present.
- Learning to trust the virtual partner.
- Balancing reliance on the AI's observations with reliance on our own instincts and wisdom.

A word of caution

Learning how to work with AI will require a whole new set of yet-to-be-defined competences. But the potential to enrich every session is significant.

While AI may at some point have the technical capability to hold a supervision session for a supervisee without human intervention, it is envisaged that for the time being AI will supplement rather than replace the coaching supervisor. We see supervision as a relational process and while humans may develop relationships with AI, knowing that the 'other' is an Artificial Intelligence will alter the quality of that relationship.

What else might need attention?

Given the newness of this way of working we are limited in knowing what working with AI might involve. However, we might assume that contracting will need to take into account that a third party (the AI) is part of the process. Where the AI stores information arising from the supervision work there will need to be clarity on how this data is handled and protected.

What other uses are there for this approach?

Experiments with AI therapists reveal that they can be more accurate in diagnosis and perceived as less judgemental than their human counterparts (Tieu, 2015).

Very basic coaching – predictable, relating to frequent patterns of circumstance and behaviour – can already be provided by coachbots and basic AI.

Reference

Tieu, A. (2015) We now have an AI therapist, and she's doing her job better than humans can. [online] Available at: https://futurism.com/uscs-new-ai-ellie-has-more-success-than-actual-therapists [Accessed 25 September 2019].

Further reading

Birch, J. and Welch, P. (2019) *Coaching Supervision: Advancing Practice, Changing Landscapes*. Abingdon: Routledge.

Hall, M. (2017) Herts NHS trust trials CoachBot digital coaching. *Coaching at Work*, 12 (6), p. 7.

Whitehouse, E. (2019) Would you let a Chatbot coach you? [online] Available at: www.peoplemanagement.co.uk/long-reads/articles/would-let-chatbot-coach-you [Accessed 25 September 2019].

~ ~ ~ ~ ~

40. Using vision boards

Liz Ford

Where can this be used?				Typical level of supervisee experience required	

When is this used?

Vision boarding is particularly relevant to the developmental purpose of supervision (Hawkins and Smith, 2006). It can help the supervisee gain motivation towards a goal or vision such as completing accreditation, starting a coaching business or planning their coaching development. The technique can also be used for a more resourcing purpose to explore boundaries, work-life balance and wellbeing.

What is the technique?

Vision boarding involves creating a visual representation of a goal, desire or place/state you want to get to. When this is placed in a space where you can look at it regularly, you are essentially doing short visualisation exercises throughout the day. It helps to focus the mind and can create incredible energy and motivation.

Step 1: Help the supervisee decide what the vision board is for, identify its purpose.

Step 2: Discuss what size of vision board is wanted and what the base will be (cork board, scrap book, art canvas, flipchart paper ...).

Step 3: Assist the supervisee to collect pictures, quotes, symbols, mementos and photos that capture the essence of what they want to achieve, how they want to feel and the steps they need to take.

Step 4: Encourage the supervisee to assemble the resources collected into a collage.

Step 5: As the supervisee creates their board, the supervisor can help by exploring their choices with questions such as:

- What would you like to achieve?
- How would you feel if you achieved that?
- What symbolises that for you?
- What would that look like?
- How do these link?
- What amount of space would you like this to take up in your work/life

Step 6: When finished, encourage the supervisee to display the vision board in a place where they will see it often.

How to work with the technique ...

It can be useful to have vision board examples and a variety of crafty resources available in a supervision session to assist the supervisee to get started. If working remotely, then talking through examples you can share on screen is helpful. It's worth encouraging the supervisee to be as creative as they wish, adding anything relevant that means something to them. It's important that they feel drawn to the creation so content, colour and layout are all important. For example, a supervisee who likes clean lines and order, could mirror this on their vision board using defined areas for each business quarter. Conversely those who want more fun and spontaneity in their practice or life, might set their board out quite differently. If a supervisee wants more space in their diary, or their coaching sessions its important that their board reflects this and isn't rammed full of words, sayings or pictures.

Creating a vision board is usually started in a supervision session and continued at home afterwards. Often the supervisees will send the supervisor a picture of how it is developing so that it can be referred to in future sessions.

Although it is possible to use online tools such as Pinterest to create a collage, the tactile process of choosing pictures and symbolic references and sticking them in place can be more powerful. Plus having the vision board in plain sight can have a bigger impact.

A word of caution

The purpose of a vision board is to help the supervisee move towards something. Just having it displayed won't make this happen, actions will also be needed. Supervision discussions can help the supervisee really understand what they want to achieve and why, as well as the steps they need to make to get there. The board will then not only represent the destination, but also the journey.

What other uses are there for this technique?

This technique can also be used for individual and team coaching.

Reference

Hawkins, P. and Smith, N. (2006) *Coaching, Mentoring and Organisational Consultancy Supervision and Development*. Maidenhead: Open University Press.

Further reading

Ford, L. and Matthews, K. (2019) Using vision boards in supervision. *Coaching Perspectives*. July 2019, Issue 22, pp. 44–45.

Schuck, C. and Wood, J. (2011) *Inspiring Creative Supervision*. London: Jessica Kingsley Publishers.

~ ~ ~ ~ ~

41. Writing the labyrinth

Jackee Holder

Where can this be used?				Typical level of supervisee experience required	

When is this used?

Most useful for reflecting on client sessions, for thinking through a supervision problem or dilemma. It is a useful tool for changing perspective on an issue and presents a different approach to supervision themes. It can also be used to reflect on broader matters for example, one's coaching style or coaching development.

What is the technique?

The labyrinth is two printable templates that facilitate individual written reflection (see Resources below). Through completing each one in different directions different thinking is generated. *Writing into* the labyrinth you unravel your presenting issue. Then you explore solutions and new ideas through *writing out* from the centre back to the entrance of the labyrinth.

Step 1: Set aside some quiet time where you can work uninterrupted – allow a minimum of 20 minutes so that you can complete your reflections thoroughly.

Step 2: Using a pencil (or coloured pens if you prefer) begin with the page title 'Writing In.' Start at the entrance of the labyrinth and following the pathway write about the matter you are reflecting upon inside the labyrinth pathway. Be descriptive and include all the facets that come to mind, what you have done so far, current impact, include how you were feeling about it at the time. When you have exhausted all that you can write, if there is still space until you reach the centre, draw a line to take you there.

Step 3: Metaphorically 'stand back' and look at what you have written, digest it as though you were meeting it for the first time. Capture any new thoughts that emerge.

Step 4: Now turn to the 'Writing Out' page. Starting at the centre, repeat the exercise this time working outwards. Write about your current thoughts and feelings and start to include what ideas you have for solutions or alternative ways to progress or respond to your issue. When you have exhausted all that you can write, if there is still space until the entrance, draw a line to take you there.

Step 5: Repeat Step 3 then consider what you notice now and what sense you are making about the matter you reflected upon.

Step 6: Make a note of your thoughts and reflections along with any actions you intend to take, including what additional reflection or supervision could be beneficial.

Step 7: File your work so that you can add to your reflections over time. Periodically review a number of reflections to see what patterns you notice. Good questions to ask yourself could be:

- How is writing the labyrinth different to other reflective approaches?
- How does this help me shift perspective and generate new ideas?
- What do I tend to reflect upon most often?
- What do I tend not to reflect upon?
- What happens to my intentions to act/work differently over time?

How to work with the technique ...

It often generates a sense of surprise and unexpected solutions tend to emerge through the active reflection of writing around the labyrinth. By working with it, individuals discover how they can best utilise it, many noticing a preferred direction of working.

It can be particularly useful as a preparation and reflection upon a supervision session itself. For example, the supervisee might complete it privately at the start of the session, then prior to session close use it to capture their learning.

What else might need attention?

This tool when used routinely or used alongside other reflective activities can help supervisees map what kind of issues they tend to reflect upon, or not. These themes provide useful insights for sharing with a professional supervisor to stretch their reflective practice further.

A word of caution

Reflection is valuable, and our intention here is to prompt a difference in how we practice. Step 6 of reflecting back on what you have written is an essential component of the process.

What other uses are there for this technique?

This can be used in groups as an arrivals exercise with each group member clarifying what they would like to bring to supervision. If reflecting as a group at the end of a session you might invite individuals to share the impact of engaging in the exercise rather than sharing the content of their reflections. Groups often marvel at the cathartic experience of physically moving the paper as they complete the labyrinth, it serves to connect the group with a more reflective and creative energy.

The labyrinth template could also be offered to clients to aide their reflection.

Further reading

Holder, J. (2013) *49 Ways to Write Yourself Well: The Science and Wisdom of Reflective Writing and Journaling*. Brighton: Stepbeach Press.

Holder, J. (2014) The write stuff. *Coaching Today*, January 2014, pp. 28–33.

Holder, J. (2014) Notes to self. *Coaching at Work*, 9(2), pp. 38–41.

Holder, J. (2014) *Slow Hand*. London: MSLEXIA, pp. 18–19.

Holder, J. and Levin, S. (2016) *Writing with Fabulous Trees: A Writing Map for Parks, Gardens and Other Green Spaces*. London: Writing Maps.

Holder, J. (2019) Creative forms of reflective and expressive writing in coaching supervision. In. E. Turner and S. Palmer (Eds.), *The Heart of Coaching Supervision: Working with Reflection and Self Care*. Abingdon: Routledge, Ch. 7, pp. 125–146.

Turner, T., Lucas, M., and Whitaker, C. (2018) *Peer Supervision in Coaching and Mentoring: A versatile Guide for Reflective Practice*. Abingdon: Routledge, pp. 34–35 & 46.

Resources

Holder, J. (2011) Writing the labyrinth - Guidance notes. Download free template. [pdf] Available at: www.jackeeholder.com/wp-content/uploads/2015/06/Writing-the-labyrinth-April15.pdf [Accessed 19 August 2019].

Chapter 2

An existential approach to coaching supervision

Ernesto Spinelli

How is this philosophy described?

Existential philosophy is concerned with exploring questions that centre upon existence and, more broadly, what it means to be human. Its ideas rapidly exerted a significant influence upon psychology and psychotherapy (Spinelli, 2005, 2015a; van Deurzen-Smith, 1988; Yalom, 1980). More recently, practitioners have argued that an existentially informed perspective on coaching would be similarly influential (Spinelli, 2018; Spinelli and Horner, 2018; van Deurzen and Hanaway, 2012).

What are the underpinning principles and beliefs of this philosophy?

Existential philosophy argues that humans are meaning-making beings. We construct meanings for those things or events that impinge themselves upon our experience and with which we are in relation. This meaning-making emerges through a foundational *relatedness*. It is not the separate and isolated individual who generates meaning. Rather, it is always the relationally embedded 'being-in-the-world' who makes meaning. Further, because of this foundational relatedness, all meanings being maintained by any individual can never be said to be final or complete. Instead, even the most significant meanings, such as those focused on one's values, beliefs and identity, will always be open to challenge, re-interpretation or rejection. From this existential perspective, all meanings are inevitably open-ended, or *uncertain*. As such, our lived, or embodied, experience of existing in a relationally uncertain meaning-world is always imbued with *anxiety*. Existential anxiety may be a debilitating, disruptive or problematic presence, but it can also be the source to all creative and original insight and decision-making.

These three foundational principles – *relatedness, uncertainty* and *anxiety* – form the basis to existential philosophy's approach to the basic givens of our existence, such as choice, freedom and responsibility (Cohn, 2002; Jacobsen, 2007; Yalom, 1980). Obviously, these concerns are of substantial relevance to many of the issues that clients bring to the coaching encounter. Just as obviously, these same issues might well arise during the course of any coaching supervision.

However, it is principally *the way* that applied existential theory explores these issues that distinguishes it from other models and approaches. This way centres upon a descriptively focused investigative enquiry. Its aim is that of opening up or making explicit that which is implicit in statements expressing any particular lived, or *embodied* experience. Embodied stances include rational (and irrational), emotional, behavioural and feeling based values, beliefs, assumptions and biases. Together, they make up, or structure, any given lived experience in that they seek to express how it is for an individual to live or 'be-with' any identified experience (Spinelli, 2005, 2015a).

When applied to coaching supervision, this descriptively attuned, experientially focused mode of enquiry immediately raises the most basic of questions: 'Just what is coaching supervision? What is its purpose?' Various existential practitioners have addressed these questions regarding the supervision of psychotherapists and counsellors (du Plock, 2007, 2009; Mitchell, 2002; Spinelli, 2015b; van Deurzen and Young, 2009). This chapter proposes that the clarification and reconsideration of these implicit assumptions is of equally pivotal importance to coaching supervision.

What is the role of the coach supervisor in the context of this philosophy?

For the great majority of supervisors and coaches, *supervision suggests an act of over-seeing*. From this standpoint, supervision emphasises notions of guiding, judging and/or interpreting *from above*. In doing so, it contains the implicit assumption of the supervisor's superiority in expertise, status and power. From this over-seeing standpoint, supervision concerns itself primarily with formative, normative and restorative functions as identified by Proctor (1991).

The formative function focuses upon a broadly educational enterprise in that the supervisor seeks to improve the supervisee's understanding of any particular coaching theory and its associated skills and techniques.

The normative function concerns itself with the protection of clients through the supervisor's 'policing' of the coach's professional behaviour and maintenance of ethical standards.

Finally, in applying its restorative function, the coaching supervisor encourages the supervisee to concentrate upon the issues raised by a specific client that are impacting upon the supervisee's focus and energy for the work. The impact that these issues are having upon the whole coaching dynamic is then viewed via the lens of the supervisor's and/or coach's preferred model of coaching.

In general, the over-seeing focus places the discussion of the supervisee's clients, and their concerns or aspirations, centre stage so that they can be identified, examined and interpreted during supervision.

However, as Simon du Plock has pointed out, an all-too-obvious but nonetheless often missed pivotal point arises: *the client who is the primary focus of the over-seeing supervisory encounter is not actually present.* Rather, it is the coach who is recounting the experience of coaching the client who is the one who is present in the supervisory encounter. And it is that coach's experience of the encounter that is, more accurately, being discussed in supervision (du Plock, 2007, 2009).

This existentially focused view of supervision, which emphasises the key principles summarised above, does not sit easily with over-seeing dominated perceptions and assumptions. How can a coherent alternative view of existential coaching supervision be formulated?

Expanding upon du Plock's argument, an existentially attuned approach proposes that *supervision suggests an act of seeing-over.* From this focus, coaching supervision invites supervisees to *review from the standpoint of their embodied stance* that which they experienced as coaches in their encounter with the client. For instance, how did the coaching encounter impact in some noticeable – typically disruptive, disturbing or distressful – way upon the coach's currently maintained meanings regarding 'being a coach'? This exploration brings to light the coach's beliefs, values, assumptions and biases associated with 'being a coach.' In brief, this approach focuses on a number of key questions for the supervisee:

1 How are my values/beliefs/assumptions about being a coach and doing coaching being challenged in this particular client encounter?

2 In what ways am I experiencing the client's way of being with me, or their response to my challenges and interventions as 'wrong'? How does this serve me (be it professionally and/or personally)? How does it impact upon the possibilities of our encounter?

3 How might my concerns about my client serve to validate and maintain my overall coaching (or personal) embodied stance? What, if anything, am I protecting?

This seeing-over approach attempts to explore and make explicit that which blocks coaches' ability to stay with, assist and challenge the supervisee to the best of their ability. More generally, it clarifies that the primary aim of existential coaching supervision is to explore the supervisee's embodied stance toward the coaching model they espouse and seek to apply. By doing so, it exposes those aspects of that stance that are experienced as problematic and which, in turn, create obstacles for their willingness and ability to be present for their clients.

How would you prepare yourself to work congruently with this approach?

Existential coaching supervision, in common with existential coaching in general, is primarily a descriptively focused exploratory process. Description sounds like an easy enterprise - until one attempts it. In doing so, it becomes evident how rarely we stay with description and, instead, how rapidly explanation, judgment and a desire to change 'what is there' are introduced. Supervisors follow various methods of descriptive investigation that assist them in 'staying with' the supervisee's currently lived experience rather than directly focusing on ways to move the supervisee toward an assumed better or more desirable way of being a coach. Broadly, these aims follow a method of phenomenological investigation. This method urges existential coaching supervisors to:

a) Attempt to set aside or 'bracket' their initial biases and prejudices and to suspend expectations and assumptions all presuppositions regarding the supervisee.
b) *Describe, don't explain* so that they may more adequately stay with the 'what and how' of the supervisee's experience rather than seek to explain its 'why'.
c) Avoid jumping to conclusions as to what really matters to the supervisee or, indeed, what it may be that the supervisee is seeking to address and resolve. Instead, supervisors are urged to treat all statements made by supervisees as being *initially* both unclear as to their meaning and of equal importance with regard to what concerns the supervisee is attempting to express through them.

Phenomenological investigation provides the means for reviewing (or seeing-over) the supervisee's embodied stances as experienced in the coaching encounter under discussion. In general, existential practitioners argue that description, in and of itself, changes that which is being described - though what changes, and how that change is experienced remains an uncertainty.

In order to remain within a descriptively focused framework, however, the existential coaching supervisor needs to be willing to abdicate a great deal of the power and authority that accompanies an over-seeing stance. Instead, the supervisor's attempts are to *meet the supervisee where they are*, rather than seek to move the supervisee to a space of better practice or understanding. One immediate consequence for the supervisor is that this alternative is far less concerned with the explicit dissemination of existential theory and practice. Instead, the supervisor's primary attempt is that of embodying an existential attitude or *way of being* regarding the descriptive disclosing of what is there for the supervisee as they discuss the issues being brought to supervision.

This attempt places both supervisor and supervisee in an uncertain context wherein what will emerge from their discussion and how it will be experienced by either or both of them remains uncertain and unpredictable. Such engagements are likely to have an anxious quality about them. For the supervisee, they might provoke the experience of feeling the weight of their choices, or to sit with the discomfort of recounting aspects of their coaching encounter that they judge to be problematic, inappropriate, embarrassing or even shameful in some way. In addition, they might highlight previously unacknowledged issues centred upon the supervisee's desired way of being a coach. For the supervisor, the attempt to engage in a more fluid emergent exploration might point out contradictory instances of their power or authority as a supervisor. For both, this uneasy and uncertain enterprise may generate disorienting and challenging anxieties. Equally, their encounter might be the source to a highly valued sense of a shared, mutually-respectful learning experience.

Anything else you need to consider before applying an existential approach?

It must be acknowledged that any coaching supervision that falls under the current guidelines set by professional bodies must, in some way, pay heed to the formative, normative and restorative functions of supervision – which is to say, existential coaching supervision cannot avoid or deny its over-seeing aspects.

The existential view under discussion is *not* suggesting that an over-seeing stance is inappropriate or incorrect. What *is* being questioned is whether coaching supervision must *only* be considered from its over-seeing aspects. Instead, the proposal here is that the seeing-over stance advocated by an existentially-focused approach to coaching supervision provides an important alternative.

The tension between existential supervision's over-seeing and the more typical seeing-over interpretations need not be understood as yet another case of either/or options. Issues surrounding the formative, normative and restorative functions of supervision cannot - nor should not - always be dismissed nor denied. For instance, it would be absurd to suggest that considering the client's concerns from various theoretical and/or practical perspectives should be avoided within the supervisory discussion. But even when this happens, such discussions can still retain their principal seeing-over focus. In short, the challenge remains for both the existential coaching supervisor and supervisee to find the means to hold the tension between these two interpretations of supervision and to find their way to best navigate between them.

How might this way of working be particularly useful to the supervisee?

Existential coaching supervision maintains the challenging, questioning and revealing spirit of all existential inquiry. Such resonances reveal a significant link between existential supervision and the processes of existential therapy and coaching. *Although it is not coaching or therapy per se, existential coaching supervision can often be experienced by coaches as personally illuminating (or, in its broadest sense, therapeutic).* Nonetheless, it remains the case that issues may be touched upon in the course of existential coaching supervision that are experienced by the supervisee as having wider ramifications extending beyond the professional to the personal. In such cases, the supervisor can always encourage a focus that assists the supervisee to explore how such broader insights might be impacting upon the particular coaching encounter under discussion.

Existential coaching supervision need not be restricted solely to supervisory encounters between existentially attuned and trained supervisors and coaches. Insofar as its primary concerns rest upon the descriptive exploration of the coach's embodied stance regarding being a coach and practising coaching, existential coaching supervision can be a valuable experiential alternative to more over-seeing modes of supervision *regardless of the coach's preferred model of coaching.*

Ultimately, existential coaching supervision is less concerned with training supervisees to be better existential coaches than it is about encouraging supervisees to *embody* the model they espouse. In doing so, existential coaching supervision remains true to its experiential 'being-focused' emphases. At the same time, it both challenges and expands our understanding of what coaching supervision can be and what it may be able to offer, seeking to enhance the coach's experience of being a coach and practising coaching.

References

Cohn, H.W. (2002) *Heidegger and the roots of existential therapy*. London: Continuum.

du Plock, S. (2007) A relational approach to supervision: Some reflections on supervision from an existential-phenomenological perspective. *Existential Analysis*, 18 (1), pp. 31–38.

du Plock, S. (2009) An existential-phenomenological inquiry into the meaning of clinical supervision: What do we mean when we talk about 'existential-phenomenological supervision? *Existential Analysis*, 20 (2), pp. 299–318.

Jacobsen, B. (2007) *Invitation to existential psychology*. London: Wiley.

Mitchell, D. (2002) Is the concept of supervision at odds with existential thinking and therapeutic practice? *Existential Analysis*, 13 (1), pp. 91–97.

Proctor, B. (1991) Supervision: A co-operative exercise in accountability. In: A. Marken and M. Payne. Eds. Undated. *Enabling and ensuring: Supervision in practice*. Leicester: National Youth Bureau/Council for Education and Training in Youth and Community Work, pp. 21–23.

Spinelli, E. (2005) *The interpreted world: An introduction to phenomenological psychology, 2nd ed*. London: Sage.

Spinelli, E. (2015a) *Practising existential therapy: The relational world, 2nd ed*. London: Sage.

Spinelli, E. (2015b) On existential supervision. *Existential Analysis*, 26 (1), pp. 168–178.

Spinelli, E. (2018) Existential coaching. In: E. Cox, T. Bachkirova, and D. Clutterbuck. Eds. *The complete handbook of coaching, 3rd ed*. London: Sage. pp. 81–94.

Spinelli, E. and Horner, C. (2018) The existential-phenomenological paradigm. In: S. Palmer and A. Whybrow. Eds. *The handbook of coaching psychology: A guide for practitioners, 2nd ed*. London: Routledge, Ch.13, pp. 169–179.

van Deurzen, E. and Hanaway, M. (Eds.) (2012) *Existential perspectives on coaching*. London: Palgrave Macmillan.

van Deurzen, E. and Young, S. E. (Eds.) (2009) *Existential perspectives on supervision: Widening the horizon of psychotherapy and counselling*. Basingstoke: Palgrave Macmillan.

van Deurzen-Smith, E. (1988) *Existential counselling in practice*. London: Sage.

Yalom, I. (1980) *Existential psychotherapy*. New York: Basic Books.

~ ~ ~ ~ ~

42. Deliberately self-centred supervision

Michelle Lucas

Where can this be used?				Typical level of supervisee experience required	

When is this used?

This is for mature supervisees who are interested in exploring themes and patterns in their work. It relies on the tenet of the self being an instrument of our coaching work (Bachkirova, 2016).

What is the approach?

Building on individual reflection, the supervisor facilitates a meta-reflection to explore how their client work is shaping their identity and vice versa.

Step 1: Appropriate contracting is necessary if the entirety of the supervision session is held in this more developmental frame.

Step 2: Prior to the session, supervisee(s) are invited to reflect on the question 'What is your client work telling you, about you?' Typically, supervisees will notice patterns and themes arising in their work, they might also notice shifts and differences in their current clients compared to what they experience as their 'norm.'

Step 3: Only the lightest of facilitation is needed. Each group member takes a turn to use the space to share their reflections in an unhurried manner.

Step 4: In a longstanding group, once a member has voiced their reflections the other members tend to naturally respond. If needed, some useful prompts could be:

- What's resonating for you?
- What are you noticing that you would like to share?
- How did you experience XX's reflections?
- What dissonance or surprise did you experience?

Step 5: To help ensure there is space for all members the supervisor may interject at appropriate points, inviting the supervisee to summarise their learning. A useful question could be 'So, where has that taken you to?'

Step 6: Signpost opportunities to move focus to another group member, seeking permission from the group to do so.

Step 7: At the end of the whole group session, pause to allow consideration of what implications the supervision work may have for their clients.

Step 8: Before closing prompt consideration of the group process. Some interesting questions could be:

- When did our encouragement or reassurance stray into collusion?
- Where did our empathy/resonance blind us from nuanced difference?
- When did we side-step challenge for fear of denting our relationships?
- How did we share the time today, what might that say about our group dynamic?

How to work with this approach ...

This approach generates deep and personal work and so the set-up of the group and of the session needs to be considered and bespoke. Given this work is strongly connected to our authenticity, the set up cannot be scripted. Perhaps the supervisor may choose to role model vulnerability, sharing something of their current personal developmental journey as a lens for the upcoming supervision session. This is intended as a catalyst not a directive, with participants being at liberty to attend or ignore this prompt as they engage in their own reflections.

In order for the work to be unhurried, it can be helpful to contract for an emergent session, agreeing that while the time will be shared, it may not be equally divided. Mature groups tend to recognise the passing of time and self-regulate. With newer groups, the supervisor might be tempted to take more control, this is not recommended. It is better to let the session unfold in its own way, drawing attention to how time was attended to in Step 8.

What else might need attention?

The set-up of this work assumes that individuals will engage in other forms of reflective practice to understand and explore more practical client conundrums.

A word of caution

To work at this depth - the group needs to establish a high level or rapport and trust. However, the supervisor needs to ensure that the group does not slip into collusion or group think. To ensure the work resides in the supervision rather than a 'coaching the coach' space, the supervisor needs to encourage the group to keep their ultimate clients in mind. Step 7 is therefore an essential part of the supervisor's 'due diligence'.

What other uses are there for this approach?

The question outlined in Step 2 may be used in a more traditional supervision arrangement. In these instances, spot contracting can be useful, seeking permission for the dialogue to move from a more client-focused discussion to a more introspective one.

This is not recommended for use with client work.

Reference

Bachkirova, T. (2016) The self of the coach: Conceptualization, issues and opportunities for practitioner development. *Consulting Psychology Journal: Practice and Research*, 68 (2), pp. 143–156.

Further reading

Lucas, M. (2017) Applying the oxygen mask principle to coaching supervision. *International Journal of Mentoring and Coaching*, Special Issue October 2017, pp. 13–20.

~ ~ ~ ~ ~

43. Harnessing self-doubt

Michelle Lucas

Where can this be used?				Typical level of supervisee experience required	

When is this used?

When an experienced supervisee appears to be seeking reassurance. At a practical level, perhaps something didn't go as well in a session or something feels elusive. Energetically, perhaps a more child-like quality manifests in the supervisee.

This approach diverts the energy away from a normative conversation towards a deeply personal and developmental one.

What is the approach?

While creating an environment where the supervisee feels 'safe enough', the intention of the supervisor is not to reassure nor to help the supervisee remove their self-doubt, rather to embrace the potential of the self-doubt for the learning it may hold.

Step 1: Often, the work begins when the supervisor is directly asked or notices the supervisee seeking reassurance from them.

Step 2: The supervisor surfaces their felt sense of the encounter and seeks permission to work at a deeper level, contracting carefully to clarify how each of you will know if the boundary of unhelpful discomfort is reached.

Step 3: Invite the supervisee to describe in more detail the sense of doubt they are experiencing. Useful questions could be:

- What kind of doubt is it?
- Which part of you notices the doubt the most?
- What might the doubt want you to know ... perhaps something you hardly dare hear?
- If there was a nugget of truth in the doubt, what might it be?

Step 4: Deepen the enquiry by helping the supervisee articulate their experience of exploring their doubt. Useful questions could be:

- How are you experiencing this work right now?
- What are you noticing about your awareness? What's already known to you? What is not yet known?
- How far away is the boundary of your discomfort? How might we get closer to it?

Step 5: Offer a pause for the supervisee to rest and to process the emerging information.

Step 6: Check how the supervisee would like to use the remaining time and respond accordingly.

How to work with this approach ...

This is a particular way of holding the supervisee in their sensation of uncertainty and perhaps their rising anxiety too. The steps above are therefore an approximation to how a dialogue will unfold. While not offering reassurance, it is helpful to offer a supportive presence, as often the questions land with a forensic quality.

The supervisor can facilitate the dialogue by role modelling their own self-doubt and uncertainty. This requires a language that holds both credibility and not knowing in equal measure. A parallel process or resonance may also occur. If, when offering questions, you are using tentative language and you notice a gentle anxiety in your own somatic response, then you are probably working in a helpful space.

Resist the temptation towards the end of the exploration to move the discussion to what may feel like a safer, lighter more positive space. The point of this approach is to sit in the discomfort, to describe the experience such the discomfort is processed more fully and to see what learning emerges.

What else might need attention?

Often, this enquiry raises awareness of personal narratives that have the potential to impede the supervisee's client work. Sometimes the connections happen within the session but more often it will occur following further reflection or work. Therefore, encourage the supervisee to continue to process the experience while also highlighting that fuller awareness may not yet be within their grasp. You may need to prepare them to sit with that discomfort too.

A word of caution

The importance of contracting cannot be underestimated – so give it the time it takes. Re-contracting can be an interesting piece of work on its own, i.e. clarifying how the supervisee manages the boundary of their comfort and discomfort. Hold your own curiosity lightly and ensure you always work in service of your supervisee.

This approach navigates the edges of the supervisees awareness and therefore should only be done in the context of an established and ongoing relationship. The work requires a developmental not an intellectual shift. Awareness cannot be rushed, it will occur in its own time and in the context of a supportive and developmental relationship.

What other uses are there for this approach?

When used within a group setting, it may generate an additional level of vulnerability. This should be reserved therefore for mature and established groups with a supervisor who holds deep experience of group dynamics. By exception this could be useful for coaching clients – conditional upon psychological safety in the relationship.

Further reading

Lucas, M. (2017) From coach to coach supervisor – A shift in mind-set. *International Journal of Evidence Based Coaching and Mentoring*, 15 (1), pp. 11–23.

~ ~ ~ ~ ~

44. Intentions and interventions

Benita Treanor

Where can this be used?				Typical level of supervisee experience required

When is this used?

As we cultivate a deeper understanding of self as the 'instrument' of change, we need to welcome our blind spots and be awake to our intentions such that we make conscious choices in how we intervene with our clients.

Developed by Heron in the 1970s, the Six Categories of Intervention provides a toolkit for how we intervene. It is used to enhance clarification at the level of *intentions* rather than loosely identifying *behavioural* outcomes. It sets out to establish a place of 'witness' (internal supervisor) within the awareness of the supervisee, increasing ability to self-regulate their practice, recognising the 'gap' between results and intentions. It enhances the supervisees ability to be aware of *what* they are doing, as they are *doing* it.

What is the approach?

The six categories provide a range of styles, supporting agility through switching interventions to meet the emerging context. 'An "intervention" is an identifiable piece of verbal or nonverbal behaviour that is part of the practitioner's service to the client' (Heron, 1991, p. 3). Within each style, the emphasis is on intention, what drivers or motivators are behind the intervention.

There are two basic styles for describing how we intervene (Authoritative and Facilitative), each sub divided further as outline in Table 2.1 below.

Table 2.1 Heron's Six Categories of Intervention with examples

Authoritative taking responsibility for and on behalf of the supervisee.	
Style	**Example**
Prescriptive – directing behaviour, giving advice, taking a hierarchical stance	Your cancelation policy is not clear therefore you need to reclarify with your client.
Informative – giving instructions through conveying knowledge, information, meaning	When you challenge in that way so soon after meeting, and with little rapport, it could be unhelpful
Confronting – Give constructive feedback in order to raise the supervisees awareness or blind spot	You seem to have introduced your own solutions rather than allow the client to find their own
Facilitative encouraging/affirming supervisee, self-awareness	
Cathartic – releases tensions, recognising emotions, freeing up energy	How did it feel when your client cancelled their session for the second time?
Catalytic – encourages self-discovery, self-directed learning and problem-solving	How have you dealt with this on previous occasions?
Supportive – Valuing, affirming capability and qualities, compassionate and kindness	You really stayed present with your client as they worked through their frustrations

Step 1: In listening, notice which of the six styles are in play. Authoritative or facilitative? Hold this in your awareness.

Step 2: Ask your supervisee questions:

- What was their intention by intervening?
- How might this have been received?
- How are their actions impacting the intention of the work?

Step 3: Work more consciously to understand what styles are in play.

- Did the supervisee accomplish what they set out to do?
- The supervisor might offer observational or developmental feedback?

How to work with the approach ...

This level of observation can be challenging. Care needs to be given in how this approach is introduced. Consideration of purpose and clarity of contract is vital.

In group supervision peers can add a 'third position' to notice any disconnects between intention and interventions. Peers may need gentle encouragement to challenge their counterparts in this way, and it is a useful parallel for how they might challenge their own clients with similar observations.

A word of caution

Our actual intervention may be at odds with our intention. This may signal further attention needs to be given. For example, the supervisor may notice the supervisee's a tendency to avoid following their instincts, perhaps fearing they might get it wrong, be rejected or lose rapport. The supervisee might need encouragement to reconnect with their good intention and to take a risk, whilst also exploring how they might mitigate or deal with the perceived risks.

What other uses are there for this approach?

Supervisors can be mindful of their own interventions. In slowing down, articulating both our intention and our behaviour, taking an educative stance role models self-awareness and vulnerability. Similarly, coaches can raise awareness with client interventions and impact on outcomes.

Reference

Heron, J. (1991) *Helping the client: A creative practical guide.* London: Sage Publications.

Further reading

Heron, J. (1976) Six category intervention analysis, *British Journal of Guidance and Counselling*, 4 (2), pp. 143–155.
Heron, J. (2001) *Helping the client, 5th ed.* London: Sage Publications.

Resources

Visit John Heron's South Pacific Centre for Human Inquiry, website: www.human-inquiry.com/jhcvpubl.htm [Accessed 4 September 2019].
Oasis School of Human Relations Intervening in Human Relations [online] Available at: www.oasishumanrelations.org.uk [Accessed 5 September 2019].

~ ~ ~ ~ ~

45. The value of noticing

Diane Hanna

Where can this be used?				Typical level of supervisee experience required	

When is this used?

This approach is helpful in the check-out of a supervision session. It can sometimes be used within a reflective practice session with a coach or group of coaches when they have a reaction to the work of supervision.

What is the approach?

The intention of this approach is to build the self-reflective skills of the coach and build self-awareness at a cognitive, emotional and felt sense level.

Step 1: Encourage introspection with the supervisee(s).

Step 2: Quietly encourage self-reflection on the question:

- What did I notice about myself in this session?

Step 3: Continue to encourage the supervisee to self-reflect further with questions such as:

- How do I respond to what I noticed?
- Perhaps consider what thoughts you may have had?
- What emotions were evoked in you?
- What sensations came into your awareness?

Step 4: Finally, encourage supervisee to self-reflect and write down the answer to the questions like:

- What does my response tell me about me?
- Perhaps consider what feels familiar or conversely new to you?
- Cast your mind backwards, might this reflect common themes in your practice or wider life?

Step 5: Supervisor asks: 'What has changed?' and 'How will this inform your practice going forward?'

Step 6: By way of closing, invite the supervisee to consider what further reflection they will engage in independently.

How to work with this approach ...

This approach can be a deceptively simple way of encouraging deep reflection on the part of the supervisee. It provides a rigour to the check-out process of supervision and more readily allows coaches to access themselves on multiple levels. Encourage the supervisees to write down their responses and then talk about them, rather than just talking them through, as this generates deeper learning and the use of more senses in this process. When working in groups, this also allows individual supervisees to process their reactions to another group member so that they can share their response in a thoughtful manner rather than sharing their more visceral reaction. In a group setting these questions often require a significant pause as they are challenging to answer. Having spent the bulk of the session with the support and challenge of their fellow supervisees in mind it requires work to shift awareness to think and experience themselves again.

What else might need attention?

On occasion this exercise can lead to deeper introspection and supervisees being overly critical of themselves. It is important to attend to the restorative aspect of supervision in this exercise and ensure that the supervisee is leaving renewed and restored to their best coach self and not doubting their capabilities. Asking 'How does this inform your practice?' or 'How can you be more of your best self as a coach?' are great questions to ensure a resourceful coach state.

Should the supervisee find they have nothing to reflect on, hold the silence to allow the inner work to happen. Alternatively, change the state in the conversation for a few moments and go back to the reflective exercise much as you may do with a coach client.

A word of caution

As this is a check-out activity it is important not to be rushed at the end of a session. Ensure you allow a proportionate amount of time to this process, in line with the length of the session itself. Another consideration is to ensure that the coaches leave the session with a positive energy and restored to be their best self as coach.

What other uses are there for this approach?

You can usefully use these questions with clients and encourage self-refection as part of sessions with clients so that they better understand themselves.

Further reading

Hay, J. (2007) *Reflective practice and supervision for coaches.* Maidenhead: Mc Graw Hill.

Morgan, K. and Watts, G. (2015) *The coaches casebook: Mastering the 12 traits that trap us.* Cardiff: Inspect & Adapt Ltd.

Passmore, J. (2011) *Supervision in coaching supervision, ethics and continuous professional development.* London: Kogan Page.

~ ~ ~ ~ ~

46. Working with shame using embodied coaching

Tsafi Lederman and Jenny Stacey

Where can this be used?				Typical level of supervisee experience required	

When is this used?

Useful when there may be a shame process in the supervisory system. This way of working can be used to increase the supervisees awareness of their shame triggers and discover a place of Self-Acceptance.

What is the approach?

The Embodied Coaching method expands awareness by addressing implicit, non-conscious knowledge; something we 'know' but cannot easily express in words. This knowledge can be accessed through two primary pathways; body process and exploring emerging images and metaphors through the use of the Arts.

Step 1: Contract appropriately for the depth of work.

Step 2: Ask the supervisee to imagine a situation of Shame. For example:

'What is your image or metaphor for this situation? What do you notice in your body as you describe it?'

Step 3: Invite the supervisee to choose a place in the room to represent the situation of shame and go there. Ask the supervisee to adopt the 'body shape'/posture that represents being there. Ask:

'What do you notice in your body?'

Step 4: Invite the supervisee to move away from the place of shame and 'shake off' the embodiment. Ask:

'What did you notice about that experience? What was the trigger that took you into this situation?'

Remember their shame trigger could be non-verbal, e.g. a facial expression or tone of voice.

Step 5: Now ask the supervisee to imagine a place/situation of Self-Acceptance. Ask:

'What is your image or metaphor for this place? What do you notice in your body as you describe it?'

Step 6: Invite the supervisee to choose a different place that represents Self-Acceptance and go there and put their body into a shape that represents being there. Ask:

'What do you notice?'

Step 7: In the place of Self-Acceptance, invite the supervisee to remember a time when they achieved an important objective. Ask:

'What did you learn about your skill, abilities and what you are capable of achieving?'

Then ask them to take up a body position of fulfilment and/or satisfaction and to make some statements from that position.

Step 8: Moving away from both positions. Ask:

'Thinking about the original issue now, what is your understanding? How has this changed your view? What would you like to take away with you?'

How to work with the approach ...

It can be hard to know how to begin this work. The impetus may come from the supervisee becoming aware that they are feeling shame but more likely the supervisor might wonder aloud if it is present. There needs to be a safe, trusting and ongoing relationship between the supervisor and supervisee. The attitude of the supervisor needs to be one of unconditional positive regard and empathy for the supervisee and the system in which they work.

Convey that shame is a feature of our human existence - a collapse of self-esteem - which may impact our relational patterns. Shame is often triggered by self-talk from the Inner Critic, and this approach encourages an exploration of the experience of shame without necessarily seeking to reduce or remove it, rather to examine its 'being there' and what that might illuminate. On occasion it might be entirely appropriate to feel shame. Additionally, connecting with a more positive self-image can provide further understanding of the supervisee's process.

Through parallel process shame can be mirrored in the coach–client relationship and echo shame in the wider system. When the supervisee understands how shame manifests for them and how to manage it constructively, they are in a much clearer position to identify and work with any shame in the client system.

It is important for the work to end in the place of Self-Acceptance. Where appropriate, the supervisor could start at Step 5.

What else might need attention?

The origin of shame is often laid down in early life. Further personal work may be needed outside the supervisory relationship.

A word of caution

Shame is often experienced in the coaching supervision relationship, but it can be difficult for the supervisor to notice, as we all strive to keep shame hidden. The supervisee may use protective strategies, e.g. withdrawing contact, being overly compliant, self-critical or aggressive. There are often non-verbal clues that may help the supervisor identify shame, e.g. the supervisee looking away, blushing, change of posture and energy level.

In this embodied way of working the supervisor needs to notice how the supervisee is reacting in the different positions. The supervisor's skill is in bringing this into attention without inadvertently shaming the supervisee. Offer neutral observations and questions such as: 'What are you noticing in your body now and how does it feel?'.

What other uses are there for this approach?

This approach can be expanded by using the Arts. Simply ask the supervisee to draw or find an image to represent both places.

An image can offer a tangible representation of the unconscious dynamics and shame triggers in the supervisory process. It can give a different perspective and offer 'super' vision.

Further reading

Lederman, T. and Stacey, J. (July 2014) Embodied coaching: Pathways to implicit knowledge using the arts and somatic process. *Coaching Today*, (11), pp. 6–9.

Chapter 3

A gestalt approach to coaching supervision

Julie Allan and Alison Whybrow

How is this philosophy described?

A gestalt (translated from German) is a shape, pattern or configuration, distinguished as a separate 'figure' against the 'ground' of the context(s). The famous candlestick-face illusion demonstrates figure and ground at work in our process of seeing. However, a figure need not be concrete (e.g. a person) but could be, for example, a sensation, or an experience of confusion.

Gestalt approaches focus on awareness, gained through attention and experiment, to enable a healthy and potent experience of life and its challenges. A gestalt practitioner regards people as fundamentally healthy in that, when all is taken into account, they are doing/being their best as well as being a work in progress. Support, challenge and exploration are offered to enhance, rather than to fix perceived failings.

Gestalt practice, developed through psychology and therapy, encompasses organisational consultancy and, in more recent years, draws key aspects of each into coaching and supervision practice. Gestalt coaching continues to evolve, and to contribute to other approaches, while staying close to core elements (Allan and Whybrow, 2019; Bluckert, 2015; Siminovitch, 2017; Simon, 2009; Spoth, Toman, Leichtman and Allan, 2013).

The importance of awareness, relationships and holism, with acknowledgement of complexity, is a good fit with today's ecologically minded conversations about challenges across scales from individual to biospheric. Gestalt's biological and phenomenological aspects give a fertile space to explore somatic knowing, sense- and meaning-making, cognitive development and neuropsychology. Other adult-developmental perspectives have areas of compatibility: Berger and Johnston (2015), Scharmer (2016), Laske (2007, 2008, 2015), Kegan (1980, 1994), Rooke and Torbert (2005) and Torbert et al. (2004), among others. The psychology of wisdom in coaching and supervision contexts is relevant (Allan, 2013; Kilburg, 2006), as is Nora Bateson's (2015, 2017) continuing articulation of the intricacies of our mutual learning in relationships.

What are the underpinning principles and beliefs of this philosophy?

Awareness is both goal and methodology. Yontef (1981) describes three principles of gestalt therapy, also relevant in gestalt coaching and coaching supervision. Each of the three, when fully understood, is held to encompass the others.

First, phenomenology, seeking to understand situations through the full breadth of what can be immediately experienced (Allan and Whybrow, 2019). Gestalt supervisors need to be able to hold the frame for phenomenological enquiry in a way that distinguishes sensation from interpretation, for example.

Second is the principle of dialogic existentialism. In coaching supervision, this is the here-and-now dialogue happening at the 'contact boundary' between supervisee and supervisor, reflecting the similar space between a supervisee and their clients. In dialogue, from the Greek *dia* and *logos* (meaning flowing through), attention to the relationship and a spirit of enquiry means that something can emerge that was not in the minds of either party at the start (see Allan and Whybrow, 2019). This is a creative space and, through the principle of holism (see below), encompasses the wider contexts.

The third principle is holism and includes field theory. We exist, indeed develop, in a wider field of contexts and we cannot be understood without that contextual reference. This highlights the importance of the supervisor-supervisee relationship and attention to how multiple overlapping and entwining contexts may be showing up in the moment. The supervisor and supervisee are part of each other's fields.

Two other philosophical stances inform gestalt work in particular ways.

1 The paradoxical theory of change (Beisser, 1970): change occurs in the process of becoming more fully what is rather than in trying to become other. This is an aspect of awareness – full attention and contact with how things *are* has the result that change naturally arises.
2 Everyone is fundamentally healthy. The focus is on enabling the continuing progression of an inherently healthy organism. The Gestalt Cycle is a guide for noticing and addressing 'blocks' or 'resistances' to that healthy progression, so that full and rounded 'contact' is made.

Clarkson (1989) explains this cycle of awareness, from the first indicators of something attracting our attention, through full engagement, then an ebbing and a rest time before the next item arises. This underpinning cycle is found in gestalt practice across the world, developed from Perls (1965) and the Polster and Polster (1973) and sometimes known as the Cycle of Experience or Cycle of Change. The Cleveland Institute uses 'Unit of Work' to denote a full cycle during coaching (Spoth, Toman, Leichtman and Allan, 2013, p. 397). Somebody can become stuck at any point of the cycle because of an 'interruption to contact'. These interruptions can be noticed by a skilful supervisor, as they would be by a skilful gestalt coach for their client. Perspectives on the cycle, the interruptions and useful actions can be found in Allan and Whybrow (2019) and Leary-Joyce (2014).

What is the role of the coach supervisor in the context of this philosophy?

The very creative experimentation that forms the basis of gestalt practice is ever present in the process of coaching supervision.

Supervision through a gestalt lens intends to provide a full, open opportunity to work consistently with the principles described as part of the explicit process of practice development through experiment and awareness. So, the definition of supervision in use for this text might be amended in order to:

- Emphasise mutual learning in the relationship.
- Allow for change that is other than incremental improvement.
- Be consistent with the field theory view that any 'systems' are not objectively separate from the supervisor or supervisee – they show up through them.

Perhaps:

> Coaching supervision is *a relationship* facilitating supervisees and supervisors to grow their reflective practice, *to extend their capabilities and expand their capacities while attending to* client safety. *It considers the multiple contexts and interrelated 'systems'* surrounding *or showing up through* the supervisee and their client work and seeks to bring value to *those relationships.*

The supervisory stance is one of exceptional curiosity and action enquiry (e.g. Fisher, Rooke and Torbert, 2003). Together, we might notice where curiosity stops, or a rigid belief applied, where a contradiction occurs, or a polarity emerges. We might explore different perspectives, stepping 'out' to see the patterns in a bigger landscape, or stepping 'in' to feel what it is like being 'in it' through a range of senses. This attention to shifting perspectives grows capacity for perspective taking and can create a felt sense of self-as-instrument within and between the supervisee and supervisor.

Given that our experience of 'reality' is subjective, inviting curiosity using descriptive and metaphorical language provides a counterpoint to other forms of possibly analytical enquiry (Clarkson, 1989) or depth psychology. You might invite a supervisee to unpick what's in the foreground, or to repeat a phrase or a word and connect with the sensations evoked, bringing that sensation into full awareness. In gestalt thinking, words are also actions.

A supervisor adopting a gestalt approach will aim to support the supervisee in:

- Becoming more fully aware in their work and, in particular, of their use of self in the here-and-now of their practice. This 'presence' has been written about quite extensively in relation to coaching (e.g. Siminovitch, 2017) and is true of supervisory work.
- Increasing their capacity and capability for noticing their own process and using it. So, the supervision may bring particular attention to developing metacognitive awareness (Efklides, 2008; Flavell, 1979) – thinking about the type of thinking that is happening, for example, in the room and outside it; learning about the learning. In gestalt, metacognition includes emotion as much as cognition, and encompasses perspectives from individual to planetary.
- Using the present moment to help emerge and explore each needed focus from a presumably infinite array of possibilities or gestalt figures arising for the supervisee. Times past and projected futures are brought to the present. Embodiment and practical wisdom are both in the field as thoughts, feelings, sensations and different outer contexts are attended to as in-forming.

The question of what constitutes professional and ethical practice will always be in the supervision space as a lived enquiry. The supervision partnership grows and develops awareness of differing norms, for example, and of the frames the supervisee brings to their ethical navigation.

How would you prepare yourself to work congruently with this approach?

As with other gestalt-based work, it is at the contact boundary, in the relationship between supervisor and supervisee, that learning occurs. As supervisor, you offer to become an instrument of change, with the purpose of awareness, through relationship (Whybrow and Allan, 2014). The lens of curiosity and enquiry, then, is not just 'out there' but also 'in here': what's happening for me, what am I noticing, what's shifting for me, what am I able to listen to, when am I less curious? And bringing that openness and contained vulnerability to the supervision process in service of supervisee growth. Both parties are impacted.

Preparation to work in this way is captured well by Mee-Yan Cheung-Judge (2001), who identifies two key features:

- Owning your own instrumentality by devoting time and energy to knowing yourself.
- Dedicating time to the maintenance of your self-understanding and capability by developing lifelong learning habits, working through issues of power and control, building emotional and intuitive self-awareness and committing to self-care.

Nevis devotes a chapter 'The Desired Skills of a Competent Intervenor' (Nevis, 1987, pp. 88–104) to the description of the skills required, based on the needs of the gestalt cycle, related to attention, observation, focus and curiosity. Supervisors working in a gestalt way need good capacity and capability regarding what rises moment by moment, including their own responses. Philosophically, they need to be comfortable with not 'fixing' their supervisee, who is deemed to be in a positive process of growth and development, as is the supervisor. And, of course, they need to be alert to ethical navigation and relevant professional or legal standards.

How might this way of working be particularly useful to the supervisee?

We do not claim a gestalt lens is intrinsically more useful to a supervisee than any other. However, as we use this lens often in our work, we find it highly valuable for:

- The opportunity to use the relationship to fully and transparently work from the principles described. This attention to how the work is being constructed, and to what is in play in the space of the relationship, noticing points of connection and disconnection (i.e. cycle of experience) attunes the supervisee to the gestalt lens and its use in practice.
- The modelling, practice and support for the supervisee to explore their self-as-instrument patterns.
- The emphasis on experiment, emergence and enquiry. This helps develop a stance that is flexible in the face of common challenges, such as perceived uncertainty or environmental complexity. It can also encompass ways of working from other theoretical perspectives.

Anything else you need to consider before applying a gestalt approach?

For those supervisees less used to this way of working, it can be very useful for the supervisor to articulate how work on self is a way into the work 'out there'. This is not always a straightforward journey, as educational processes have typically emphasised objectively measuring 'this' and fixing 'that'. Indeed, this is often what we have been most rewarded for in successful careers.

A supervisor using themselves as the instrument for their work will need to make sure they have the supervisory space in which they also can explore, experiment and grow. They have the challenge to model becoming more fully 'what is' while remaining fully in service of the supervision. Also, as supervisors we notice that a good portion of supervision is conducted on-line, via video conference, bringing the challenge to learn how the visceral, contactful aspects of relational practice are retained in this format.

Working in a gestalt way is fundamentally not about tools and techniques; the notion of an 'experiment' is more congruent. Resnick (1984) was very succinct in speaking about gestalt therapy; the same applies in gestalt coaching and supervision:

> Every Gestalt therapist could stop doing any gestalt technique that had ever been done and go right on doing Gestalt therapy. If they couldn't, then they weren't doing Gestalt therapy in the first place. They were fooling around with a bag of tricks and a bunch of gimmicks.
>
> (p. 19)

Given the focus on experiential learning, a group setting for gestalt supervision can be fruitful in extending the possibilities for interaction and experiment.

References

Allan, J. (2013) Metacognition: Why supervision isn't super without it. *4th International Coaching Psychology Congress*. Edinburgh, 2013.

Allan, J. and Whybrow, A. (2019) Gestalt coaching. In S. Palmer and A. Whybrow (Eds.). *Handbook of Coaching Psychology: A Guide for Practitioners*. Hove: Routledge, Ch. 14, pp. 180–194.

Bateson, N. (2015) Symmathesy – A word in progress: Proposing a new word that refers to living systems. *Journal the International Society for Systems Sciences – 59th Meeting,* 1 (1), pp. 1–22. Available at: <http://journals.isss.org/index.php/proceedings59th/article/view/2720/886> [Accessed on 8 October 2019] and Available at: <https://norabateson.wordpress.com/2015/11/03/symmathesy-a-word-in-progress> [Accessed on 8 October].

Bateson, N. (2017) *Small Arcs of Larger Circles: Framing through Other Patterns*. Axminster: Triarchy Press.

Beisser, A.R. (1970) The paradoxical theory of change. In J. Fagan and I. Shepherd (Eds.). *Gestalt Therapy Now*. New York: Harper and Row, pp. 78–80.

Berger, J.G. and Johnston, K. (2015) *Simple Habit for Complex Times: Powerful Practices for Leaders*. Stanford, CA: Stanford University Press.

Bluckert, P. (2015) *Gestalt Coaching: Right Here, Right Now*. Maidenhead: McGraw Hill.

Cheung-Judge, M.-Y. (2001) The self as instrument: A cornerstone for the future of OD. *OD Practitioner*, 33 (3), pp. 11–16.

Clarkson, P. (1989) *Gestalt Counselling in Action*. London: Sage.

Efklides, A. (2008) Facets and levels model of metacognitive functioning in relation to self-regulation and co-regulation. *European Psychologist*, 13 (4), pp. 277–287.

Fisher, D., Rooke, D., and Torbert, W.R. (2003) *Personal and Organisational Transformations: Through Action Inquiry*, 4th ed. Edge/Work Press.

Flavell, J.H. (1979) Metacognition and cognitive monitoring: A new area of cognitive-developmental inquiry. *American Psychologist*, 34, pp. 906–911.

Kegan, R. (1980) Making meaning: The constructive-developmental approach to persons and practice. *Journal of Counseling & Development*, 58 (5), pp. 373–380.

Kegan, R. (1994) *In Over Our Heads: The Mental Demands of Modern Life*. Cambridge, MA: Harvard University Press.

Kilburg, R. (2006) *Executive Wisdom: Coaching and the Emergence of Virtuous Leaders*. Washington, D.C.: American Psychological Association.

Laske, O. (2007) Contributions of evidence-based developmental coaching to coaching psychology and practice. *International Coaching Psychology Review*, 2 (2), pp. 202–212.

Laske, O. (2008) On the unity of behavioural and developmental perspectives in coaching. *International Coaching Psychology Review*, 3 (2), pp. 125–146.

Laske, O. (2015) *Dialectical Thinking for Integral Leaders: A Primer*. Tuczon, AZ: Integral Publishers LLC.

Leary-Joyce, J. (2014) *The Fertile Void: Gestalt Coaching at Work*. St Albans: AoEC Press.

Nevis, E.C. (1987) *Organisational Consulting: A Gestalt Approach*. New York: Gardner Press, Ch. 5, pp. 88–104.

Perls, F.S. (1965) Three approaches to psychotherapy: Gloria. Part II: Frederick Perls. Founder of Gestalt Therapy. Available at: www.youtube.com/watch?reload=9&v=8y5tuJ3Sojc. [Accessed 21 October 2019].

Polster, E., and Polster, M. (1973) *Gestalt Therapy Integrated: Contours of Theory and Practice*. New York: Brunner/Mazel.

Resnick, R.W. (1984) Gestalt therapy East and West: Bi-coastal dialogue, debate or debacle? *Gestalt Journal*, 7 (1), pp. 13–32.

Rooke, D., and Torbert, W.R. (2005) Seven transformations of leadership. *Harvard Business Review*, 83 (4), pp. 66–76, Harvard Business School Publication Corp.

Scharmer, O. (2016) *Theory U: Leading from the Future as It Emerges*. Oakland: Berrett-Koehler.

Siminovitch, D.E. (2017) *A Gestalt Coaching Primer: The Path towards Awareness IQ*. Toronto: Gestalt Coaching Works, LLC.

Simon, S.N. (2009) Applying Gestalt theory to coaching. *Gestalt Review*, 13 (3), pp. 230–240.

Spoth, J., Toman, S., Leichtman, R., and Allan, J. (2013) Gestalt Approach. In J. Passmore, D.B. Peterson, and T. Friere (Eds.). *The Wiley-Blackwell Handbook of the Psychology of Coaching and Mentoring*. Chichester: John Wiley & Sons, pp. 385–407.

Torbert, W.R., Fisher, D., and Rooke, D. (2004) *Action Inquiry: The Secret of Timely and Transforming Leadership*. Oakland: Berrett-Koehler.

Whybrow, A., and Allan, J. (2014) Gestalt approaches. In J. Passmore (Ed.). *Mastery in Coaching: A Complete Psychological Toolkit for Advanced Coaching*. London: Kogan Page, pp. 97–126.

Yontef, G. (1981) Gestalt therapy: A dialogic method. In P. Clarkson (Ed.). (1989). *Gestalt Counselling in Action*. London: Sage, p. 26.

Further reading

Gillie, M. (2011) The Gestalt supervision model. In J. Passmore (Ed.). *Supervision in Coaching: Supervision, Ethics and Continuous Professional Development*. London: Kogan Page, Ch. 4, pp. 45–64.

Houston, G. (1995) *The Now Red Book of Gestalt*. London: Rochester Foundation.

Kuhn, L., and Whybrow, A. (2018) Coaching at the edge of chaos: A complexity informed approach to coaching psychology. In S. Palmer and A. Whybrow (Eds.). *Handbook of Coaching Psychology: A Guide for Practitioners*. Hove: Routledge, Ch. 31, pp. 413–423.

Perls, F.S. (1967) *Ego, Hunger and Aggression*. New York: Random House.

Perls, F.S., Hefferline, R., and Goodman, P. (1994) *Gestalt Therapy: Excitement and Growth in the Human Personality*. London: Souvenir Press Ltd.

Varela, F.J., Thompson, E., and Rosch, E. (1993) *The Embodied Mind: Cognitive Science and Human Experience*. Cambridge, MA: The MIT Press.

~ ~ ~ ~ ~

47. Giving an object a voice

Michelle Lucas

Where can this be used?				Typical level of supervisee experience required	

When is this used?

This can be useful where the supervisee might benefit from taking an observer perspective such that they distance themselves from their own experience and in doing so open up their thinking. It can therefore be particularly useful when there is some 'stuckness' to be explored.

What is the experiment?

Influenced by the work of Joyce Scaife (2010), supervisees are invited to consider what objects are typically present as they work that could bear witness to what happened. The idea is a perceptual positions experiment – playing with the notion that if we take a different position (even that of an inanimate object!) we might access new information.

Step 1: Create a supervision focus for the enquiry in a way that is authentic for you. The approach could be used both with very specific client situations or when seeking to understand themes or patterns in a supervisee's work.

Step 2: Invite the supervisee to consider which objects are routinely with them as they work, then choose one.

Step 3: Ask the supervisee where their chosen object was when the topic being explored was playing out; use some visioning techniques to help bring this to life. So if they chose their pen, you might invite them to consider where was the pen at that point in time? How were they holding it? What was the colour of the ink that was flowing onto the page? What sounds could they hear as they used it or held it?

Step 4: Become playful – invite some exploratory questions along the following lines:

- What might [object] have noticed that you might not yet have noticed?
- If the [object] had a voice what might it be saying? To who? And how?
- What advice might the [object] be giving you right now?

Step 5: Allow some reflection time and encourage the supervisee(s) to consider what is emerging for them now that might not have been attended to before.

Step 6: Bring the exploration back to the original supervision focus if this has not naturally happened within Step 5.

Step 7: Invite the supervisee(s) to reflect on the process, what did they notice about their response to this approach.

How to work with the experiment ...

This requires an 'out of the box' mindset and for that reason it can be helpful if the supervision relationship is firmly established. It will work best when the supervisor takes an emergent approach, working with what is generated in the moment. For example: one supervisee felt their phone would advise them 'to take a break, to stop being so serious all the time' ... so the supervisor built on this and enquired 'so if your phone sent you on holiday, where would it send you?' Interestingly, the prospect of going on holiday without the phone, even hypothetically, evoked anxiety ... and in noticing that, laughter. This visceral awareness prompted the realisation of how enmeshed they had become with their work. The supervisee then committed to resolve this through engaging in peer coaching.

The experiment intends to help the supervisee to think more speculatively and hypothetically, so the supervisor's question needs be posed tentatively. In Step 4, notice the use of the word 'might' rather than 'would' - this encourages possibility and options rather than implying certainty or any assumption that an answer should be known.

What else might need attention?

Some supervisees can struggle to engage with this kind of abstract activity, and this is useful information. Where rapport is good, it may be possible to enquire how the struggle with this approach might say something about what they struggle with in their client work. For example, How do they manage ambiguity? How easily do they play? This could then become a topic for the supervision discussion or a matter for individual reflection.

A word of caution

Despite its playful nature it is not suitable as an ice-breaker - it can prove disorienting for those more comfortable with logical and analytical approaches. Even in more established groups it needs careful positioning and contracting to ensure supervisees are open to new ways of working and to seeing this as an 'experiment'.

What other uses are there for this experiment?

The idea of tapping into external perspectives could be used in many situations. It could be used with coaching clients provided that it is contracted for clearly and the practitioner feels that the client would enjoy seeing what it might bring.

Reference

Scaife, J. (2010) *Supervising the Reflective Practitioner: An Essential Guide to Theory and Practice*. East Sussex: Routledge, pp. 98–99.

~ ~ ~ ~ ~

48. Inner noticing

Julie Allan and Alison Whybrow

Where can this be used?				Typical level of supervisee experience required	

When is this used?

This approach is used to expand the parameters of enquiry, bringing to awareness information that the body is offering. It can be adapted for many supervision questions, such as: 'Why am I so challenged by this client?' or, 'What will make for a good client contract in this particular situation?' Perhaps most obviously suited to the initial phase of the gestalt cycle, it can serve throughout.

What is the experiment?

The approach pays attention to sensation, physiology and (optionally) emotions. It includes the 'felt sense' that is central to Gendlin's Focusing (Gendlin, 1978).

First, ensure that the supervisee is sitting or standing comfortably, using your preferred approach for becoming centred. From this starting point, the process, to be lightly facilitated, is along these lines:

Step 1: Inviting.

- Bring to mind the situation you want to give attention to. Let your mind's eye wander around it, see it from different places. Perhaps you hear conversational snippets.
- As you are doing this, become curious about what you experience and notice.
- Notice any sensations in your body, with curiosity and enquiry. Some people find themselves associating with scents or tastes. This may take some time, and it may also be that things are a bit foggy; that is also information.

- What draws your attention? Do you find yourself using any emotional labels?
- In a relaxed way, notice all these elements and sit with them. What seems clear? What seems less so?

Step 2: Receiving.

- Imagine there are two or three important messages for you in that inner world gathering. These things will be useful to have noticed in relation to the situation you are exploring. Allow yourself to sense what these are. Some may seem very clear, others less so.
- If it helps you to say out loud what is coming forward for you, do so. Explore rather than judge. If there isn't a word for it then you can make an expression with your face, or a sound. You can even ask out loud, 'Is this/are these what it will help to have noticed?' or 'Is there anything else?'

Step 3: Acknowledging.

- When you feel settled that your attention has been drawn to the foremost aspects to work with today, even if a bit puzzling, take a moment to notice what you have noticed and to say a thank you to everything that showed up. Also invite the gathering to disperse.
- Come back to the outer world with your new awareness.

You then work with the information gained from the inner noticing in whatever way seems appropriate. This may simply be quiet reflection. Note that in Step 2, people might say things such as: 'There is something here I am associating with fear; for some reason I am aware that my neck is sore; I am also noticing three people involved in this that I hadn't thought about before.'

How to work with this experiment ...

The work of the noticing is to pay attention in a more full way than people often do when puzzling about an issue, and to stay close to sensation, although encompassing any arising emotion. Ensure distinctions are made between, for example, sensation and emotion, or either of these and judgements. The invitations of the supervisor to 'notice' is best done in an easeful and relaxed manner. Different individuals will have different pacing, so acute attention is required to a supervisee's readiness to move on. Be guided by the supervisee rather than the clock.

A word of caution

Work to a depth that is appropriate to the question and suits the capabilities and capacities of the supervisor and the supervisee.

Check that the 'felt sense' arising from the enquiry is not hanging around in an unhelpful way to promote rumination or worry. This is the reason for asking the metaphorical gathering to disperse, having expressed appreciation.

What other uses are there for this experiment?

There are many uses for a similar format as the intention is always to tap in to our wider ways of knowing/understanding, to notice in a phenomenological way, and to make a conversational space for our own embodied process of making sense. When we experience ourselves noticing and learning, we also start to explore our own filters, translations and co-evolution of our contexts, and this is usually helpful. Coaching clients benefit similarly.

Reference

Gendlin, E.T. (1978) *Focusing*. New York: Everest House.

Further reading

Stelter, R. (2000) The transformation of body experience into language. *Journal of Phenomenological Psychology*, 31 (1), pp. 63–77.

Varela, F.J., Thompson, E., and Rosch, E. (1993) *The Embodied Mind*. Cambridge, MA: The MIT Press.

Resources

Gendlin's Focusing:

International Focusing Institute. Available at: (www.focusing.org/sixsteps.html) [Accessed 8 October 2019]

Gendlin film clip; *Focusing with Eugene T. Gendlin. PhD.* Available at: www.youtube.com/watch?v=Bjhf_qUklSc [Accessed on 8 October 2019]

And any basic sources on phenomenology according to Husserl and to Merleau-Ponty.

~ ~ ~ ~ ~

49. Supervision and sensing

Claire Davey

Where can this be used?				Typical level of supervisee experience required	

When is this used?

This technique is useful when a supervisee is curious about working beyond talking and thinking and wishes to explore and experience sensing, tapping into their inner wisdom that often gets overlooked, dismissed or drowned out. It might also serve a supervisee that is stuck, enabling them to ground themselves and access a different perspective.

What is the technique?

It is a form of meditative self-enquiry, guided by the supervisor. It is influenced by the wisdom tradition, yoga nidra.

Step 1: Establish the area the supervisee wants to enquire into and agree a timeframe in which you will work. Explain that time can get distorted and you will be the guardian of the process. This enables the supervisee to drop deeper into the experience.

Step 2: If working individually set up two chairs opposite each other, when working in a group, a circle of chairs with you as part of the circle. Adjust as appropriate if working remotely.

Step 3: Ask the supervisee(s) to make any final adjustments in how they are sitting to settle into the space, with their eyes open or closed. For example, some people like to take their shoes off to feel their feet connected with the floor.

Step 4: Using your own words, guide participants into the practice, for example:

> *'Get comfortable in your seat, allowing the body and mind to settle, feeling your feet against the floor, your back against the chair, clothes against the skin ...'*

You might then turn the supervisees attention to their breath, to release any residue of tension in the body, grounding them into the now and surrendering to the core of being. Take the time to do this step fully, typically between five and 15 minutes.

Step 5: Guide the supervisee(s) to bring into their awareness the focus of their enquiry. Invite them to welcome in what emerges, letting go of judgement or assumptions and suspend immerse themselves in enquiry. Offer some of the following:

a) *'Notice any sensations surfacing in the body...'*
b) *'Where in the body are you experiencing sensation...?'*
c) *'Are there any emotions co-arising with the sensation/s...'*
d) *'If yes, what's the opposite of that emotion ... and does that opposite emotion reveal sensation in the body ....'*
e) *'Can you sense between these two emotions, moving from one to the other ...?'*
f) *'Can you experience both emotions simultaneously in the body ...?'*

Step 6: Close out the exercise, for example:

'When you are ready, come back to the breath, come back into the room, slowly opening your eyes, move or stretch in a way that feels natural as you reorient.'

Step 7: Invite supervisee(s) to capture their immediate reflections in silence.

Step 8: Once the individual or group are ready, pose questions such as:

- How was your experience?
- How has it informed your dilemma/question/issue/relationship?
- What might you continue to enquire into?
- What action/s does it feel important to take?
- Are you aware of any patterns or themes that it's important to acknowledge for future sessions?

How to work with the technique ...

As supervisor, it's important you are able to ground yourself to hold the space, the silence, use intuitive pausing and pacing, tone of voice and utilise any emerging sounds to maintain the flow.

It is helpful to work with authenticity, avoid reading from a script and create your own 'live' narrative, based on the context you are experiencing. Additionally, sharing your somatic responses from the exercise (Step 8) may generate insight for individual and group process.

Initially supervisees might hesitate to close their eyes, closing yours might help to ease them in.

If working in a group, at Step 7 observe people's behaviour and energy, and hold the silence until everyone is ready to move on.

A word of caution

If supervisees are not familiar with mindfulness or meditation they may experience frustration with the process, your voice etc. On the premise that their experience is their experience just as it is, encourage them to explore this in their reflections.

What other uses are there for this technique?

Steps 1–4 can be used to ground a supervisee or client at the start or end of a session.

Further reading

Kline, J. (1984) *The Ease of Being*. Durham, NC: The Acorn Press.

Miller, R. (2010) *Yoga Nidra: A Meditative Practice for Deep Relaxation and Healing*, 2nd ed. Louisville, Colorado: Sounds True Inc.

~ ~ ~ ~ ~

50. Transformative explorations through objects and metaphor

Sue Congram

Where can this be used?				Typical level of supervisee experience required	

When is this used?

Typically, this approach will help take the supervision dialogue to a transformative level. It can shift energy when the process is stuck, or going around in circles. It can provide an alternative perspective where the supervision is overly logical/rational (out of balance).

What is the experiment?

This technique uses objects and metaphor to discover what is not yet known, through a here-and-now exploration. This is one of many creative ways of working, influenced by arts-based and transformative learning philosophies (Lahad, 2000; Mezirow and Taylor, 2009).

Step 1: Brief the group to listen to the supervisee's case as a freshly emerging narrative, paying attention to the content, the way they describe the case, and to notice their own response to it. Small nuances are as important as the big story.

Step 2: The supervisee brings their client scenario.

Step 3: Invite the supervisee to explore elements of the scenario through metaphor. For example:

'You said that you were feeling stuck with this client, would you be interested in exploring your scenario in a different way, by using objects and metaphor?'

Step 4: Ask the supervisee to quickly choose objects in the room to represent elements for exploration. Encourage them to be instinctive, without making meaning of the objects.

Step 5: Guide the supervisee to describe one object at a time, using that same description as metaphor for what it represents. For example:A supervisee chose a small vase to represent the client and a pebble for them self. (Other elements from the narrative may have been chosen.)

Supervisor:	Tell me about what you have chosen.
Supervisee:	The vase is round, green with a swirl pattern inscribed on it. It is small, for small flowers. There are no flowers in it, it is an ornament today.
Supervisor:	Now use the same description as metaphor for your client.
Supervisee:	My client is small, green, with a swirl pattern inscribed and has no flowers inside, they are an ornament today.

Supervisor: What is happening for you as you describe your client in this way.

Supervisee: I feel hollow.

Step 6: Invite further expansion, staying curious about the words used. Attend to the immediacy of this exploration, moments of insight and new information. The example above might lead to ... 'It's as though they arrive every time as an empty vessel, an ornament, a token of leadership, they do not come with flowers inside.'

Step 7: repeat Steps 5 and 6 with the remaining object(s).

Step 8: Next, invite the supervisee to position the objects in relation to each other, sharing what they notice about how the objects are positioned. In this example the supervisee had previously noticed a 'small flaw' in the pebble, which now had discretely been hidden from view. Interestingly, they had positioned the objects such that the client would not be able to see the flaw. Noticing this became insightful, which fuelled further exploration.

Step 9: Group members may now share something they noticed, in particular, revealing personal reactions and images from the process that might reflect alternative perspectives.

How do you work with this experiment?

With experience the spontaneity of the moment will shape the intervention. To begin with, three core principles offer guidance:

- Stay present to the here-and-now process.
- Become fluent and at ease with the richness of metaphor.
- Allow the process to emerge without the constraints of control (or the technique).

This last point is fundamental; perhaps the supervisee will choose two or three objects to represent their client. Every choice point is open for inquiry, the number of objects and the choosing may present the most insightful exploration. Work with experiment emergently rather than prescriptively.

A word of caution

Highly rational and logical people may not find this way of working helpful. If this was not anticipated and you are already in the flow, exploring the here-and-now process is usually rich in learning.

What other uses are there for this experiment?

Groups and teams could use this experiment to enrich their group process, by each choosing an object, describing and sharing the metaphors, and then placing all the objects in relation to each other as representative of the group. It can be used in both coaching and supervision contexts.

References

Lahad, M. (2000) *Creative Supervision: The Use of Expressive Arts in Supervision and Self-supervision.* London and Philadelphia, PA: Jessica Kingsley.

Mezirow, J., and Taylor, E.W. (2009) *Transformative Learning in Practice.* San Francisco: Jossey-Bass.

Further reading

Congram, S. (2008) Arts-informed learning in manager-leader development. In R.A. Jones, A. Clarkson, S. Congram, and N. Stratton (Eds.). *Education and Imagination: Post-Jungian Perspectives.* London: Routledge, Ch. 10, pp. 160–177.

~ ~ ~ ~ ~

51. Two-chair experiment

Alison Whybrow and Julie Allan

Where can this be used?				Typical level of supervisee experience required	

When is this used?

When there is more than one perspective to explore, this way of experimenting-and-reflecting raises awareness of the present moment and emerging possibilities. It is typically used when working with one person, although could be undertaken in group supervision. Constellations work is a highly expanded version of this type of experiment.

What is the two chairs experiment?

Simply put, this experiment is about creating a space in the supervisee–supervisor dialogue for a third perspective. This third perspective could be another person (for example, the supervisee's client, a peer, a HR buyer, a family member).

Step 1: Noticing the consistent presence of another person.
As a supervisor, you might hear your supervisee frequently mention an individual in a way that infers some difficulty or stuckness in their relationship.

Step 2: Inviting the person in.
This experiment works from the premise that the other person is already 'in the room,' that they are already in the field. Here, we pay attention to that presence and create a space for them in the dialogue. Invitation often comes in the form of a question to the supervisee along the lines of 'Shall we invite XXX into the conversation?'; or perhaps, 'What do you imagine XXX might think, say or do if s/he were here?' Followed by, 'shall we invite them in?' In crafting the invitation to your supervisee, you are testing whether they are willing and ready to work with an experiment of this nature.

Step 3: Encouraging engagement.
Having created the space, there is purposeful shift as the supervisee addresses the imagined person sitting in the chair as if they are in the room.

Step 4: Supporting dialogue.
Invite your supervisee to speak to the empty chair, using 'I' for themselves and 'you' for the other person. They may want to revisit some of the things they have already brought to the session about the person or the issue at hand. The supervisor then invites the supervisee to 'embody' the person in the other chair by physically moving into the 'empty chair' and hear what has been said as if they are the person that has just been spoken to. The supervisee then speaks and responds as if they are the other person.

This process of embodiment provides useful insight and awareness. The supervisee can move chairs, occupying their own position and the position of the other person, as much as is useful.

Step 5: Holding the enquiry.
The supervisor may reiterate some phrases or words to allow greater attention, and may ask some curious, enquiry-based questions such as:

- What does it feel like to hear that as the supervisee/as the other person?
- What more needs to be said?
- What are you now aware of?

Step 6: Closing.

The experiment continues as long as is necessary and no longer. At an appropriate point, the supervisor invites the supervisee to move back to their original chair, reconnect with themselves, stepping out of the process of moving between chairs and reflecting on any new awareness.

How to work this experiment ...

As with all gestalt experiments, there is no set way and no set process. The intention is to illuminate and raise awareness. The process of moving about can itself absorb attention which could be a distraction for those new to this approach. Contract carefully, and discard what isn't helpful. The experiment can sometimes explore unexpected territory. Be prepared to stop if you notice an unhelpful level of discomfort, and de-brief sensitively.

What else needs attention?

It might seem obvious but it's important to consider the room that you are working in. Room to move as well as solid walls (for privacy) enable people to engage in physical movement. You may need more chairs for additional perspectives.

A word of caution

It is helpful to have experimented in some way with this approach, either as a recipient or in a practice group, before using with supervisees.

What other uses are there for this?

This works well within supervision groups in an experimental way to allow exploration and deconstruction so that supervisees can start to build their own capacity to use it with their coaching clients. This approach can also be used when reflecting on your own practice.

Further reading

Houston, G. (1995) *The Now Red Book of Gestalt,* 7th ed. London: Rochester Foundation.

~ ~ ~ ~ ~

52. Working with blocks

Julie Allan and Alison Whybrow

Where can this be used?				Typical level of supervisee experience required	

When is this used?

The purpose of this type of exercise is to explore the nature of what might be going on when somebody is experiencing a 'block' or 'resistance' in relation to something important for them. They may be stuck at some point in the gestalt cycle, for example. Each part of the cycle comes with an accompanying way in which resistance can show up – these are known as 'interruptions to contact', and the intention is to address such interruptions in a way that allows progress.

From a gestalt frame, being in full contact with the 'block' would of itself be the completion of a cycle within the greater cycle(s). See Figure 3.1. This approach allows an embodied type of exploration that can be informative and contactful, including the benefits of working somatically (with body), whether there are words for this block or not. It can produce a shift that enables movement.

What is the experiment?

The experiment involves using a wall or other immovable part of the room, to serve as an embodiment of this block. It can be done standing or seated, as appropriate. Brief the supervisee along the following lines:

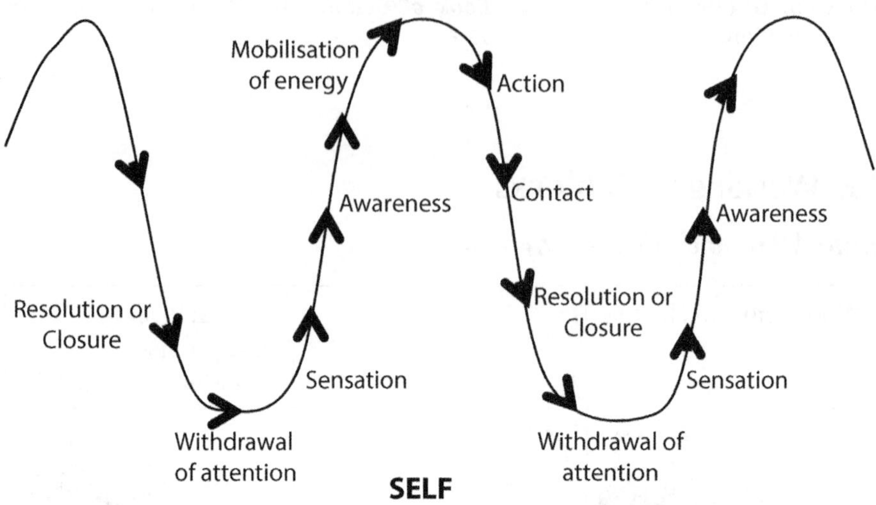

Figure 3.1 The gestalt cycle of awareness adapted from Zinker (1977)

Step 1: Set-up.

- Place your back against the wall. Bring to mind the situation about which you feel stuck.
- You can have your eyes open or closed, whatever suits you. The wall represents the 'stuck'.

Step 2: Explore.

- Feel the wall behind you, experiment with leaning against it more or less heavily, shifting weight from side to side, being straighter or less straight, back of hands or palms to the wall, all the different ways you can find.
- Notice any sensations. Notice how things change when you adjust your position. Do any colours, places, images come to mind?

Step 3: Explore more.

- If you like, you can experiment in other ways. What if the wall felt soft? What if it was a tree? What if ...?

Step 4 (optional)**: Expanding safely beyond the block.**

- Imagine a safe bubble for yourself as you lean there. What would it be like to extend that bubble behind you to include the wall and everything behind it? If you try it, stay a while and then bring the bubble back to this side of the wall.

Step 5: Consolidate awareness.

- When you are ready, disconnect from the wall. What do you notice now?

How to work with this experiment ...

As with many gestalt experiments, light facilitation is used to enable somebody to explore. Consider that this way of working may not suit everyone and could be experienced by some as confusing or annoying. Such a response is also part of the field and potentially informative, but whatever a supervisee chooses to work with is their choice; an experiment is just that - an experiment, not a mandate in which choice is over ridden by a supervisor's inappropriately strong attachment to a specific process or outcome. So, if a supervisee wishes to explore the nature of the 'nothing' or 'annoyance' they feel, that is fine, and it is equally fine for them to say they don't think they are getting anything from it and do not want to continue.

A word of caution

Resistance is normal and can be functional. The task is not to eradicate but to explore, and in so doing expand awareness of what the resistance is like, what it is serving and whether it is still needed. It may need to stay but change form.

What other uses are there for this experiment?

With skilled clients and supervisors in a group setting, it can be interesting to sit back to back and become a living 'block' for the partner. This gives the possibility of some careful exploration of a moveable, living block and indeed of experiencing self in the role of block. What is that like? It is important to de-role after this.

Exploration of blocks in this way can also be used in coaching, with previous supervised learning or training.

Reference

Zinker, J. (1977) *Creative Process in Gestalt Therapy*. Toronto: Vintage Books, p. 77.

Further reading

Allan, J., and Whybrow, A. (2019) Gestalt coaching. In S. Palmer and A. Whybrow (Eds.). *Handbook of Coaching Psychology: A Guide for Practitioners*, 2nd ed. London: Routledge, Ch. 14, pp. 180–194.

Clarkson, P. (1989) *Gestalt Counselling in Action.* London: Sage, Ch. 3, p. 29.
Spoth, J., Toman, S., Leichtman, R., and Allan, J. (2016) Gestalt approach. In J. Passmore, D.B. Peterson, and T. Freire, (Eds.). *The Wiley-Blackwell Handbook of the Psychology of Coaching and Mentoring.* Chichester: John Wiley & Sons, Ch. 20, pp. 385–406.

~ ~ ~ ~ ~

53. Working with gesture

Alison Whybrow and Julie Allan

Where can this be used?				Typical level of supervisee experience required	

When is this used?

This approach is used to augment psycho-physical awareness, the dynamic link between the mind and body. Perhaps as a supervisor you have noticed a particular lack of movement or a repetitive movement by your supervisee, perhaps around a certain topic. The intention is to illuminate the impact of posture and gesture on the landscape of perspectives and energy available to the supervisee.

What is the experiment?

One way of experimenting with gesture is to strengthen the link between physical action and/or physical sensation and a specific psychological intention or psychological awareness. For example, a supervisee might find they are leaning forward and focusing narrowly; almost becoming 'stuckness.' In expressing the intention to take a wider perspective, the supervisee might slightly shift to be more upright with a more open gaze. Picking up on this, augmenting and cementing the link between body posture and mental focus, can assist the supervisee to intentionally shift their physical stance on other occasions – and this may result in a different energy and focus with clients. Noticing and working with a tiny, almost imperceptible gesture can be transformational.

We share one way of working with gesture, purposeful anchoring below, and suggest another in the notes at the end.

Step 1: Notice a pattern that your supervisee wants to change. Building on the example above, the supervisee may report finding themselves becoming narrowly focused on their client or their client's context, being drawn in. They might notice that this results in them losing perspective, 'getting lost' in the detail. Notice your supervisee's posture as they describe this pattern.

Step 2: Ask your supervisee what they want to happen instead of the 'getting lost', what is their psychological intention.

Step 3: Pay close attention to the small physical movements that your supervisee makes as they focus on this new intention.

Step 4: Ask, 'What is the physical movement or gesture that captures this intention?'. Alternatively, you can demonstrate the physical movement you have noticed and ask them to repeat it.

Step 5: Test out the movement a few times. How well does it fit with the psychological intention? What happens as a result of the movement? Ask your supervisee to pay close attention to the sensations evoked.

Step 6: Ask your supervisee to identify a way to experiment with this shift. It might be in any kind of conversation with others rather than only in a coaching session. This helps dissipate an old habit in favour of other options, making the gesture more easily accessible.

Step 7: The supervisee may need to adapt the moment to one that is smaller, one that is meaningful to them, but not distracting in an everyday context.

How to work with this experiment ...

As with all gestalt work, this a co-created experiment with the aim of generating greater awareness.

In Step 5, you might need to invite your supervisee to really augment a physical gesture in order to fully experience the sensation, before making the gesture small enough to be easily incorporated into a day to day movement.

A word of caution

Be constantly guided by your supervisee. It's important not to judge or impose your own perspective; the movement is the right movement for your supervisee, even if you would have made a different choice in that or a similar situation.

What other uses are there for this?

This approach can also be used as described above with coaching clients.

Another way of working with gesture is to support your supervisee to become aware of any physical gestures that accompany a particular thought or situation. In this sense you're using the same link between physical movement and psychological impact, the difference being that you are working directly with gesture, rather than expressed intent. For example, you might notice your supervisee using a vertical chopping motion each time they describe a particular coaching client. Replaying the gesture and linking it with the events or phrases they are describing can help them explore the sensory and psychological impact of the gesture. In this example, they may become aware of a critical emotion or pattern, potentially an unintended display of anger. Quite what the gesture is associated with will emerge through attending to the gesture and enquiring into it. This enquiry into their own gestures might also help them understand their client's response.

Having raised awareness, there might be a further experiment to devise, going back to the seven steps outlined above – or raising awareness might take the supervision into a different direction.

Further reading

Leary-Joyce, J. (2014) *The Fertile Void: Gestalt Coaching at Work*. St Albans: AoEC press, Ch. 7.

Chapter 4

A person-centred approach to coaching supervision

Linda Aspey

How is this philosophy described?

The psychotherapist Carl Rogers (1902–1987) developed the person-centred approach from the late 1940s. It was based on a philosophy that people are unique, intrinsically resourceful, capable of insight, and motivated to fulfil their potential. As the name infers, he put the person right at the centre of his work.

This positive, optimistic, humanistic approach contrasted with some of the prevailing ideas from earlier psychoanalysts such as Freud (1856–1939) who believed that unconscious desires and forces control us. Rogers was strongly influenced by Otto Rank (1884–1939); once a staunch follower of Freud, Rank came to reject deterministic, analytical approaches in favour of a relational approach between the client and the therapist.

What are the underpinning principles and beliefs of this philosophy?

1 *The person is a client not a patient*

Unusually, in that era, Rogers used the term 'client' rather than 'patient' believing that people seeking therapy weren't helpless or sick but actively taking personal responsibility and already working towards change. Compassion was central to his therapy; people were doing the best they could, even if to others their efforts made no sense. His humanity and warmth were in stark contrast to the detached neutrality of other mainstream therapies of the time and inspired several more humanistic approaches.

2 *People have an innate drive to self-actualise*

Rogers believed that people have a natural drive to 'self-actualise' a term first coined by Abraham Maslow (Maslow, 1943), in his hierarchical theory of human motivation. Only when our physiological, safety, love and belongingness and esteem needs are met, can we seek to fulfil our potential. Rogers viewed 'becoming' as a lifelong process; an innate motivation within every individual, even under difficult circumstances. His vivid metaphor of potatoes stored in the basement, below a distant window, describes this well:

> The conditions were unfavourable, but the potatoes would begin to sprout - pale, white sprouts, so unlike the healthy green shoots they sent up when planted in the soil in the spring. But these sad, spindly sprouts would grow two or three feet in length as they reached toward the distant light of the window. The sprouts were, in their bizarre, futile growth, a sort of desperate expression of the directional tendency I have been describing. They would never become plants, never mature, never fulfil their real potential. But under the most adverse circumstances, they were striving to become. Life would not give up, even if it could not flourish.
>
> (Rogers, 1980, p. 118)

Rogers rejected the idea that therapists should be experts that analysed, diagnosed, or treated the illness. Instead he felt that if people had developed their personalities and behaviours prompted by unfavourable conditions, they were equally capable of making positive change in the presence of favourable ones. People were the best experts about themselves, and for that expertise to flourish, he believed a non-directive approach was essential.

Applying this to coaching supervision, coaches want to grow professionally and personally. They too are reaching for the light. For example, if they recount a coaching intervention that seems odd to the supervisor, instead of pointing out the error, the supervisor invites the supervisee to consider what they were aiming for, so that both may seek to understand the intention behind the actions.

3 *The role of the therapist is to create favourable conditions in which the client can change and grow.*

Rogers believed that individuals have within themselves vast resources for psychotherapeutic change or constructive personality changes which could include 'greater integration, less internal conflict, more energy utilisable for effective living; change in behaviour away from behaviours generally regarded as immature and toward behaviours regarded as mature' (Rogers, 1957, p. 95). These could best be tapped if a 'definable climate of facilitative psychological attitudes can be provided' (ibid). Rogers hypothesised that 'significant positive personality change does not occur except in a relationship' (Rogers, 1957, p. 96) and suggested six 'necessary and sufficient' conditions for this to occur. Note: Much of the existing literature on Rogers' work associates *empathy, congruence* and *unconditional positive regard* as his three core conditions yet this term was not his, rather adopted by the British person-centred movement in the 1970s/1980s. We include here all six, adapted to reflect the intended relationship between the person-centred supervisor and the supervisee:

1 A psychological 'contact' between them; both present and aware of being in a relationship with the other.
2 Coach incongruence where the supervisee is conflicted between how they feel or behave and how they think they *should*, particularly if it means that others may perceive them as they really are.
3 Supervisor congruence or genuineness, where the supervisor is real, human, transparent, accepting of their feelings about the supervisee, and expresses these appropriately in the relationship.
4 Supervisor unconditional positive regard where the supervisor fully accepts the supervisee without pre-conditions or judgement, seeing them as doing the best they can, and wanting to thrive.
5 Supervisor empathic understanding where the supervisor deeply wants to understand the supervisee's inner world so they can share the journey.
6 Coach perception where they perceive the supervisor as genuine, empathetic in their understanding and not imposing conditions of worth on them.

Rogers believed that these conditions would inevitably result in movement or change towards potential, and that people who continually strove to self-actualisation could become 'fully-functioning' (Rogers, 1963, p. 17). By this he meant congruent and living in the moment, open to experience, able to live in harmony with others, with a flexible self-concept, an unconditional self-regard, and the self-esteem and confidence to live to their full potential.

What is the role of the coach supervisor in the context of this philosophy?

The supervisor needs to attend to the key functions of supervision in a way that honours the supervisee's inherent resources. Starting a session with an open invitation such as 'What would you like to spend our time together working on?' signals to the supervisee(es) that they, not the supervisor, are in charge of the session content. They then focus on providing the conditions that allow the supervisee to access their own innate knowledge and to grow. Rogers's own style was relatively conversational in line with his desire to be real, rather than analysing or offering hypotheses (as was prevalent at the time); he reflected back to the client what he heard, or asked a question that invoked insight. The person-centred supervisor would do the same. If the supervisor shares knowledge for resourcing or learning purposes or steers the supervisee away from unethical choices, that would not be treating them as inherently resourceful. By holding in their awareness that the supervisee is in a state of 'becoming' (just as the supervisor is, actually), it will reduce the likelihood of seeing them as 'wrong' or lacking in resources.

So, if the supervisor has any feelings of anxiety or discomfort about the supervisee's work, they will share appropriately: for example,

> *I have an observation and a question which I would like to explore with you. Just now, I noticed feelings of confusion and concern in myself as you were relaying your responses to your client. And I wondered about your client's possible feelings. Do you have any thoughts?*

This is not laden with judgement, but it is being congruent and real in sharing feelings.

How the supervisee might respond to that would depend on context; it could be received as inviting and exploratory, or challenging, and perhaps the latter more so if asked during group supervision. Edmonson (1999) found that teams performed more highly where 'psychological safety,' i.e. being able to show and employ one's self without fear of negative consequences of self-image, status or career (Kahn, 1990, p. 708) was high. In such an environment people believed that it was safe to make a mistake, to not know, to not understand or to disagree. She believed this is key to learning and it underscores the importance of creating a climate where people are comfortable in being and expressing themselves. We could hypothesise that this could equally apply to individual and group supervision.

Where the supervisor creates a safe environment, the supervisee can acquire new courage to take risks. Without that safety, feelings of fear, ignorance, inadequacy or vulnerability could ferment and stunt their capacity for reaching their potential. Where the supervisor shares concern congruently, the likelihood of the supervisee coming to an insight is higher than when nothing is said but concern is still present in the dynamic.

How would you prepare yourself to work congruently with this approach?

The person-centred approach is a way of being, or a set of attitudes, not a set of techniques. Supervisor preparation could include considering what they might or might not do, or be, to provide the right conditions for the supervisee to take an active role.

The supervisor needs to make it possible for the supervisee to step into uncertainty, so that insight and learning can occur. This may mean letting go of our need to be expert and to instead step back to enable the supervisee to be or become the expert, an idea explored by the author in a blog post (Aspey, 2016).

It could be said that in person-centred supervision work it is the relationship that provides both the welcome nourishment and the safe vessel for the supervisee's journey. In setting out the intention to create the best possible relationship, the supervisor can ask themselves similar questions to Rogers' own questions in the famous 'Gloria' tapes (1965): Can I be real, genuine, congruent? How can share my philosophy of supervision so they know what is happening at any given moment and can take the lead in the session? How can I express my feelings without imposing on them? What do I mean by unconditional positive regard and how will I convey it, so the supervisee perceives it and believes it? Will I be able to put aside my own questions and ideas for long enough to understand their inner world, and without analysing them or treating them as deficient in some way?

If the supervisor does not feel congruent in so doing, this could impact on their reactions and what they convey in words, tone or body language, and this can impact on how the supervisee responds, opens up and connects. However, this in itself need not be an obstacle to doing good work. When we can hold in mind that *both* the supervisor and supervisee are in a state of 'becoming' we are more able to let go of anxiety about being perfect. Instead we enter into a territory where we explore what it means to be imperfect together.

If the supervisor can prepare themselves in this way, knowing that they will be setting aside their toolbox of exercises, techniques and theories, they can offer a wonderful foundation for working with this unique, inherently resourceful and positively motivated person: the supervisee.

How might this way of working be particularly useful to the supervisee?

Good contracting is vital. The supervisee and supervisor both need to be willing to step into a place full of possibility, co-creation and potentially, uncertainty. This can be a pleasant or an unpleasant surprise to a supervisee who has previously experienced a more directive or more structured approach. It can be a relief to be attended to in this way, or feel risky to be so exposed, invited to share thoughts, responses, opinions, actions.

Any resulting movement or change for the supervisee is not intended to be therapeutic change but something akin to and something signalling growth. It could be an insight that leads to new learning. It may lead to a change in the supervisee's internal world (e.g. a more accurate self-concept, or more confidence in their judgment). Or it could be a change in the way that they respond to their coaching clients (for example, in managing boundaries, being genuine and authentic with their client). Because this work starts with the individual themselves, these shifts can equally be useful for the coach when delivering other developmental work such as facilitation, training, consultancy and so forth. Indeed, everything that happens in the supervision session can apply in parallel to the way the coach is with their client.

Anything else you need to consider before using a person centred approach?

Having experienced this way of working the supervisee is well positioned to help their clients to strive towards their own light, their own potential. It is a reciprocal process; as we aid someone else to become, we become more, also.

References

Aspey, L. (2016) *Coaching Supervision: Who is the Expert in the Room?* [blog] Available at: www.aspey.com/blog-posts/coaching-supervision-who-is-the-expert-in-the-room [Accessed 6 August 19].

Edmonson, A. (1999) Psychological Safety and Learning Behavior in Work Teams. *Administrative Science Quarterly*, 44(2), pp. 350–383.

Kahn, W.A. (1990) Psychological Conditions of Personal Engagement and Disengagement at Work. *Academy of Management Journal*, 33(4), pp. 692–724.

Maslow, A.H. (1943) A Theory of Human Motivation. *Psychological Review*, 50(4), pp. 370–396.

Rogers, C.R. (1957) The Necessary and Sufficient Conditions of Therapeutic Personality. *Journal of Consulting Psychology*, 21, pp. 95–103.
Rogers, C.R. (1963) The Concept of the Fully Functioning Person. *Psychotherapy: Theory, Research & Practice*, 1(1), pp. 17–26.
Rogers, C.R. (1980) *A Way of Being*. Boston: Houghton Mifflin.

Further reading

Rogers, C.R. (1961) *On Becoming a Person*. Boston: Houghton Mifflin.

Resources

Rogers, C. (1965) [film] Directed by Everett. L. Shostrom. *Three Approaches to Psychotherapy, Part I.* (aka The Gloria Tapes) California: Psychological and Educational Films. Available at: www.youtube.com/watch?v=24d-FEptYj8 [Accessed 21 October 2019].

~ ~ ~ ~ ~

54. Exploring congruence

Michelle Lucas

Where can this be used?				Typical level of supervisee experience required	

When is this used?

This enquiry is likely to be offered when the supervisor notices a persistent somatic discomfort in response to a supervisee's account of their client work. The intention is to prompt a normative discussion exploring how the supervisee is enacting their espoused approach or model of coaching.

What is the enquiry?

The supervisor's surfaces their own sense of discomfort (practitioner congruence) to raise the supervisee's awareness of possible inconsistencies between their model and their practice (task congruence).

Step 1: Bring the sensation of discomfort into awareness.

While keeping a non-directive stance, the supervisor invites a pause for the supervisee to 'rewind' to an earlier part of the discussion. For example:

> .... might we pause for a moment? When you were talking about XXX I noticed the sensation of something tugging at my belly, often that signals to me something in the system may have been overlooked. How would you feel about re-visiting this to see if anything else comes into our awareness?

Step 2: Invite a more granular review.

Once the moment is captured and located by both supervisor and supervisee, the supervisor poses gentle questions, such as:

- What is your sense of how XXX came about?
- What were you aware of at the time, that you may or may not have attended to?

Step 3: Consider how their practice maps to their coaching approach.

Paradoxically, it is not necessary to know your supervisee's coaching approach. In fact, when it is known, a supervisor can be drawn to a more interrogative position. So, pose questions from a position of genuine discovery:

- Can we explore what you tell your clients about how you work?
- Which aspects of your coaching approach would you say most influenced you in that moment?
- Which parts might not have been attended to?
- What's your sense of why your work unfolded in the way it did?
- As you hear yourself talk about your worked on that day, how might you describe your coaching model now?

Step 4: Allow a new equilibrium to emerge.

For most experienced supervisees, this type of enquiry will bring into their awareness a need for adjustment. Unless an ethical issue has surfaced that needs more direct attention, simply allow space for fuller independent reflection.

How to work with the enquiry …

When working with this enquiry, offer the fullest respect for your supervisee. Remember, you were not in the room at the time. Honour your supervisee and trust that they were working with good intent and to the best of their ability. With this as an over-arching attitude, questions are framed in a gentle way, helping the supervisor to be experienced as someone seeking to facilitate a fuller understanding, rather than to highlight poor practice, or to diagnose or problem solve.

When inconsistency is identified it can provoke a tussle for the supervisee, considering how they wish to work and how they work effectively. Many coaches aspire to be 'pure and non-directive' and yet in truth they offer their clients an effective blend of coaching, mentoring and consultancy. Through using this enquiry, we help supervisees to be more accurate and more articulate in how they bring value to their clients. A supervisor will, of course, have a duty to their supervisee's clients (are they getting what they were promised?), but additionally they have a duty to the coaching profession (are coaches properly explaining what they do?).

What else might need attention?

In order to check for consistency, the supervisee needs to have considered how to articulate their coaching approach. If not already done, it could be developed as part of the supervision work.

A word of caution

It is for the supervisee to decide whether they want to *change the way* they work or *change what they say* about how they work. The role of the supervisor is only to highlight the difference (and where agreed, hold the supervisee to account for creating greater consistency) not to direct what needs to change.

What other uses are there for this enquiry?

This could be adapted to work with coaching clients who have developed a personal leadership brand and who want to review how they are embedding new ways of working.

Further reading

Counselling Training Liverpool. (2015) *Being Congruent – What Does It Mean?* [online] 23 November. Available at: www.counsellingtrainingliverpool.org.uk/blog/being-congruent-what-does-it-mean# [Accessed 7 September 2019].

~ ~ ~ ~ ~

55. Supervisee-led supervision

Louise Sheppard

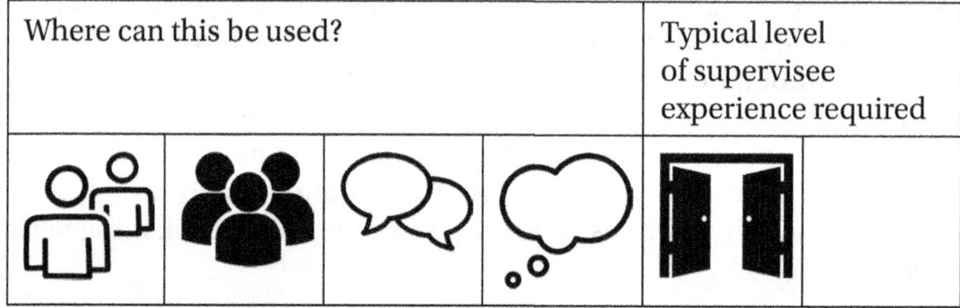

Where can this be used?
Typical level of supervisee experience required

When is this used?

Supervisee-led supervision is a strategy that can be used throughout coaching supervision. Supervisors use supervisee-led supervision when they adapt, accommodate and attune to the supervisee's personal preferences and focus on maximising the supervisee's learning. Supervisees use it to take ownership for their supervision and engage fully with their learning.

What is the approach?

The concept of supervisee-led supervision was introduced by Michael Carroll (2014) and developed by Sheppard (2016) who studied what supervisees do that helps and hinders them during supervision. She created a framework for how supervisees can get the most from the process (see Figure 4.1) along with guidelines for its use.

The framework is specifically designed for supervisees with an intention to become active participants in their supervision. Thus, 'supervisee-led supervision' is at the heart of the inner circle. The outer circle of the framework depicts the possible underlying mechanisms that affect

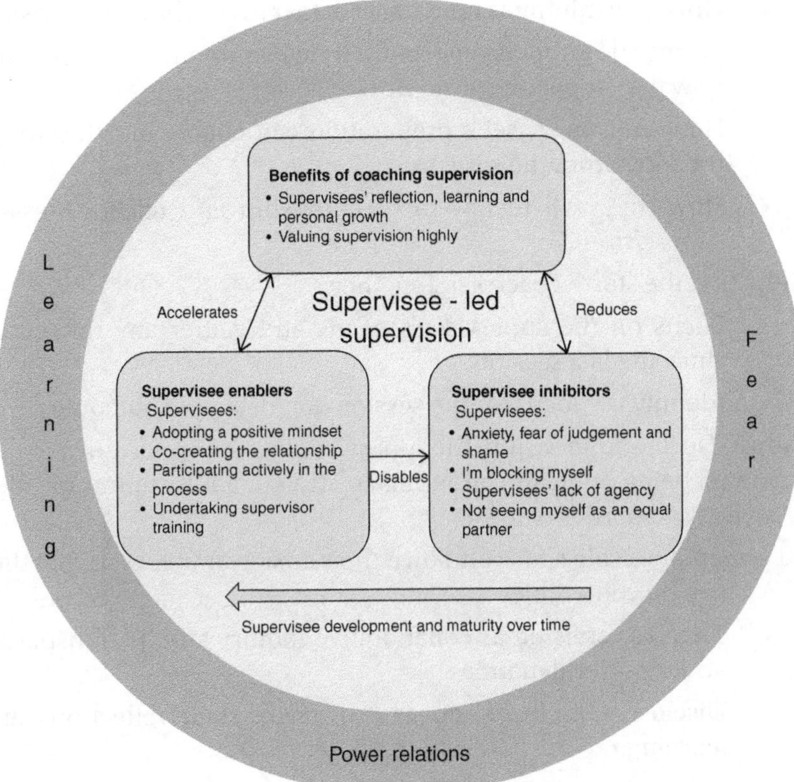

Figure 4.1 Framework for supervisee-led supervision by Sheppard (2016)

coaching supervision – our natural desire for learning, power relations and fear. Inside the circle lie the benefits of coaching supervision, as well as what supervisees can do to enable or inhibit their supervision experience. The small arrows between the boxes illustrate that the benefits of supervision accelerate supervisees' desire to enable their supervision and reduce their tendency to get in their own way and inhibit their supervision. The larger arrow represents supervisee development and maturity over time.

Step 1: Both parties co-create the supervisory relationship by discussing:

- What assumptions and beliefs they are holding about their respective roles and responsibilities.
- How they can acknowledge power relations and establish an equal partnership.

- How they minimise the impact of fear in coaching supervision.
- Where the supervisee is in their development as a coach and how that might affect the work.
- How the supervisee's preparation can enable him/her to get the most from the session.
- How they will review the relationship and effectiveness of supervision.

Step 2: At the start of each session, they:

- Focus on the supervisee's needs and gather any reflections since the last session.
- Identify the focus for the session and desirable outcomes.

Step 3: During supervision, the supervisor has the opportunity to role model being open and adopting an adult to adult communication style. Both parties will

- Create a safe space and own their anxiety and fear so that they can be vulnerable.
- Treat supervision as collaborative inquiry and be transparent about power dynamics.
- Disclose their experiences and share their reflections and learning.
- Review how they experienced the session - what was helpful and what could be done differently going forward.

Step 4: At regular intervals, they:

- Review the effectiveness of the supervision, how the supervisee's supervision needs are developing and how the sessions might change accordingly.
- Explore if the supervisee has outgrown the supervisor and/or would benefit from an alternative perspective.

How to work with the approach ...

The framework is not intended to be a complete guide to conducting a supervision session, rather a checklist for adopting a supervisee-led approach. The supervisee-led supervisor will set a tone of collaboration in every aspect of the relationship - from setting appointments to navigating the work.

What else might need attention?

Using supervisee-led supervision does not prevent supervisors from fulfilling the normative part of their role and calling out ethical issues. The approach necessitates an adult-to-adult way of communicating, thereby enabling open and honest conversations about differences in perception, options and potential consequences.

A word of caution

Using supervisee-led supervision is challenging and requires a high degree of self-awareness and courage for both parties. For example, where the supervisor is taking too much power, perhaps by being too 'expert', it is vital that the supervisee steps into their authority and points this out.

What other uses are there for this approach?

Supervisee-led supervision can be used in workshops, webinars and guidelines on how to get the most out of coaching supervision. It is also useful for supervisor training programmes as the current supervision models are often based on the supervisor perspective.

The principles of supervisee-led supervision can be applied in a coach-client context by contracting with the client about how to acknowledge and minimise the impact of anxiety and fear and power dynamics and maximise learning.

References

Carroll, M. (2014) *Effective Supervision for the Helping Professions*. London: Sage.

Sheppard, L. (2016) *How Coaching Supervisees Help and Hinder Their Supervision: A Grounded Theory Study*, PHD, Oxford Brookes University.

Chapter 5

A positive psychology approach to coaching supervision

Carmelina Lawton-Smith

How is this philosophy described?

The term 'positive psychology' was coined after Martin Seligman as chair of the American Psychological Association in 1998 observed that psychology seemed to have become pre-occupied with the study of dysfunction and distress. For many years, psychologists had studied mental illness and cognitive malfunctions as a route to discovering how the mind works. Some argued that you would not seek to learn about the secrets of a happy marriage by asking a recently divorced couple, so why were we looking for the secrets of human functioning among the forests of mental illness? Surely, we need to study those who are thriving in life in order to discern the secrets to higher human functioning. So began the interest in taking a more positive view of psychological research. Researchers began to ask questions like, what helps people be resilience, what makes for a happy life, or how to promote optimism and well-being? Positive psychology is therefore described by Seligman and Csikszentmihalyi (2000) as the 'scientific study of optimal human functioning [that] aims to discover and promote the factors that allow individuals and communities to thrive.' It is this focus on optimal functioning that demonstrates clear synergy with coaching and makes it of interest to the coaching community.

What are the underpinning principles and beliefs of this philosophy?

There are three key principles that underpin this approach:

1 *Taking a strengths-based approach to development:*

As practitioners we have frequently fallen into the same trap as the psychologists. We often treat development as a gap analysis focusing on weaknesses that need to be corrected. In organisational review processes it is common to overlook what people do well and focus on how to correct their perceived short-falls. Coaches, too, fall into the same pattern, for example by asking clients about the 'issue' they want to address. This is often mirrored in supervision. Supervisees tend to come with current challenges they are facing or looking to resolve problems they are experiencing.

Positive psychology takes a different starting point by seeking to identify what is good and can be built upon. Most notably, the 'strengths' movement emerged arguing that we can learn and develop just as much by focusing on strengths we already have and using these more effectively to overcome our potential limitations in other areas. For example, someone with excellent people skills could leverage them in order to develop their lack of creativity. They will likely find it a more effective strategy to bring people together in problem solving groups to help them generate creative ideas, rather than to read a book on creative problem-solving. The logic of the argument rests on the fact that to constantly work on things that are hard, in which you often feel inadequate is neither stimulating nor motivating. By contrast, applying your natural strengths feels more authentic and natural, brings energy and is more likely to end in success because you have a natural capability in that domain. This generates positive emotions that can be harnessed to good effect.

2 *Leveraging the benefits of positive emotions.*

It has long been known that positive emotions are correlated with certain hormonal reactions. For example, oxytocin is released in response to touch and signals trust, and serotonin is associated with feeling a sense of recognition or confidence. However, the wider purpose of these positive emotions has long puzzled researchers. Negative emotions have a clear survival benefit, when we feel fear the body prepares physiologically for fight or flight. Emotion researchers commonly assumed that all emotional reactions were linked to an 'action-tendency' so were in effective a trigger for a survival behaviour. Yet positive emotions seemed to generate a desire to *do* nothing. The contentment that can be felt when lying by the river on a sunny day seemed to convey no evolutionary advantage. Since there was no apparent benefit, Barbara Fredrickson (2009) argued that scientific principles dictate that these feelings were unnecessary and should, by now, have died out and yet they are still part of our experience. She started to research what possible purpose these emotions might have to explain their endurance in evolutionary terms. She identified three key benefits of positive emotions and her research led to the 'broaden and build theory'. This states that positive emotions:

- Enhance our breadth of options, making us more innovative and creative when problem solving or facing new challenges. People are effectively more free thinking and innovative when happy and not stressed.
- Make it more likely that you will build relationships with others, promoting social interactions which creates a safer environment because it builds support and coalitions. Not an unsurprising finding, that happy people find it easier to attract friends.
- Help 'undo' or reverse the physiological effects of stressful negative emotions. Laughing at a funny joke or film will help the body to more quickly restore a normal blood pressure and hormonal state after a stressful event. We will all have experienced how humour can sometimes diffuse a difficult situation, so these findings are in line with what we perhaps knew anecdotally.

3 *Promoting well-being through balance and authenticity.*

It is this link to things 'we knew all along' that has caused positive psychology to attract criticism. It has been derided in the media as a statement of the obvious or simply positive thinking. But the tenets of positive psychology should not be confused with the self-help literature that proclaims a positive attitude can cure all ills! Positive psychology does not seek to deny the existence of bad things, in fact the study of Meaning, for example the work of Ben-Shahar (2008) has revealed that it is often experiencing significant difficulty that makes something meaningful: running a marathon is meaningful precisely because it involves hardship and struggle to the edges of capability. Rather, positive psychology seeks to rebalance our knowledge and understanding by promoting our ability to focus on the good as well as the bad. We are all hard-wired to notice and attend to negative things as priority because they are the most likely to do us harm, but this can mean that the positive gets over-looked. Positive psychology attempts to combat this negativity bias – it promotes acceptance of the bad, rather than denial of it. The aim is to help individuals build a strong sense of well-being by understanding and accepting their authentic self.

The scope of positive psychology therefore extends to many topics of value and interest to developing coaches and the techniques in this chapter will demonstrate some of these. Many techniques concentrate on ways to enable positive conversations in order to generate positive emotions, such as a focus on strengths, successes or positive events. Others deal with an understanding of emotions and self-awareness where the supervisee can develop their emotional intelligence and build their personal resilience. Another important aspect in positive psychology is to understand the importance of meaning and values in our daily life and how to achieve congruence and authenticity in our work. All these concepts can support coach development and make it a useful addition to the supervisory toolbox.

What is the role of the coach supervisor in the context of this philosophy?

We know that supervision has three core functions in respect of supervisees. These are to enhance development, to encourage self-care and to promote quality in the profession. Working within a positive psychology paradigm will enhance development by harnessing the power of positive conversations to build motivation and self-belief, and also exposes the supervisee to the impact of a positive approach. This means they can evaluate how and when that same positive focus might be of value in their own practice. However, the positive approach can also help significantly in the role of encouraging self-care. Positive psychology has a strong focus on resilience, on acceptance, self-compassion, and achieving psychological well-being, all areas that can support coaches in their ability to practice effectively and minimise the chances of burnout.

According to Ryff and Keyes (1995) psychological well-being is made up of six principles:

1 Personal Growth.
2 Environmental Mastery.
3 Self-Acceptance.
4 Purpose in Life.
5 Autonomy.
6 Positive Relations with others.

It could be argued that supervision shows significant synergy with all these principles. The developmental role of the supervisor aims to support personal growth and mastery in the supervisee's coaching role. When encouraging self-care there is often a focus on self-acceptance and uncovering key values that give their coaching a sense of purpose. Yet the supervisory interaction also aims to provide a positive relationship that promotes personal autonomy. The supervision process therefore seems to show alignment with positive psychology principles and would appear to be a valuable way to support the psychological well-being of coaches.

How would you prepare yourself to work congruently with this approach?

As a supervisor there are two significant considerations for working in this way:

1 This is not an approach you can use convincingly unless you have experienced the benefits and believe that it is valuable. It requires a belief in the approach as valid, so beware of creating a self-fulfilling prophesy, if you feel it is based only on fashionable hype, the techniques are likely to fail. There is a lot of evidence showing the benefits these ideas can bring but they will not work for all of your supervisees, all of the time. Test out the ideas and techniques on yourself and willing volunteers who can give you feedback. Discover which approaches work for you, and which do not, then be selective in what you choose to apply. Use only those you really believe in.

2 The positive approach does not require you to be Pollyanna personified! Pollyanna was always interminably cheery and this can prove exhausting and irritating for others. Positive psychology looks for the good but not to the exclusion of the bad. There must still be space for the supervisee to be authentic and reveal concerns, doubts and failures in the environment of non-judgemental acceptance. Positive may not always mean happy. When working with positive psychology, you try to look for and focus on the good to support development, there is no need to fix a smile or talk only of happy events.

How might this way of working be particularly useful to the supervisee?

We know that focusing attention on and discussing positive events will release positive emotion, which can help people become more creative, build relationships and reduce stress. Therefore, mobilising these benefits in supervision could be of benefit to the supervisee in a number of ways. First, a focus on strengths and positive experiences in the early stages of the supervision relationship can help build connection and trust. Second, the creativity and innovation released can help the supervisee think more freely when investigating issues and possible solutions.

With the reduction in stress, the mind is more able to wander, it does not need to focus on the imminent threat and can be more receptive to new ideas. Third, it can help supervisees create more balance in their practice for themselves and their clients. For supervisees who are overly critical of their own performance it can give them techniques for managing this negativity-bias and support self-care. Supervisees who are more used to working with a deficit mindset may be surprised by the positive developmental impact this philosophy can have. By using a positive psychology approach in supervision, it helps raise the supervisee's awareness of how frequently the focus of coaching becomes a problem-solving approach. This awareness can support the development of a wider set of options for the supervisee to try in their own practice, perhaps testing or adopting some of the approaches with their own clients. Ultimately, releasing more positive emotion in the supervisee is likely to support confidence, release energy and enhance engagement in the supervision task.

Anything else you need to consider before using the techniques that follow?

There are many techniques that sit within this philosophy. Remember to consider whether the language and terminology is appropriate for the context. Talking about a gratitude diary may cause some supervisees to dis-engage from the process, whereas asking them to complete an appreciation journal may be more acceptable. The discourse and language linked to positive psychology can become a hindrance, so it is perfectly acceptable to adapt the language and remain true to the underpinning principles. Bear this in mind as you consider the techniques that follow. Your own context of work may require you to make adaptations to the presentation or language of techniques.

While a focus on the positive aspects of a situation can be of value, an inflexible and ill-considered use of these approaches can come across as single-minded and unresponsive. There are always times when to ask about the 'positives' might be insensitive and inappropriate, so be mindful of this. The positive approach is not one for every day, nor every situation. However, it can offer a refreshing and energising alternative to the problem-focussed starting point of many supervisory sessions.

References

Ben-Shahar, T. (2008) *Happier*, New York: McGraw Hill.
Fredrickson, B. (2009) *Positivity*, New York: Crown Publishers.

Ryff, C.D. and Keyes, C.L.M. (1995) The structure of psychological well-being revisited, *Journal of Personality & Social Psychology*, 69, pp. 719–727.
Seligman, M. and Csikszentmihalyi, M. (2000) Positive psychology: An introduction, *American Psychologist*, 55, pp. 5–14.

Further reading

Biswas-Diener, R. and Dean, B. (2007) *Positive Psychology Coaching*, Hoboken, NJ: Wiley.
Boniwell, I. (2012). *Positive Psychology in a Nutshell*, 3rd ed. Maidenhead: Open University Press.
Boniwell, I. and Kauffman, C. (2018) The Positive Psychology Approach to Coaching. In: E. Cox, T. Bachkirova and D. Clutterbuck (Eds.) *The Complete Handbook of Coaching*, 3rd ed., London: Sage. Ch. 11, pp. 153–166.
Buckingham, M. and Clifton, D. (2004) *Now, Discover Your Strengths*, London: Simon and Schuster.
Corrie, S. (2009) *The Art of Inspired Living*, London: Karnac.
Driver, M. (2011) *Coaching Positively*, Maidenhead: Open University Press.
Green, S. and Palmer, S. (2019) *Positive Psychology Coaching in Practice*, Abingdon: Routledge.
Linley, P.A. (2008) *Average to A+*, Coventry: CAPP Press.
Seligman, M. (2017) *Authentic Happiness*, London: Nicholas Brealey.

~ ~ ~ ~ ~

56. 5% sentences

Carmelina Lawton Smith

Where can this be used?				Typical level of supervisee experience required	

When is this used?

Originally developed by Branden (1994) to support the growth of self-esteem, this 'sentence completion' approach can be a useful way to raise supervisee awareness about their growth potential. It is most valuable in three possible contexts. First, when a supervisee is becoming habituated to the supervision process or with a specific client context. The supervisor can use this to open a discussion about going beyond their existing comfort zone. Second, when the supervisee puts unnecessary constraints on their development, e.g. 'I can't do that', in such a situation the request to just imagine a 5% shift can be an acceptable way to push those boundaries. Lastly, it can be a useful approach when looking at the longer-term development potential for supervisees or as part of an annual review. It can identify areas for future focus and the potential impact of what might initially seem quite achievable increments.

What is the technique?

The technique involves setting out a set of sentence stems that often include a 5% change. Working quickly, the supervisee generates at least six endings to complete the sentence stems with whatever comes up. There is then a period of exploration and reflection on the completed statements.

Step 1: Prepare the supervisee.

Provide an overview of the approach and ensure the supervisee is happy to explore their topic under focus in this way.

Step 2: Prepare the stems.

Stems can take many forms and you can get ideas from the References below but here are some you may consider:

- If I accept myself 5% more ...
- If I bring 5% more awareness to my coaching ...
- If I bring 5% more integrity to my coaching ...
- If I operate 5% more purposefully in my coaching ...
- If I become 5% more authentic in my coaching ...
- If I become 5% less of a perfectionist ...
- If I become 5% more realistic ...
- If I appreciate my successes 5% more ...

Step 3: Explore meaning.

The simple process of reading and reflecting on the statements can be valuable but any further discussion should allow the supervisee considerable autonomy in their choice of focus.

- What does this suggest to you?
- Which areas would you like to explore further?

- How can I best help you?
- What do you take from the statements?
- What do you want to do with this information?

Step 4: Ensuring the work serves your client.

As a final step it can be valuable to relate the learning back to their coaching context.

- How might this serve your clients?
- What might be the impact with your coaching work?

How to work with the technique ...

As you prepare the supervisee in Step 1, this might reveal some sensitive areas. It may therefore be helpful to include a caveat to allow them to choose which to explore with the supervisor, and which they prefer to reflect on in their own time.

Where the supervisee struggles with confidence even a 5% shift may seem daunting, play with the figure accordingly until the supervisee feels that the size of the shift can be contemplated.

A word of caution

This may not be suitable to do in a group setting unless the written reflections remain private or are discussed in a subsequent 1:1 supervision context.

What other uses are there for this technique?

These questions are useful material for individual reflection and could be offered by way of preparation for a supervision session. It is then up to the individual how much of their thinking they share with the supervisor or the group.

Tal Ben-Shahar has also expanded this approach and alternative formulations can be used. For example:

- If I give myself permission to make mistakes ...
- If I give myself permission to fail ...
- When I reject my emotions ...
- If I remain loyal to the values I truly believe to be right ...
- I fear that ...
- I hope that ...
- I am beginning to see that ...

This could also be a useful approach for coaching clients, where there is a good level of trust in the coaching relationship. Because the technique can elicit divergent thoughts, the coach needs to be prepared to manage boundary issues and to have the skills to harness emerging topics while keeping the coaching goals in mind.

Reference

Branden, N. (1994) *The Six Pillars of Self-Esteem*, London: Bantam.

Further reading

Ben-Shahar, T. (2009) *The Pursuit of Perfect*, New York: McGraw-Hill.

~ ~ ~ ~ ~

57. eMotive cards

Peter Duffell

Where can this be used?				Typical level of supervisee experience required	

When is this used?

An understanding of emotion is a key element of building personal resources in positive psychology. Research (Duffell and Lawton-Smith, 2017) has shown that supervisors frequently encounter emotions with supervisees and strongly believe that emotion should be explored to facilitate coaches' personal and professional development. For some this emotional exploration can be difficult; the eMotive cards have been developed to enable a more tangible and objective discussion.

They help raise awareness of the potential source and impact of emotions on both the coach and their clients. They are particularly useful where the supervisee:

- Is finding it difficult to describe their emotions.
- Relies upon metaphor to convey a sense of their emotional situation.
- Is able to externalise or objectify their emotions and wants to enrich the supervision discussion.

What is the technique?

The technique relies on getting the supervisee to choose those word cards that describe either their current emotional state, or an event evoking an emotional response that they wish to explore in supervision.

Step 1: Selection.

Invite the supervisee to select all relevant words, by either:

- Spreading the cards out with the large words facing upwards.
- Handing the cards to the supervisee and invite them to look through them.

The supervisee chooses a number of emotion descriptors; in our experience, it can be helpful to pause at five cards. The cards have a large word on one side and four similar words on the other. If none capture the feeling, supervisees can write their own words in the blank box (dry-wipe pens enable the plastic coated cards to be reused). Extra blank cards are also included offering a lot of flexibility in how emotions can be named.

Step 2: Drilling down.

Explore the personal meaning of the chosen emotion. Typically, this helps them to clarify or uncover how they personally experience this emotion and also prevents the supervisor making assumptions. In some ways this is similar to values elicitation where a supervisee and supervisor may share the same value but have completely different views of what this means to them personally. Use questions like:

- How would you describe this emotion for you?
- How did it manifest in this situation?

Step 3: Emotional impact and management.

Once the emotion is understood the supervisor can explore the impact of that emotional state and discuss management strategies. For example, a supervisee 'anxious' about their client work could be asked to quantify this on a 1–10 scale. The supervisor can then explore how the supervisee might reduce their anxiety score. Alternatively, there could be an exploration of what might have given rise to that emotional reaction so that preventative strategies could be put in place.

- How might that emotion affect your coaching?
- When did you first notice the emotion?
- What steps might help you prevent/manage/reduce this emotional impact?

How to work with the technique ...

Given the exploration is of the supervisee's emotion experience, it can be helpful to facilitate this lightly. Allow the supervisee to control the exploration; there is no need to enforce rules about 'how many' cards or whether words are grammatically correct. Indeed, some of the most impactful explorations occur when the supervisee creates their own language for their emotions.

A word of caution

Ensure the supervisee is allowed to name their emotions without contamination from the supervisor. The value of the tool is in helping the supervisees to understand their emotions in their own words (Duffell and Lawton-Smith, 2015).

What other uses are there for this technique?

Supervisors are encouraged to develop their own way of using the cards; most often used in individual supervision, they can also be used in group settings. For example, peers could listen to the scenario brought and listen out for the feelings that they noticed being expressed or un-expressed. The cards could be used as the vehicle for offering feedback. The alternative words on the reverse of the card can make it easier to accept feedback as they have the ability to tailor what has been offered; the supervisee may also find them useful to use with their own clients. They are particularly helpful to open up a discussion about emotion in a more concrete way.

References

Duffell, P. and Lawton-Smith, C. (2017) Once more with feeling, *Coaching at Work*, 12(3), pp. 6–40.

Duffell, P. and Lawton-Smith, C. (2015) The challenges of working with emotion in coaching, *The Coaching Psychologist*, 11(1), pp. 32–39.

Resources

Cards available from www.westwoodcoaching.co.uk [Accessed 7 September 2019].

~ ~ ~ ~ ~

58. FeedForward

Carmelina Lawton Smith

Where can this be used?				Typical level of supervisee experience required	

When is this used?

This technique uses positive past experiences to raise awareness and draw lessons from other contexts, which can then be related to the current situation they are facing. It draws on the idea of when they are 'at their best' and how to leverage that knowledge by taking positive lessons from similar experiences. It can be used to help supervisees deal with issues or to engage in self-care by identifying the conditions that need to exist for them to achieve the desired aim.

What is the technique?

The approach relies on the supervisee being able to recount a past success, which might have been in a different context when they were 'at their best' in relation to the topic. For example, a supervisee might explain that they do not feel a connection with a particular client. The supervisor might elicit a story about when they 'did' experience a strong connection with another person to identify what might be required to bring about this state. This raises self-awareness and lessons can be drawn to inform the actions the supervisee feels it is appropriate to take forward, or maybe just increase understanding and self-acceptance. The approach is taken from the work of Kluger and Nir (2010), which was adapted for coaching by McDowall et al. (2014).

Step 1: Elicit a success story.

Working with the topic the supervisee has brought, ask for a story of when they felt 'at their best.' This story might be from a work or a personal context. Ask questions that focus on positive emotions, encouraging them to re-live the experience in as much detail as possible.

- When do you feel you have been 'at your best' in your coaching work?
- Thinking back, including other contexts, when have you felt frustration, yet been able to manage it?
- When have you previously successfully managed your anxiety when approaching an unfamiliar task?

Step 2: The peak moment.

Draw attention and focus to the 'high-point.' Concentrate on positive self-evaluation and emotions.

- What made it a high point?
- How did it feel at the time?

Follow up with questions like:

- Tell me more about that experience – what did you see, or hear or sense?
- What else was happening?

Step 3: Clarifying the conditions.

Ask questions that engage the supervisee in an evaluation of the facilitating conditions, such as the environment, their own state or the involvement of others.

- How was this achieved?
- What was the most important factor for you at the time?
- What skills and attributes helped you achieve that?

Step 4: FeedForward to the future.

Now that there is an understanding of their optimal performance conditions, the supervisee can be encouraged to make comparisons with the current situation. To move towards personal action planning based on the learning, the supervisor might offer questions like:

- What could you borrow from your prior experience that could be useful to you now?
- What would need to shift in your current situation to mirror more closely your prior experience?
- Which parts of you contributed to your success before, which need to be harnessed for you now?

How to work with the technique …

The essence of this technique is helping the supervisee to re-live their experience in order to identify key factors. Therefore, in both Steps 1 and 3, minimise the focus on dates times and facts, rather help them to re-experience that event, so ask questions about emotions, senses, such as sight or smell. Ensure your enquiry is holistic - consider all the possible ways of experiencing and all the possible sources of knowing as we need to be mindful that our supervisees preferred processing style may be different to our own.

A word of caution

If the supervisee cannot elicit a past success it is appropriate to question the wider context and experiences but if no examples are forthcoming move on to an alternative approach. To labour their lack of success in this topic will otherwise only serve to de-motivate them even further.

What other uses are there for this technique?

It is possible to draw attention to this process as a technique the supervisee can use with clients, especially when clients get stuck or seem to be overlooking their resourcefulness.

References

Kluger, N.K. and Nir, D. (2010) The FeedForward interview, *Human Resource Management Review*, 20, pp. 235–246.

McDowall, A., Freeman, K. and Marshall, S. (2014) Is FeedForward the way forward? A comparison of the effects of FeedForward coaching and Feedback, *International Coaching Psychology Review*, 9(2), pp. 125–146.

Further reading

Itzchakov, G. and Kluger, A. (2018) *Giving Feedback: The Power of Listening in Helping People Change.* [online] Harvard Business Review (Published 17 May 2018). Available at: https://hbr.org/2018/05/the-power-of-listening-in-helping-people-change [Accessed 2 September 2018].

~ ~ ~ ~ ~

59. Give yourself an 'A'

Clare Norman

Where can this be used?				Typical level of supervisee experience required	

When is this used?

This technique is used at the start of supervision, typically after the first session, to enable the supervisee to set their intentions for what success would look like for them at the end of the programme.

What is the technique?

The supervisee writes a letter, looking back over their supervision series, stating why they got an A. Zander and Zander (2000) wrote about the technique in their book *The Art of Possibility*; Benjamin Zander had used it at the start of term, telling his students that they had already got an A, and the only requirement was for them to write him a letter, dated the end of term, outlining why they deserved this grade. By the end of the term, they had met or exceeded their own expectations of success.

Step 1: Brief supervisees as follows:

You will 'get an A' for the six months of this supervision series. There is one requirement that you must fulfil in order to earn the grade. Write me a letter dated [end of supervision series], which begins with the words ...

'Dear XX, I got my A because ...'

Share as much detail as you can, the story of what will have happened to you as a coach by that time which is in line with this extraordinary grade. Place yourself in the future, looking back, and report on all the insights you acquired and milestones you attained during those months, as if those accomplishments were already in the past. You are part of multiple systems, so tell me about the impact that you will have on those systems and how you will be achieving that. Phrases like 'I hope', 'I intend', 'I will' must not appear. I am especially interested in the person you will become by then and the attitude, feelings and world view of that person who will have done all you wished to do or become everything you wished to be. I want you to fall passionately in love with that person you describe in your letter. You can choose to send it to me, but more important is that you keep it for yourself, as your commitment to yourself. You'll be amazed at what happens as a result.

Note: Based on Zander and Zander's *The Art of Possibility* - see pp. 25–53.

Step 2: At the end of the supervision series, ask supervisees to look at their letter and compare where they are today to where they had started.

Step 3: Debrief with additional questions such as:

- Who are you now as a coach?
- What has changed in the way you feel as a coach?
- What is your attitude now towards your work?
- What is your world view now as a coach?
- What is the impact you now have on the people you work with?
- And the impact on their systems?
- And the impact on the world?
- What have you learned about yourself as a result of this exercise?
- What is possible for you as a coach now?

How to work with the technique ...

Supervisees choose whether to write this letter or not. However, we can reassure them about its value, in visualising the future they desire and the likelihood that it will come to pass once they have articulated it. On the rare occasion that they fall short of their A, encourage them to consider what they could do differently to make supervision a success for them.

What else might need attention?

The original technique is individually focused and yet we work with people who are part of larger systems, so the version here makes reference to this systemic perspective. You may wish to debrief further about how else the supervisee, intentionally or otherwise, has an impact for example:

- How does your philosophy of life have an impact on your coaching?
- How much do you challenge your clients about the impact of their choices on, for example, diversity and inclusion?
- What is your ethical stance regarding the impact of your client's actions on society and the world, for example climate change?

A word of caution

Where there is a lack of resonance with some of the words in the briefing (for example 'falling passionately in love with yourself'), adapt them accordingly.

Bear in mind also that this is not literally about the supervisee receiving an A from the supervisor; it is a personal quest, a striving to be the best coach and making the most of the supervision opportunity.

What other uses are there for this technique?

You can use this for any programme that takes place over a period of time, whether that is individual work or team coaching, teaching etc.

Reference

Zander, R. and Zander, B. (2000) *The Art of Possibility*, Boston: Harvard Business Press.

~ ~ ~ ~ ~

60. Good news

Michelle Lucas and Carol Whitaker

Where can this be used?				Typical level of supervisee experience required	

When is this used?

This technique provides a counterbalance to our tendency to consider what could have been better and can therefore be useful in at least two scenarios. First, where the supervisee feels something went well and they would like to affirm and 'savour' (see Peterson, p.71) the experience. Second, where the supervisee lacks confidence, is being overly self-critical or is catastrophising.

Typically a group technique, it can be adjusted to work with individuals. Originating from positive psychology, it encourages the supervisee to look for what went well, even if overall the situation was imperfect. It prompts supervisees to generate both an affirmation and to dig deeper to consider how strengths developed.

What is the technique?

Step 1: As you listen to the supervisee notice what (small or significant) they did well. Remember even where there is room for improvement – many elements of the work are likely to be worthy of affirmation.

Remind the group that when they notice something the supervisee did well, consider why this might have been so? There are three potential sources:

1 It could be connected to an earlier action. For example, *'the client sounded really open with you, and I notice how well you contracted.'*

2 Offer a hypothesis, *'the client sounded really open with you – I imagine you helped them feel safe.'*

3 You have information from other sources. This is common amongst colleagues, for example, *'I've always thought you were very respectful, and it seemed that was how you were with this client.'*

Step 2: The supervisee is invited to talk through the client case. Before other contributions are given, the supervisor encourages the supervisee to consider what they could celebrate in their work, and what they already know that enabled this.

Step 3 (a): Each group member is invited to offer an affirmation, where possible their best guess on how that came about. Reassure them that it is to have multiple endorsements of the same thing, repetition can be particularly powerful.

Step 3 (b): The supervisee is invited to say 'thank you' to each peer and to make a note of affirmations for future reference.

Step 4: The supervisor returns to the supervisee, a pause is helpful, allowing time for digesting the feedback. A useful question is 'What's been the impact on you?'

Step 5: The intention is not just to receive affirmations, but to understand how strengths came about. Before closing this round of supervision, check which of the affirmations are best understood (i.e. Do they already know how this capability developed?) and which would be helpful to explore further.

How to work with the technique ...

Step 2 can be challenging for self-critical supervisees. With encouragement, people usually find something to celebrate. This principle reminds the supervisee that they have the capacity to recognise their own strengths and integrate external feedback. Without some foundation, the supervisee could discount affirming feedback as peers 'just being nice.'

Contributions should be statements not questions. We are seeking to affirm more than explore.

What else might need attention?

When a supervisee chooses this technique more often than anything else, particularly when working as a group, this may be an indication of defensiveness (not wanting to discuss mistakes) or that some power play is going on (a desire for others to know of their brilliance). This may indicate that a return to the contract may be timely.

A word of caution

Cultural nuance can mean some people find this technique challenging, believing that ignoring areas for development would be foolhardy. If this occurs, try using Affirmations and Alternatives (see pp. 10–12) as it provides greater balance.

Given this lack of balance the supervisor may decide not to offer their own 'Good News' as it could be perceived as favouritism.

What other uses are there for this technique?

This can be a useful method for coaches to offer their clients; many people discount those qualities that come easily to them and this technique helps give greater awareness or 'conscious competence' to the client.

Reference

Peterson, C. (2006) *A Primer in Positive Psychology*, New York: Oxford University Press.

~ ~ ~ ~ ~

61. Personal strengths review

Carmelina Lawton Smith

Where can this be used?				Typical level of supervisee experience required	

When is this used?

This is a useful approach when a supervisee has a tendency to appraise their skills as a gap analysis, focusing on their lack of expertise. It can help boost confidence to consider what strengths they already have that they can bring to their coaching.

It might be especially useful when working with a new supervisee to build rapport with a positive focus by asking about their strengths in coaching, rather than starting with their issues or a simple bio. Because this approach builds positive rapport, it can be valuable with groups in the early stages of their work together and would be suitable for peer groups with minor adaptation of the questions.

What is the technique?

The technique is based on an open discussion about the strengths they bring to coaching. Linley (2008, p.9) defines a strength as 'a pre-existing capacity for a particular way of behaving, thinking, or feeling that is authentic and energising to the user, and enables optimal functioning, development and performance.' Therefore, by revealing the supervisees natural strengths it is likely to lead to greater energy and authenticity in their coaching.

Step 1: Achievements.

Ask them to tell a short story about an achievement that demonstrates a key strength. Avoid asking simply 'What are your strengths?' as this can be hard to answer and might lead to a superficial discussion. Use questions like:

- What would you describe as your most significant accomplishments?
- What key strength(s) does it highlight?

Step 2: Elicit strengths stories.

Follow up with a more general discussion about strengths - some sample questions are shown below. You may want to explain what a strength is and why it is important. This section can also be done in small groups or pairs in group supervision as an icebreaker.

- What makes a great day for you? Tell me about the best day that you remember having?
- When would your friends and family say you are at your happiest?
- If you could plan a day that would leave you feeling energised, what would you do?
- What sort of everyday things do you enjoy doing?
- When you are at your best, what are you doing?
- What gives you the greatest sense of being authentic and who you really are?
- What do you think are the most energising things that you do?

Note: Adapted from Linley (2008).

Step 3: Application to coach development.

Invite the supervisee to consider what strengths they have noticed through telling their stories. Then consider how these could be applied to their coaching work.

- How can you apply these strengths in your coaching?
- What are the implications for your coaching practice?
- How might your coaching clients experience you utilising these strengths?
- What key strengths do you want to make more use of?

How to work with the technique …

In a group setting this might need careful positioning and group management to ensure no one dominates the discussions and that all strengths are seen as equally valuable. It is best to introduce clear group contracting stating the unique nature of strengths and explaining the expectations from a group working perspective. You might want to set clear time limits for each speaker and say something like 'obviously everyone may have very different strengths and it is important we each value the diversity'. You could then either set out some response guidelines or ask the group something like 'How can we ensure as a group that we are supportive of each other's strengths?'

A word of caution

Beware of a very superficial conversation that focusses on skills, e.g. 'I am very organised'. The aim is to raise awareness of core strengths highlighting energy and transferable capabilities. You could continue probing through acknowledging what they offer initially, then inviting them to extend their thinking. For example, 'OK, so when you are very organised, what other qualities start to reveal themselves?'

What other uses are there for this technique?

This approach can be applied in a similar way to case discussions asking about how they can apply the strengths that they have used in previous accomplishments to the current situation.

Reference

Linley, P.A. (2008) *Average to A+*, Coventry: CAPP Press.

~ ~ ~ ~ ~

62. Strengths cards

Carmelina Lawton Smith

Where can this be used?				Typical level of supervisee experience required	

When is this used?

This technique can help supervisees define their personal coaching style as they often find it hard to formulate an explanation of their coaching philosophy for prospective clients. Using cards to talk about their strengths can be a valuable starting point.

It can also be a good way to address unhelpful behaviours or traits by describing 'strengths taken to excess' rather than weaknesses. This approach helps them be true to their core nature but to appreciate the need for balance in the application of key strengths. The conversation may then inform a development plan.

What is the technique?

The technique uses a set of cards or words to facilitate a discussion about 'strengths.' One of the best known is the Values in Action Inventory (VIA) that lists 24 strengths, shown below.

1. Creativity	9. Enthusiasm	17. Modesty
2. Curiosity	10. Love	18. Prudence
3. Open-mindedness	11. Kindness	19. Self-regulation
4. Love of learning	12. Social Intelligence	20. Appreciation of beauty
5. Perspective	13. Teamwork	21. Gratitude
6. Bravery	14. Fairness	22. Optimism
7. Perseverance	15. Leadership	23. Humour
8. Integrity	16. Forgiveness	24. Sense of purpose

Create or buy a set of cards – one strength should be listed on each card. Some of the words may not be appropriate for your context so they can be substituted accordingly. The key value is in the supervisee explaining what the specific term means to them.

Step 1: Selecting and discussing strengths.

Spread the cards out and ask the supervisee a set of questions such as:

- Which are your top three strengths? How do you apply these? How do they serve you?
- Which strengths most influence your coaching practice? What are the implications of this?
- Select one and articulate the key value of this to your coaching.
- How might your clients experience this strength?

Step 2: Developing strengths.

- Which strength(s) is needed but is lacking in your current coaching? What makes this important?
- Which strengths might be most useful to you in your coaching? How could you develop these?
- Which of your other strengths could facilitate this development?
- Which strength might you sometimes over-do?

Step 3: Summary.

- How would you now describe your coaching philosophy or style?
- What are the most important strengths for you to focus on?
- How could you use your strengths in new ways?

Step 4: Process review

- How did you feel talking about your strengths?
- What do you take from this conversation?

How to work with the technique ...

Be sensitive to the depth of conversation as it can uncover deeply held core values. If in a group setting this may mean advising the supervisee that the issue may be better addressed in 1:1 supervision. For example, a conversation about the importance of integrity can easily reveal an example where the supervisee did not display the integrity they would have liked, or would aspire to.

A word of caution

If a supervisee has a tendency to overstate their capabilities with limited critical reflection this may not be a useful approach. It may simply confirm and inflate their ego by focusing only on the strong points, not revealing any blind spots because they cannot identify when a strength has been taken to excess.

What other uses are there for this technique?

When a supervisee is having a crisis of confidence due to a particularly challenging client session, this approach can encourage them to consider which strengths they leveraged despite a sub-optimal experience. For example, the client may have been evasive, and yet they maintained an enquiring mindset, or tenaciously looked for new angles to explore.

This can also be used when the supervisee feels they are stuck with a client or with a situation.

- Which strengths are needed for this situation?
- Which strength do you have that you are not using?

Strengths picture cards can also useful to move people out of their cognitive pattern and offer a more creative approach.

This approach can easily be adapted for the supervisee to have a strength discussion with their coaching clients. It could be particularly useful to build confidence, to define a leadership philosophy or to support personal branding work.

Further reading

Buckingham, M. and Clifton, D. (2001) *Now, Discover Your Strengths,* London: The Gallup Organization.

Seligman, M. (2003) *Authentic Happiness,* New York: The Free Press.

Resources

There are extensive resources on-line and many psychometric-style assessments that focus on strengths if this is an area you wish to take further. Strengths cards can be obtained from: https://mindspring.uk.com/collections/strengths [Accessed: 28 October 2019]; https://atmybest.com/strengths-cards/ [Accessed: 28 October 2019].

~ ~ ~ ~ ~

63. Using metaphor to explore 'at my best'

Angela Dunbar

Where can this be used?				Typical level of supervisee experience required	

When is this used?

This technique is used to focus on strengths and to build supervisee's understanding of what they do well and how that happens. It is especially useful for building confidence and helping to form the supervision relationship.

What is the technique?

Metaphors are more than just figures of speech; we construct our thoughts using metaphors and exploring these metaphors taps into a powerful, raw experience. By using Clean Language questions, we both consolidate and deepen the supervisee's understanding of themselves at their best. This anchors the experience making it more readily accessible in the future. The questions used are 'clean' as they are non-directive and stripped of the supervisor's own assumptions, bias and metaphors.

Step 1: Invite reflection on the question *'When you are coaching at your best, that's like what?'* This could be part of their preparation, encouraging them to bring anything that could represent their answer (e.g. Written or drawn, bring an object, photograph, etc.).

Step 2: Encourage deeper reflection by repeating the supervisee's own words and descriptions exactly as they said them. This holds them in their inner experience rather than inviting a more typical two-way dialogue.

Step 3: Continue to explore by asking a series of clean language questions that build on and include the supervisee's own words. Insert the supervisee's words where the XXXs are below:

- What kind of XXX is that XXX?
- Is there anything else about XXX?
- Whereabouts is that XXX?
- And does that XXX have a shape or a size?
- And that XXX is like what?
- And what do you know about XXX?

Step 4: Focus attention on the metaphors using the same questions given above, and then, deepen the exploration of any sensory and/or symbolic language. For example:

- Supervisee: When at my best it's like I am in flow.
- Supervisor: And what kind of flow is that flow?
- Supervisee: Like a meandering river.
- Supervisor: It's like a meandering river. Is there anything else about that meandering river?

Step 5: Continue to use the same set of questions, in a fluid way. Follow the supervisee's emerging understanding by questioning in an iterative fashion, taking the output of one line of enquiry as the input for the next line of enquiry. As each new element of the metaphor emerges, explore with the Clean Language questions above.

Step 6: At this point you could wrap up learnings with further Clean Language questions, such as:

- 'And now you know it's like this when you are coaching at your best, what difference does knowing that make?'

Or, when Step 4 feels done you could move into another supervision approach, such as a real life exploration of when the supervisee last coached at their best.

How to work with the technique ...

Questions need to be asked exactly as shown, without changing the word sequence. For instance, 'That's like what?' invites a metaphor whereas 'What's that like?' is a very different question and invites a description. Even when positioned clearly some people respond without using a metaphor. Remember to remain client centred; this may not have been the response you anticipated, but your questions will still encourage deeper reflection. Also, remember metaphors come in many forms, so a response may be overtly metaphorical, e.g. 'Light at the end of the tunnel' or it may be more subtle, e.g. 'Things are looking up'.

A word of caution

This exercise works best when focusing on resourceful and positive experiences. For those not trained in Clean Language, avoid asking questions of the less positive aspects. For example, with the response 'When I am coaching at my best, I feel no fear', do not ask 'What kind of fear?' A more positive follow up would be 'What kind of feeling is that, when you feel no fear?'

What other uses are there for this technique?

Asking 'That's like what?' will invite a metaphor of any positive experience or resource. For example, if the supervisee says 'I know I need to trust more' you could explore 'trust' in metaphor using Clean Language questions: 'And when you trust more, that "trust more" is like what?' (etc.).

With practice a supervisee could use this approach with their own coaching clients.

Further reading

Dunbar, A. (2018) *Using Metaphors in Coaching.* [pdf] Available at: https://cleancoaching.com/files/2018/04/Using%20Metaphors%20with%20Coaching%20April%20'11.pdf [Accessed 1 September 2019].

Wilson, C. (2004) *Metaphor and Symbolic Modelling for Coaches.* [pdf] Available at: https://cleancoaching.com/files/2018/04/Metaphor-Symbolic-Modelling.pdf [Accessed 1 September 2019].

Smith, K. (2012) *A Clean Corner of Coaching Supervision.* [online] Available at: www.cleanlanguage.co.uk/articles/articles/318/1/A-Clean-Corner-of-Coaching-Supervision/Page1.html [Accessed 1 September 2019].

Chapter 6

A psychodynamic perspective

A developmental Transactional Analysis approach to coaching supervision

Lynda Tongue

How is this philosophy described?

Transactional Analysis (TA) is described as a social psychology developed by Eric Berne (d. 1970) and colleagues, founded in San Francisco and now practised world-wide by a diverse range of practitioners. It is a psychotherapeutic model and there are four fields of application: psychotherapy; education; organisational and counselling. Developmental Transactional Analysis (DTA) is a school in TA that encourages growth and development and is the most appropriate for those working in the organisational context.

This chapter offers an introduction to some of the many concepts used in DTA. Others, including transference and countertransference, parallel process (Berne, 1961) Ego States (Berne, 1961), Drivers (Kahler, 1975) and Working Styles (Hay, 1993) also hold a richness to understanding what might be occurring in relational dynamics and outdated cognitions. (See Further reading.)

A founding philosophical premise in a TA approach is in the recognition of how we form our 'scripts' (the narrative we write for ourselves in response to our environment and parental messages).

We are born into family systems, we co-create our 'script' with the 'big people' in our lives (parents, extended family, religious figures, teachers). We are endeavouring to make meaning: 'who am I in this world?' What other people say to us and about us can be taken on as truths and we make survival decisions based on this information.

One of the philosophical tenets of TA is that everybody can think (providing they have capacity) and therefore everybody can change. Autonomy is the aim of DTA. While we make decisions as a child, we can re-decide when we have more personal power. Once we can see we are holding on to a belief formed when young, we are able to distinguish between fact and opinion and can make new autonomous decisions based on grown up evaluation. We make choices in our response, as opposed to reacting from a 'scripty' place.

What are the underlying principles and beliefs of this philosophy?

TA has an 'I'm okay, You're okay' foundation. A stance that says 'I value you as a human being, and I invite you to value me in the same way.' These life positions illustrated in Figure 6.1 (Berne, 1972) are fundamental, core beliefs about ourselves. We aim to be in the okay/okay place, but are often in our default 'not okay' place instead.

Consciously aiming to be in the top right box allows us to be grounded, to feel more confident, to see reality rather than fantasies ('I'm not good enough'; 'people are stupid'; 'I can't fix this and neither can you').

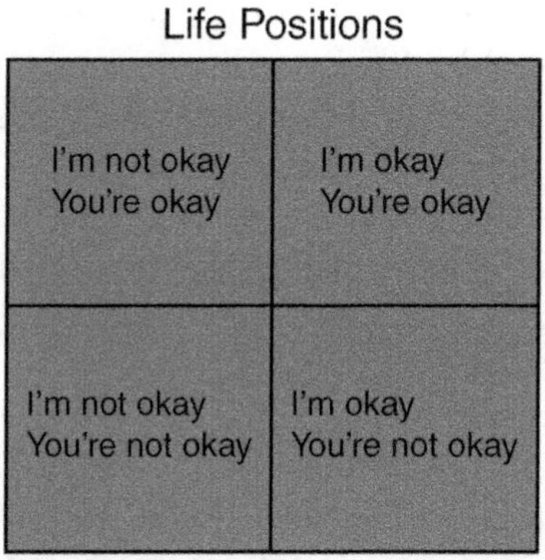

Life Positions

I'm not okay You're okay	I'm okay You're okay
I'm not okay You're not okay	I'm okay You're not okay

Figure 6.1 Life positions of Berne (1972)

The I'm okay: You're okay stance also allows for positive challenge around behaviour; for example, 'I value you as a person and there are aspects of your behaviour that I invite you to change.'

In the context of coaching supervision, this approach manifests itself in three ways. The supervisor:

1 Encourages (by asking relevant questions) the supervisee to do their own thinking.
2 Seeks to recognise game invitations, rackety displays (i.e. the supervisee unwittingly holding self-limiting beliefs) and to avoid being unconsciously diverted by the supervisee.
3 Resists telling the supervisee what to do or think - unless there are ethical considerations, or managerial aspects for the supervisee.

In effect, the supervisor takes responsibility for being the best supervisor they can be, and the supervisee takes responsibility for their own learning.

Within a coaching supervision context, it is important to understand that TA is a contractual modality. By this we mean that the supervisor constantly facilitates a process of contracting to enable clarity, accounting for all parties, identifying boundaries, avoiding psychological games and enabling progress and resourceful problem-solving. Everything that occurs in the supervision partnership holds information on the nature of the psychological contract in which it is held. The supervisor models the process and therefore knowledge of TA concepts will help the supervisor to stay in the Integrating Adult Ego State (Tudor, 2003). Their intention is to work transparently with the supervisee, contracting and re-contracting as the work unfolds.

In DTA, a robust contract helps both supervisor and supervisee stay in the 'I'm okay, You're okay' Life Position. Human beings have psychological hungers, three of which are stimulation, structure and recognition (for more information, see Berne, 1961). If these hungers are not met people can initiate, or get drawn into, psychological games. The process of contracting encourages both parties to view what is happening in the relationship, from a grounded and evaluative perspective. In doing so, each person takes responsibility for their behaviour. In DTA this is known as Accounting.

Berne (1964) identified three levels to the contract: administrative, professional and psychological. Often, there are others involved in the contract – the supervisor needs to be aware that the supervisee's client is a stakeholder. When contracting for a programme of ongoing coaching supervision, the following would be taken into consideration:

- **Administrative**: details such as timing, regularity, venue, what to do if supervisor or supervisee is ill, etc.
- **Professional**: matters of boundary management such as the competence level of supervisor and supervisee, the appropriate scope and aims of the work (supervision is not therapy). Areas such as confidentiality and ethics fit here too. A DTA supervisor may have to tell a supervisee to stop doing something if they see a breach of ethics or professional conduct.
- **Psychological**: considerations of how either person might sabotage the process; ensuring there is a sufficient level of trust between supervisor and supervisee; and enough protection is being offered for the supervisee to feel able to be open.

When considering the sessional contract, Hay (2007) suggests the supervisor considers three things – Results, Relationship and Responsibilities.

Both these formats can be used in a co-creative manner, enabling the supervisee to increase self-awareness and their ability to self-supervise.

What is the role of the coach supervisor in the context of this philosophy?

TA supervision is a meta-activity i.e. a practice that has meaning as an activity and which also has meaning as part of a wider theme or pattern of activity. It therefore requires 'meta-skills on the part of the supervisor' (Tudor, 2002, p. 40) – especially important, as the supervisor models this skill for the supervisee. In this way, the supervisee increases their awareness, their ability to reflect and then to apply their new learning when they are with clients.

Figure 6.2 offers the EDGE model, of use to both supervisors and supervisees to structure and contain the work. The parallelogram is divided into areas describing what needs to be accounted for under Ethics, Development, Growth and Evaluation. It takes the meta-perspective – both parties can hold their awareness of the four elements under the mnemonic of EDGE as they work in the moment. It can also be used to aide both preparation and reflection.

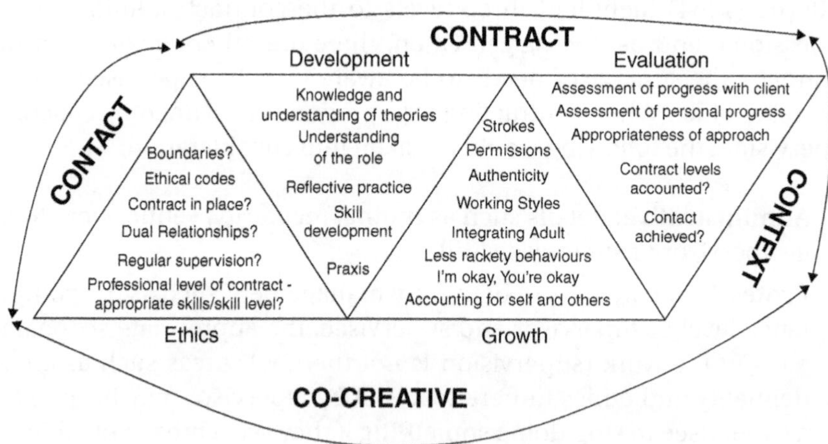

Figure 6.2 The EDGE model by Tongue
(*Source*: Author)

These elements are sited within the 4Cs:

- Contact – did supervisor and supervisee 'meet' each other?
- Contract – was the contract clear? Was it met?

- Context – was consideration given to the system of the client?
- Co-creative – was mutuality, respect and learning offered on both sides?

Coupled with using the concepts of TA to allow for reflexive practice, the supervisor is hoping to provide a safe space for learning to occur on two levels:

1 Gained without awareness (implicit memory) as through the modelling by the supervisor.
2 Consciously, cognitively as when focusing on the TA theories to analyse the situation brought by the supervisee.

In accordance with Mazzetti (2007), TA is seen as a 'practice-anchored approach' based on robust theory and is particularly applicable to the supervisory relationship.

Due to the systems approach DTA takes, a supervisor needs to be able to 'listen from multiple perspectives' (Hawkins, 2011, p. 170). In organisational contexts the DTA supervisor is aware that there may be many people metaphorically 'in the room' standing behind the supervisee as the supervisor stands beside them, enabling and facilitating the process.

How would you prepare yourself to work congruently with this philosophy?

DTA supervision takes a mutual, co-creative approach, and both supervisor and supervisee learn and develop from the process. Papaux (2016, p. 340) says that the supervisor's attitude is 'paramount to the resilience and learning process' and that the process has 'more to do with *being* a supervisor than *doing* supervision'.

Human beings are driven to get their needs met. Practitioners of TA talk about strokes, and a stroke is a unit of recognition. If we have not got our required level of positive strokes (determined and held by us unconsciously), we will do our best to create situations where we get negative strokes – because any attention is better than no attention at all. TA is a psychodynamic model – unconsciously we seek to play out our inner conflicts in our relationships with other people. Supervisors are no different, to work with more conscious awareness, supervisors also need supervision.

In order to work congruently and ethically with a TA approach a supervisor needs to understand the core concepts of TA and particularly that of discounting, psychological games and rackets. A supervisor needs to have an awareness of what triggers them to initiate or get drawn into a psychological game so that they are in a position to notice it when it occurs in the supervision relationship.

So, in preparation, the supervisor needs to make sure they are in a grounded and Integrating Adult (Tudor, 2003) space, using positive aspects of their Parent and Child as a 'here and now' appropriate response.

Practising listening for game invitations and thinking about their options when they hear one will help the supervisor to play the game in awareness, or cut across it in a positive way, i.e. 'What do you need from me in this moment?'.

Additionally, the concept of the 'Racket System' is of particular use to coach supervisors. It can be applied to both a supervisee's or a client's 'rackety beliefs'. When we hold these self-limiting beliefs about ourselves, and then behave according to those beliefs, we gain a reaction from others around us which then reinforces the self-limiting belief. We can tell ourselves we are right to think that way. What we do not see is that we are locked inside a closed-loop system of our own making. Hay (1993, 2009)) designed the BARs diagram, see Figure 6.3: it is as if we keep ourselves imprisoned behind those bars.

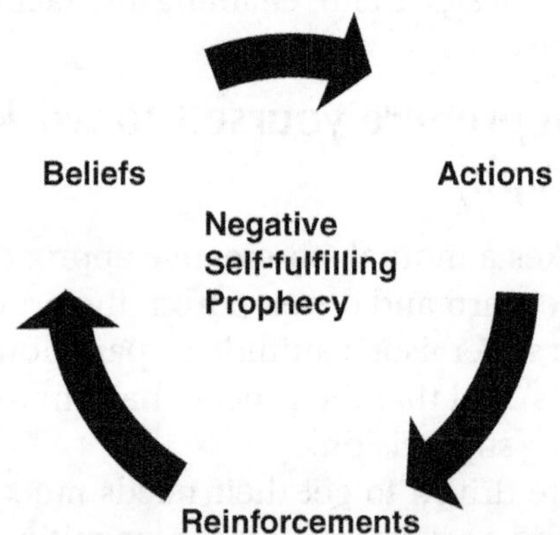

Figure 6.3 BARs diagram by Hay (1993, 2009)

The role of the supervisor is to listen carefully for the supervisee's rackets and to do so, they must also be aware of their own. A supervisee expressing sadness for the loss of some lucrative work because they were let down by a colleague may be using sadness to cover up an authentic feeling of anger. If the supervisor is not alert, they may not spot what is going on for the supervisee. They may not therefore respond with a more appropriate challenge such as 'Well, in your place I think I would feel angry ...'.

How might this way of working be particularly useful to the supervisee?

Supervisees often bring to supervision moments of their client work when they experience being out of the 'I'm okay, You're okay' life position. Supervisors ask questions to help supervisees uncover their discounting. Discounting is a concept described by Schiff and Schiff (1971); it is an unconscious process whereby we do not see what does not fit our frame of reference. If the supervisee is advanced in their TA knowledge, simply asking the question 'What might you be discounting here?' enables them to discover their discounts, and to learn a little more about discounting while they are doing so! This is a really good example of praxis (theory-to-practice) working, which TA supervision embodies.

The supervisee learns through this supervision process at a deep level. They gain insight into a particular problem, identify options for going forward and make progress both professionally and personally as they use the concepts to sharpen up their language to reflect and to deepen their understanding of human behaviour and, specifically, their own behaviour.

One of the most valuable aspects is that they learn to identify how they might invite, unconsciously, responses from others which develop into difficult situations (or psychological games). The more a supervisee understands this, the more able they are to change their behaviour, give out different, more positive invitations which enable the process to run smoothly, in a stress-free way.

Anything else you need to consider before using the techniques that follow?

In order to be of service to our supervisees we need to be in an 'I'm okay, You're okay' Life Position. Here we can identify game invitations, supervisees running their rackets or discounting themselves. In other words, we clean up our own psychological act in order to work cleanly with our supervisees.

References

Berne, E. (1961) *Transactional Analysis in Psychotherapy*. New York: Grove Press.

Berne, E. (1964) *Games People Play*. New York: Penguin books.

Berne, E. (1972) *What Do You Say after You Say Hello?* New York: Grove Press, pp. 110–114.

Hawkins, P. (2011) Systemic Approaches to Supervision. In: T. Bachkirova, P. Jackson, and D. Clutterbuck (Eds.) *Coaching and Mentoring Supervision*. England: Open University Press. Ch.13.

Hay, J. (1993) *Working It Out at Work*. Watford: Sherwood Publishing.
Hay, J. (2000) Organisational TA, Some Opinions and Ideas. *Transactional Analysis Journal*, 30(3), pp. 223–232.
Hay, J. (2009) *Working It Out at Work*. Watford: Sherwood Publishing.
Kahler, T. (1975) Drivers: The Key to the Process of Scripts. *Transactional Analysis Journal*, 5(3), pp. 280–284.
Mazzetti, M. (2007) Supervision in TA: An Operational Model. *Transactional Analysis Journal*, 37(2), pp. 93–103.
Papaux, E. (2016) The Role of Vulnerability in Supervision: From Pain to Courage, Inspiration, and Transformation. *Transactional Analysis Journal*, 46(4), pp. 331–342.
Schiff, J. and Schiff, A.W. (1971) Passivity and the Four Discounts. *Transactional Analysis Journal*, 1(1), pp. 71–78.
Tudor, K. (2002) Transactional Analysis Supervision or Supervision Analyzed Transactionally? *Transactional Analysis Journal*, 32(1), pp. 39–55.
Tudor, K. (2003) *Key Concepts in TA Contemporary Views*. London: Ego States Worth Publishing Ltd, pp. 201–231.

Further reading

English, F. (2007) I'm Now a Cognitive Transactional Analyst, are You? *The Script*, 37(5), pp. 1-2.
Hay, J. (2007) *Reflective Practice and Supervision for Coaches*. Maidenhead: Mc Graw-Hill.
Hay, J. (2011) Using Transactional Analysis in Coaching Supervision. In: T. Bachkirova, P. Jackson, and D. Clutterbuck (Eds.) *Coaching and Mentoring Supervision*. England: Open University Press. Ch. 11.
Karpman, S. (2014) *A Game Free Life: The New Transactional Analysis of Intimacy, Openness, and Happiness*: San Francisco: Drama Triangle Publications.
Searles, H. (1955) The Informational Value of the Supervisor's Emotional Experience. *Psychiatry*, 18, pp. 135–146.
Steiner, C. (1995) Thirty Years of Psychotherapy and Transactional Analysis *Transactional Analysis Journal*, 25(1), pp. 83–86.

~ ~ ~ ~ ~

64. CHECKS self supervision checklist

Lynda Tongue

Where can this be used?				Typical level of supervisee experience required	

When is this used?

This technique is used after the supervision session, as a reflective exercise. When done routinely, it also provides an interesting reference point for evaluating the processing preferences of the supervisee and also the supervision partnership.

What is the technique?

A self-monitoring checklist in the form of the mnemonic 'CHECK'.

Step 1: Familiarise yourself with the symbols and what they stand for. See Figure 6.4.

Contracting
- Was the contract clear?
- Was it met?

Here and now
- Was the process modelled?
- Did supervisee notice parallel process?
- Did supervisor stay out of parallel process?

Equal relationship
- Mutual respect shown?
- Supervisor offered I'm okay, you're okay approach – how did that manifest itself?

Challenge for growth
- Developmental guidance
- Challenge the supervisee in their learning

Key issues
- What were the key issues?
- Have they come up before?

Safety
- How was protection offered
- To the supervisee?
- To the client and client system of the supervisee?

Figure 6.4 The CHECKS-list for Supervision

Adapted from Clarkson (1991) and useful for reflection after the supervision session. This can be used by both supervisor and supervisee.

Step 2: After the supervision, work your way through the CHECKs checklist. Focus on each element in turn in a considered fashion.

Step 3: Notice when you are inclined to give yourself a tick in a box to indicate you are satisfied with your supervision experience or experience of supervision. Before making a tick consider what evidence you have that would support your decision.

Step 4: If there are boxes you cannot tick, consider why that might be. Typically, these items could then form an agenda for your next supervision session.

How to work with the technique ...

Although CHECKS is presented as a 'tick list,' it is intended as an aide for reflection. Therefore it is important to allow sufficient time and space where you can engage in a full and thoughtful response. It is not just a list of things that should be ticked off.

When done routinely over time, it is useful to keep your completed CHECKs and any notes you made while completing them. On a regular basis look at all them all side by side to see what patterns are emerging.

Additionally, it can be useful for both supervisor and supervisee to use the CHECKS list to review their partnership after a particular session (or series of sessions). It can be informative to notice which elements you saw similarly and which you saw differently. Exploring this helps both parties understand the other more fully and could identify elements of the relationship that you would like to experiment with in future.

Once familiar with the CHECKS list, the supervisor may want to add elements not listed here. Make it work for you, but at the same time make sure you are encompassing all the important elements.

What else might need attention?

Often there is a sense that something on the list is satisfactory, and yet when you consider the evidence for forming that view it is hard to pin point it. This is information in itself and could be material for future supervision. Perhaps there were some significant moments in the historical supervision relationship prior to the session being reflected upon that are getting 'carried forward'; perhaps you are making some assumptions which might benefit from more rigorous inspection; perhaps it highlights an uncertainty about how a concept actually shows up in practice.

A word of caution

Self-supervision is a very useful process and very good practice - however, it is not a substitute for live supervision with your supervisor, either face-to-face or online.

What other uses are there for this technique?

It is applicable for use in the coaching relationship.

Reference

Clarkson, P. (1991) Through the Looking Glass: Explorations in Transference and Countertransference *Transactional Analysis Journal*, 21(2), pp. 99–107.

~ ~ ~ ~ ~

65. Contracting using four Ps

Michelle Lucas

Where can this be used?				Typical level of supervisee experience required	

When is this used?

This is particularly helpful at the start of a group supervision relationship. However, it can be used in any setting where detailed contracting would be beneficial.

What is the approach?

The approach uses a model to help structure and develop the group's contract. The model see Table 6.1 stems from Julie Hay's (2007) work. Prompted by working in an organisational context, a fourth 'P' was added to help discuss the political influences on the supervision work.

Table 6.1 The four Ps of contracting adapted from Hay (2007)

Procedural	**Professional**
E.g. Logistics, protocols for time-keeping, managing distractions How will we determine the order we work in? Is it essential that everyone brings a scenario each time? What happens if someone misses a session?	E.g. What is the purpose of our work? What expectations do we have of each other? How do we want to behave? What might support and challenge look like here?
Psychological	**Political**
E.g. How will we handle comparisons with our peers? What level of trust do we have so far? What previous good and bad experiences of supervision do we bring here?	E.g. What power positions may we wittingly or unwittingly occupy? How will we make this transparent? What else could get in the way of the work?

Step 1: Generate discussion about the individual's experiences of supervision and what influences the quality of the supervision work.

Step 2: Using post it notes, ask each group member to list what they want from the group to enable them to do their best work. The rule is one idea per post it.

Step 3: Reproduce the 2 × 2 model on a flip chart. Explain what goes into each quadrant. Some suggestions are given in Table 6.1

Step 4: Facilitate the group so that one idea is shared at a time, allowing the individual to decide where their Post-it fits. Invite them to clarify their idea, then other group members add any of their post-its that feel similar. Each individual is invited to clarify any nuance in meaning.

Step 5: The supervisor then invites a contribution that is different from what has gone before, and Step 4 is repeated.

Step 6: Continue until every group member has 'led' an idea; or all the ideas are exhausted; or a time boundary has been reached.

Step 7: Invite reflection on the pattern of ideas – are they spread equally across all four quadrants or are their gaps?

Step 8: Step 7 may then generate additional ideas for the contract, or the observation of pattern may simply be acknowledged.

Step 9: Check on each group member's degree of comfort with the contract created. Where some elements cause discomfort these could be highlighted for further discussion, either in the session or at a later date.

Step 10: Take a photo of the populated flip chart for circulation amongst the group.

How to work with the approach ...

To do this fully can take an entire group session, so the supervisor needs to evaluate how much detail is appropriate with each group. It can be done more quickly if everyone places their post-it notes at the same time, then whole group reviews the output. The supervisor then scans the contributions, seeks clarity and encourages others to do similarly.

What else might need attention?

Typically, groups need encouragement to talk about the professional and the political quadrants. Sharing some personal anecdotes can highlight the subtlety of how psychological and political influences can be present. This level of vulnerability helps to role model how group members might 'say the unsayable'.

A word of caution

Some groups just want to dive in to the work. Perhaps counter-intuitively, this can be a useful strategy; simply signal the need for 'spot contracting' as and when you notice an opportunity for further clarification. For example, wait for someone's phone to ring, then use this as a prompt for discussing how they want to manage distractions.

Note: Hay (2000) in her original work included a fifth 'P' for Perceptual – the topics she works with are different from those offered here.

What other uses are there for this approach?

The model can guide dialogue in individual supervision. The approach could also inform client discussions when considering difficult relationships, the four quadrants might hold some clues about what underlies the difficulty.

References

Hay, J. (2000) Organisational TA, Some Opinions and Ideas. *Transactional Analysis Journal*, 30(3), pp. 223–232.

Hay, J. (2007) *Reflective Practice and Supervision for Coaches*. Maidenhead: McGraw-Hill, pp. 121–122.

~ ~ ~ ~ ~

66. Desert island fantasy

Michelle Lucas and Christine Champion

Where can this be used?				Typical level of supervisee experience required	

When is this used?

Useful when you are looking to inject some novelty yet depth, to the supervision work. Often helpful when there is a 'stuck-ness' in a more typical dialogue-based exploration. This playful approach will often illuminate the unconscious relational dynamics that can be missed when we use rational and logical thinking. The holistic approach helps to tap into knowledge that is just beyond our awareness.

What is the technique?

The method invites the supervisee(s) to use metaphor and images to capture themes and influences that they are noticing within their work.

Step 1: Brief the group along the following lines:

> *In a moment NAME will share with us more about their work with their client. As you listen, imagine that the coach and their client are stranded, alone on a desert island. Imagine ... where they might be on the island?*

What would they be doing? What roles are they adopting? How might they feel about this situation? How would they spend their days? When they have finished their input, we'll have about 5 minutes for you to sketch out something. Remember there is no right or wrong way to do this, so just relax and have fun with this technique

Step 2: When in a group, invite the supervisee to outline their client scenario. For talkative supervisees, put a time boundary to this or conversely pose some exploratory questions to enable more of the story to be shared.

Step 3: Pause and give time for each group member (including the supervisee) to sketch their desert island.

Step 4: Invite each person to share their sketch and to tell the story that formed in their minds, sharing thoughts and emotions as they listened to the supervisee.

Step 5: Pause after each sketch and invite a conversation amongst the group – keep the mood informal by prompting further discussion, reactions or questions to what's being presented. Sometimes new insights emerge across the different sketches and this can help determine who might go next. The supervisee presents their sketch last.

Step 6: Check in with the supervisee to consider any new insights emerging in them. Start with the metaphors offered by the group. For example, perhaps there was a rescue team mentioned in one of the peer's sketches but not in the supervisees own. So the supervisor could ask a playful question – so I'm wondering ... what happened to your rescue team?

Step 7: Move the supervisee away from metaphor to see what they might apply in a practical sense. Offer a simple open question like 'So what might this mean for your work with this client now/in future?'.

How to work with the technique ...

For some, the idea of drawing can provoke discomfort. It can be helpful for the supervisor to do a rough sketch to reinforce that this is not an art competition. When doing this with an individual, you might offer coloured pens to help them really explore and get involved in the creative expression. However, when working with a group or if working to a time constraint it is better just to use a note pad and a pen.

What else might need attention?

Group members might freeze when invited to engage with this technique, as it can feel deliberately vague and ambiguous. This could hint that rapport and/or trust needs to be strengthened in the relationship. Should this occur it might prompt an opportunity to revisit the contract and to understand how participants feel about how judgement might be impacting on the relationship dynamics.

A word of caution

This technique can be powerful in revealing higher levels of consciousness in supervisees and the depth and impact of these can be disarming. It is important there is a supportive culture in the group at these times.

What other uses are there for this technique?

This technique can work equally well in a one-to-one supervision engagement with the supervisor sketching their version of the island. One could expand on the technique, by inviting a wider story based on the evolution of the coaching relationship over time.

It can equally be applied by coaches with their coaching clients.

Further reading

Hawkins, P. and Shohet, R. (2007) *Supervision in the Helping Professions.* 3rd ed. Maidenhead: Mc Graw-Hill.

Hawkins, P. and Smith, N. (2007) *Coaching, Mentoring and Organizational Consultancy: Supervision and Development.* Maidenhead: Mc Graw-Hill.

~ ~ ~ ~ ~

67. Discounting and the steps to success

Lynda Tongue

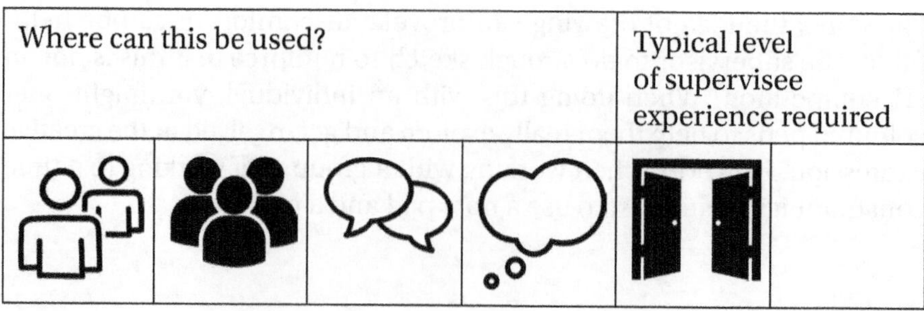

Where can this be used?				Typical level of supervisee experience required	

When is this used?

This technique is used when the supervisee appears to be 'stuck' in their thinking, perhaps because a piece of information lies outside their conscious awareness. Once the supervisor helps the supervisee to 'see' it, they are more able to solve whatever problem they were working on.

What is 'discounting'?

Discounting is a Transactional Analysis concept (see Schiff and Schiff, 1971), it is an unconscious process whereby we do not see what does not fit our frame of reference. Supervision helps bring what is being discounted into awareness. Clues that discounting may be occurring are present in the language a supervisee uses, e.g. 'They will never change' or 'I can't do anything about it'. Also, grandiosity is a sign of discounting, such as saying 'massive' (meaning fairly big) or 'disaster' (meaning mildly inconvenienced).

A distinction needs to be made between a person discounting information or skills they have but are restricting themselves by not 'seeing' them, and simply not having the required information or skill in the first place (this would be an absence of skills not a discounting of their skills).

What is the technique?

The Steps to Success model (see Figure 6.5) uses a framework to locate where the discount is taking place. There are six steps in total and the idea is to find out where the discount is and then work on the step below i.e. a place where the supervisee is not discounting.

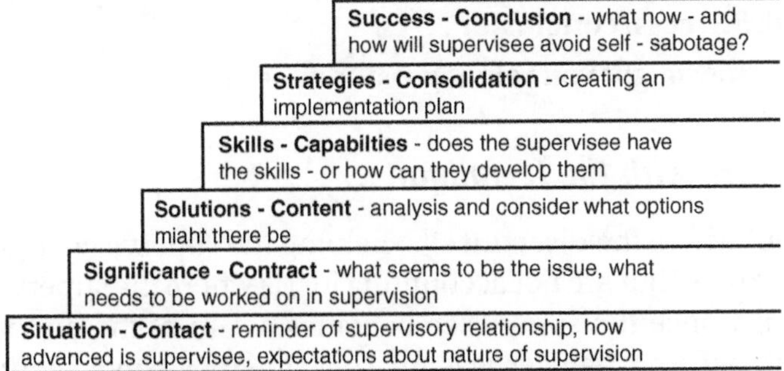

Figure 6.5 Steps to Success by Hay (2007)

Imagine that as supervisor, you are standing on the top step of Figure 6.5 then ask relevant questions to uncover where the discount might lie.

Step 1: Situation/contact.

- How robust is our supervision relationship?
- Is there anything 'unsaid' between us?
- What are you expecting of me in relation to this issue?

Step 2: Significance/contract.

What seems to be the issue here? Could it be:

- You are not accounting for your own skills (discount of self).
- You are dismissing the feelings or actions of another party (discount of others).
- You have not noticed a possible breach of ethics (discount of the situation).

Step 3: Solutions/content.

- What options have you considered?
- What options have you rejected?
- What else could you do?

Step 4: Skills/capabilities.

- What skills have you used in the past that might be useful in the present?
- What new skills would it help to develop?

Step 5: Strategies/consolidation.

What are you inclined to do now? For example:

- What will you do with your insights?
- Where will you start?
- What is the step after that?

Step 6: Success/conclusion.

- How might you sabotage your efforts?

How to work with the technique ...

Finding out where the discount sits, helping the supervisee to see something they know (but are not accounting for) is where the supervisory skill lies. Usually, once the supervisee becomes aware of the discount, they are able to access whatever was missing (i.e. they can 'account' for it) and the other steps fall into place. Sometimes further support is required by the supervisor, for example there may be more discounts further up the steps. The same process applies - ask questions and allow them to do their thinking. Typically, however, these further discounts do not then need as much work to resolve.

While the supervisee may intellectually understand what they are discounting, their language patterns often reveal that they don't yet fully own this understanding. When this occurs, the supervisor will need to go back to the level underneath the one where the discount is and 'walk' them back up the steps in the model.

What else might need attention?

Pay careful attention to your role as supervisor; avoid offering solutions (and thereby discounting the supervisee's skills) until you are quite sure they are unable to see what they are discounting.

A word of caution

Sometimes a supervisor may miss or is slow to recognise the discounting of their supervisee, instead it is 'caught' by another group member. This may suggest that the supervisor has similar areas of discounting and that the supervisor may benefit from supervision too.

What other uses are there for this technique?

The Steps to Success can be used by supervisees with their clients too. Teams can also use it for collective problem solving.

References

Hay, J. (2007) *Reflective Practice and Supervision for Coaches*. McGraw-Hill: Maidenhead, pp. 34–39.

Schiff, J. and Schiff, A.W. (1971) Passivity and the Four Discounts. *Transactional Analysis Journal*, 1(1), pp. 71–78.

~ ~ ~ ~ ~

68. Exploring the potential for collusion

Michelle Lucas and Lynda Tongue

Where can this be used?				Typical level of supervisee experience required	

When is this used?

Sometimes a supervisor may sense that the supervisee has greater empathy with one of the stakeholders in the coaching process than may be helpful. This often occurs when working in an organisational context, where the coaching assignment has undertones of being remedial work and the system draws the coach into doing part of the job of the line manager.

Alternatively, the coach may have developed a deep empathy with the individual client due to some shared history or experience and may be losing their neutrality. This approach prompts exploration of the psychological distance (see Micholt, 1992) amongst the parties and often illustrates where there is a risk of collusion.

What is the technique?

Step 1: As the supervision dialogue unfolds, keep in mind what is happening to the objectivity, neutrality or curiosity of the supervisee.

Step 2: Invite the supervisee to draw a triangle where the points of the triangle are labelled Coach; Client; Organisation – or use three post-its to create a triangle – encourage them to think about what kind of triangular shape would reflect how 'connected' they feel to each party.

Step 3: Ask them what they notice about the configuration of the triangle.

Step 4: Explore with them any comparisons where the distance is shorter or longer than others. For example: What's your sense of how the greater distance between you and the client (compared to the distance between you and the organisation) manifests in how you are working?

Step 5: Further perspective can be gained by looking at the distances from the client's and the organisation's position. Each time focusing on how that distance might be showing up in the work itself.

Step 6: Allow some reflection time and ask the supervisee to share what they are aware of now that may have been outside of their awareness before, perhaps enquire how this exploration might influence the work in future.

How to work with the technique ...

Often, as soon as the supervisee maps out the triangle, insight occurs and Steps 3–5 happen naturally. Where a supervisee maps out an equilateral triangle, it can be useful to enquire if there have been moments in the work when the triangle became lopsided in some way. Again, this typically generates insight around how different topics shift the working relationship. Occasionally, this does not provoke any further dialogue and an alternative line of enquiry will need to be found.

In most organisational situations, there may be more than three partiesinvolved, the same principles can be adopted using oblongs (four parties) or pentagons (five parties) etc.

What else might need attention?

Offering this technique is often predicated by the supervisor noticing the possibility of collusion in the system. Where the supervisee does not seem to be deriving value from the technique, remember not to get too wedded to your own insight. In this moment, it can be useful to notice how this impacts on your own sense of self and the relationship with the supervisee. A parallel process could be in play and so making transparent the distance you are currently experiencing between you and your supervisee (or any other stakeholder), may help illuminate what could be happening for the supervisee and their client in the session.

A word of caution

While supervisees of all levels could benefit from this type of exploration – those practitioners who are very tools-oriented and who work transactionally, may struggle to see the importance of subtle relationship dynamics. As always, there is a need for the supervisor to meet their supervisee 'where they are'.

What other uses are there for this technique?

Once experienced as a supervisee, the principles of this approach could be used with any clients who wish to explore relationship dynamics. When working directly with a client, the labels may be replaced with the different stakeholders they are working with.

Reference

Micholt, N. (1992) Psychological Distance and Group Interventions. *Transactional Analysis Journal*, 22(4), pp. 228–233.

Further reading

Hay, J. (2007) *Reflective Practice and Supervision for Coaches*. McGraw-Hill: Maidenhead, pp. 118–120.

~ ~ ~ ~ ~

69. Exploring transference and countertransference

Michelle Lucas and Anne Calleja

Where can this be used?				Typical level of supervisee experience required	

When is this used?

This is useful when there seems to be something 'uncharacteristic' in the coach: client dynamic that is impeding or skewing the work. Perhaps an otherwise experienced and resourceful practitioner feels 'clunky' in their work; or their sense of rapport is 'odd' in comparison to most other clients.

What is the enquiry?

Transference and countertransference are phenomenon that occur outside our awareness. They occur when relationship dynamics in the wider system ripple through into our relationship with our client. Knowing this phenomenon exists allows us to recognise and explore when it may be present.

Step 1: Take time to establish a common understanding of the terms, and seek permission to explore these concepts as a 'working hypothesis.' See further reading recommendations.

Step 2: Invite the supervisee to do a sense check and explore their physical sensations using a body scan.

Step 3: Encourage articulation, for example:

> *Describe for me in as much detail as you can about the other person that is causing a reaction in you, as well as your reaction. What thoughts, feelings and behaviours do you notice in yourself as you react to them.*

Step 4: Offer one or more of the following questions:

1. Who might they remind you of?
2. Who might you remind them of?
3. Where might your focus of attention be in the relationship?

Step 5: With this information return to the notion of transference and countertransference, reflect on any somatic sensations and thoughts arising. Consider 'who' or 'what' those reactions could be reminiscent of.

Step 6: Pause to allow the supervisee to reflect, check for new insight, identify further questions to reflect upon before co-creating a close to the exploration.

How to work with the enquiry ...

Transference and countertransference will all initially reside outside our conscious awareness. Should your supervisee become resistant this may be an indication that a defence mechanism is in operation. Work collaboratively seeking permission throughout the exploration so that the supervisee is a willing partner and does not feel pressurised to identify one of the phenomenon. Pressure will only serve to keep awareness in the unconscious domain.

Typically, when one of these processes is in play, and the supervisee is an otherwise grounded individual, the questions offered in Step 4 create a light bulb moment. Once the origins of the 'odd' relationship dynamic are understood, the supervisee's energy shifts to a more resourceful space and a sense of resolution is achieved. Where this does not occur, the supervisor needs to use their discretion whether to continue this enquiry. With experienced supervisees they are often hungry to explore beyond their initial reactions to Step 4, and will be willing to play with the idea that something might be just on the edges of their awareness.

Throughout the enquiry use tentative language – we can never know for sure what is contributing to the uncharacteristic quality of the relationship dynamic. The purpose of supervision is to explore, not diagnose. It is not uncommon for supervisees to draw a blank during the session, and then for something to shift helpfully afterwards.

Where no resolution has been found, the supervisee may be concerned about how they will hold the space appropriately in their next client session. In these cases, the supervisor may need to support the supervisee to locate a more resourceful state such that they are more grounded in the client's presence.

What else might need attention?

When working with unconscious processes, there is always the possibility that some unfinished business is triggered within the supervisee. In which case, referral to an appropriate practitioner is recommended.

A word of caution

As supervisors we might 'suspect' that one of these phenomena are in play; however, it's important that we don't become overly attached to them. Ensure you work in service of your supervisee as there may be more practical and tactical support that would be useful to explore. For example, a particularly verbose and patronising client may benefit from working with less verbal approaches regardless of what relationship dynamic is manifesting.

What other uses are there for this enquiry?

Once fully understood exploration of these dynamics could also be of use with coaching clients.

Further reading

Lee, G. (2018) The Psychodynamic Approach to Coaching. In: E. Cox, T. Bachkirova, and D. Clutterbuck, Eds. *The Complete Handbook of Coaching*. 3rd ed. London: SAGE. Ch. 1, pp. 3–16.

Sandler, C. (2011) *Executive Coaching: A Psychodynamic Approach*. Maidenhead: McGraw-Hill, p. 27.

~ ~ ~ ~ ~

70. Focus on feelings

Michelle Lucas and Carol Whitaker

Where can this be used?				Typical level of supervisee experience required	

When is this used?

This can be useful where either there is a preference for logic or rational dialogue. The approach offers a deliberate counterbalance to a fact-based discussion. It encourages an exploration of somatic sensations – it is an invitation to dive below the surface into the experience of what happened not just the content of what occurred.

What is the technique?

Step 1: Brief the group along the following lines:

> *As you listen to the supervisee try to see beyond the content of their story. Tune into what else you notice, the energy in their voice or to their body language. You may also connect with the impact that their account is having on your own emotions or somatic experience. For example, as a group member you may experience a sense of frustration or perhaps heaviness. Perhaps you will experience nothing in particular and that's a welcome observation too.*

Step 2: Invite the supervisee to talk through their client scenario. It is most helpful NOT to ask the supervisee to offer a focus for their peers.

Step 3: Each member is invited to share their experience of hearing the supervisee's scenario. Contract for this to be offered to the supervisor, not the supervisee, this allows the supervisee to be an observer to the process

Step 4: Once all contributions have been offered, the supervisor returns to the supervisee. After a pause, a useful question to ask is

'So where has that taken you?' It is deliberately vague because this technique is intended to prompt divergent thoughts.

Step 5: As this technique is rather open ended, it may be that there is no sense of resolution or completion within the time available. You may need to seek permission from the supervisee to close out the discussion. For example, 'I'm conscious that I need to move the group on, would it be OK if we leave it there for today?'

How to work with the technique ...

To help everyone (including the supervisor) move out of their heads and into their bodies, it can be helpful to prepare by engaging in short mindfulness exercise (see Quiet, pp. 71–73).

Channelling contributions through the supervisor, allows the supervisee distance should a contribution be psychologically challenging. For example, a group member may experience 'boredom' while listening to the client scenario. This might feel impertinent, so to avoid offence the group member could be tempted to dress it up; however, this would dilute the information shared. At a practical level, it discourages the supervisee responding to and rationalising the peer's contributions. This gives the supervisee reflection time and reduces the amount of time needed for this technique.

What else might need attention?

It is not unusual for one of the group to feel nothing when others do – this may simply reflect a different part of the system. However, when a group member repeatedly feels nothing, this could be a sign that additional individual work may be needed.

A word of caution

Sometimes a group member resonates with a person who has been overlooked in the system. So a contribution that initially seems 'off-track' might hold significant illumination. Should this happen, enquire where or what in the system they believe their experience is connected to.

With people who are highly cognitive, this approach can evoke a genuine performance anxiety. Some participants attempt to guess what emotions or sensations they should be experiencing. An alternative would be to invite them to notice if any images or metaphors occur to them.

What other uses are there for this technique?

With a group of mature practitioners, this technique can help access the parallel process. In this situation, at Step 3 include dialogue after each contribution so that the potential meaning can be considered.

This technique is not recommended for individual coaching clients who are highly rational. Where the client doesn't have a language for tuning in and naming their somatic responses, they are likely to resist. It is more useful in group coaching where some members are able to role model how to articulate their non-cognitive experiences.

Further reading

Turner, T., Lucas, M., and Whitaker, C. (2018) *Peer Supervision in Coaching and Mentoring: A Versatile Guide for Reflective Practice*. Abingdon: Routledge, pp. 125–160.

Whitaker, C. (2012) *Group Supervision Approaches for Coaching Supervision*. Available at: www.whitaker-consulting.co.uk/resources-and-papers [Accessed 2 August 2019].

~ ~ ~ ~ ~

71. Handling relationship conflict using the drama triangle

Julia Menaul and Lynda Tongue

Where can this be used?				Typical level of supervisee experience required	

When is this used?

This model is from Transactional Analysis. It can be used to examine and explore with the supervisees any 'hot buttons' or transference around their relationships with clients. It is especially useful when supervisees notice familiar patterns with particular clients.

What is the technique?

The supervisor offers a short explanation of the Drama Triangle, clarifying how it works and the roles of Victim, Rescuer and Persecutor. Supervisees are then encouraged to engage with experiential learning around the triangle using a technique that helps them to understand the dynamics and to explore more positive ways of behaving.

The supervisor needs to emphasise that we adopt these roles unconsciously and we can either start what is known as a psychological game or we can be invited into one. We 'switch' roles or positions and feel a negative emotion in the process. The steps below will help the supervisee to analyse where they or their client might start the game, and what happens next.

Step 1: Invite supervisee to think about a conversation that is causing some 'heat' for them.

Step 2: Plot a triangle on the floor using post-it notes with the three positions written on them, ensuring that Victim is at the bottom (See Figure 6.6).

Note: Ensure the triangle is big enough for supervisees to really feel themselves making definite moves from one position to another, while also seeing the other positions clearly

Step 3: Ask them to identify where they entered the Drama Triangle and to stand on that position. Did they start the game from here? Or did they accept the 'invitation' of the other player and enter the game here? Where is the other player?

Step 4: Stand alongside them (outside of the triangle) and not in their eye line.

Step 5: Encourage them to think about what was said next, and as they are doing so, to move to the relevant position, moving the other player to their corresponding position. At each move, ask: 'What are you feeling right now?'

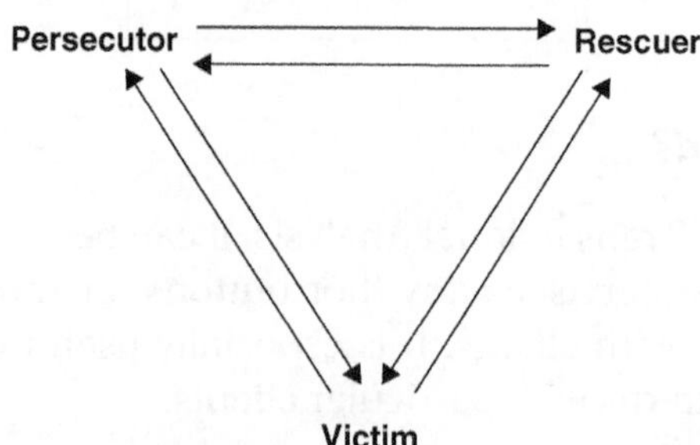

Figure 6.6 The Karpman Drama Triangle (Karpman, 2014)

Step 6: Ask them to return to their starting position:

a For the Victim corner, ask what could they do instead of Victim?

b For the Persecutor corner, ask what could they do instead of Persecutor?

c For the Rescuer corner, ask what could they do instead of Rescuer?

Step 7: Invite them to step off the Drama Triangle then pose these questions:

- What has emerged from this?
- What do they know that they didn't before?
- What first action do they need to take to achieve the best possible outcome?

How to work with the technique ...

Ask permission to introduce the model.

When working in small groups: the owner of an issue should stand on their entry point, another person to stand in the relevant place, and yet another if necessary, to take up the third role. Using the above questions; another member of the group facilitates the process. Debrief in trios between scenarios, before bringing together the large group to focus on emergent learning using questions such as:

- What tends to be your 'default' starting role, what sensations do you notice when this is happening?
- As a coach, how do you stop yourself getting into a game with a client?
- What on-going support can you arrange for yourself?

What else might need attention?

Supervisees may feel vulnerable in this activity for the personal revelations it may generate, and also the questions it raises about their relationship with the client. Emphasise that all human beings play games and this model helps us find ways of playing fewer games. This may prompt a need to explore the original contract to surface how and why this 'conflict' is occurring.

A word of caution

It can be helpful to do some spot contracting and gain permission for doing something different that may provide more challenge (albeit with support).

What other uses are there for this technique?

Small objects such as buttons could be used instead of physical movement. These can then be moved around the Drama Triangle – a good option for those with mobility issues.

This technique can also be used with coaching clients instead of supervisees.

Reference

Karpman, S. (2014) *A Game Free Life: The New Transactional Analysis of Intimacy, Openness, and Happiness*: San Francisco: Drama Triangle Publications.

Further reading

Menaul, J. (2019). *The Coach's Guide to the Drama Triangle.* Available at: www.BookBoon.com

Karpman, S.D. (1973) *1972 Eric Berne Memorial Scientific Award Lecture [pdf]* Available at: https://karpmandramatriangle.com/pdf/AwardSpeech.pdf [Accessed 30 September 2019].

Weinhold, B.K. and Weinhold, J.B. (2014). *How to Break Free of the Drama Triangle and Victim Consciousness.* South Carolina: CreateSpace Independent Publishing Platform.

~ ~ ~ ~ ~

72. Parallel process

Lynda Tongue

Where can this be used?				Typical level of supervisee experience required	

When is this used?

Typically, this exploration will be prompted by the supervisor since the phenomenon of the parallel process surfaces when the practitioner unconsciously recreates the client's issue and emotions within the supervisory relationship.

However, with more experienced supervisees who understand how parallel process may occur between the client system and their own system, they may then deliberately seek to explore this in supervision.

What is 'parallel process'?

Harold Searles (1955) highlighted this phenomenon, which has its origin in the psychoanalytic concepts of transference and countertransference. The client's transference and the coach's countertransference re-appear in the mirror of the supervisee: supervisor relationship.

What is the enquiry?

It is the supervisor's job to spot this phenomenon, and through questioning, prompt the supervisee to bring into awareness what is happening, and to then identify options for action.

Step 1: Listen carefully to the 'story' of the supervisee. How are they describing the client situation? What is the client's story?

Step 2: Be aware of what is happening in the 'interactional field' (the space between supervisor and supervisee) where the unconscious processes are taking place. Check your own responses to the story, including what is happening for you at a physical level. Trust your intuition to identify aspects of the process that belong to you, to the supervisee, and to the client of the supervisee.

Step 3: If you sense that the supervisee is recreating the client issue with you in the supervisory space find ways to highlight it to the supervisee. For instance, you may hear in the client story, that the client was 'stuck', could not decide on a course of action, and you notice that the supervisee also says *they* are 'stuck' with the client, i.e. cannot work out what happened in their relationship. (You can help to bring this into their awareness by asking 'Do you see any parallels in what you have just told me?' or if they are too caught in the grip of this dynamic you could offer more specific feedback for example 'I notice you seem to be stuck too – might that be a parallel process?'

Step 4: Model a different way of behaving so that the more positive behaviour will be passed back through the supervisee to the client (see Figure 6.7).

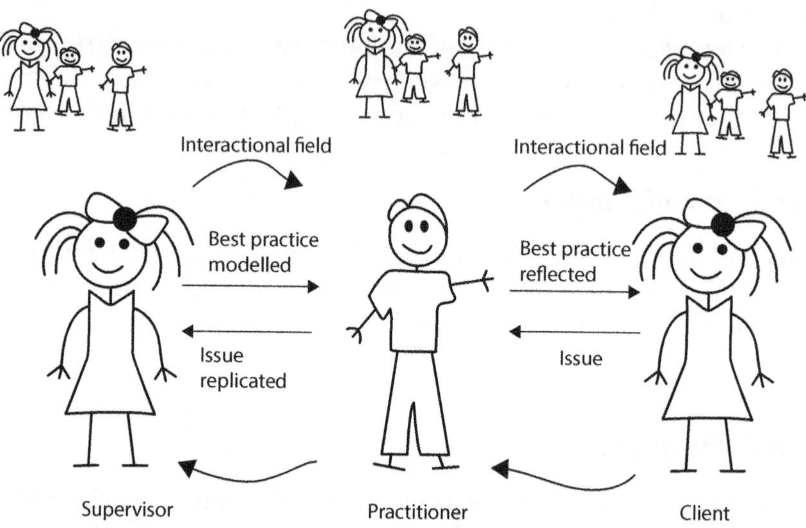

Figure 6.7 Systemic parallel process
(*Source*: Author)

How to work with the enquiry …

The supervisor needs to be on the alert at all times for the possibility of a parallel process being present. Parallel process is sometimes easy to spot, and sometimes not. The supervisor needs to have good self-awareness and good relational awareness so that they understand what their default reactions are likely to be with this particular supervisee. Variations to that default may offer clues to a parallel process being in play. The supervisor also needs to be skilled in their own reflective process, in order to be able to stay in the 'here and now' such that they do not get drawn into a 'script' (see pp. 213–214).

The parallel process can also be put to positive use. The supervisor can model different behaviour. In this example the supervisor shows they are not stuck by asking questions; those questions serve to free up the supervisee who is then well place to free up their work with the client.

What else might need attention?

Once the supervisee realises that they have been drawn into a parallel process the next phase would be to determine actions. However, these actions are not always to do with what they next do with the client. The supervisee may instead need to work through how they manage themselves to be centred and 'clean' when working with the client.

A word of caution

It is very easy to get caught up in the parallel process as a supervisor. Take your work to supervision so that you remain at a meta-level, making choices in your interventions in the here-and-now.

What other uses are there for this enquiry?

There is a 'systems' aspect to parallel process. Positive ways can counter negative unconscious processes which ripple out into the work, family, friendship etc communities of the supervisor, the practitioner and the client.

Reference

Searles, H. (1955) The Informational Value of the Supervisor's Emotional Experience. *Psychiatry*, 18, pp. 135–146.

~ ~ ~ ~ ~

73. STEPS for supervision

Lynda Tongue

Where can this be used?				Typical level of supervisee experience required	

When is this used?

This model is particularly useful to use during supervision; however, it could also be used to aid reflective practice after the supervision session.

What is the technique?

STEPS is a mnemonic to help the supervisor pay attention to various elements during the supervision. It comes from the psychodynamic body of concepts known as Transactional Analysis (representing the 'T' in the model). However, this could be replaced by 'Technique' by supervisors using different modalities.

How to work with the technique ...

Step 1: Prior to the supervision session, write 'S T E P S' down the left hand side of an A4 sheet

Step 2: Remind yourself what STEPS stands for (see Figure 6.8)

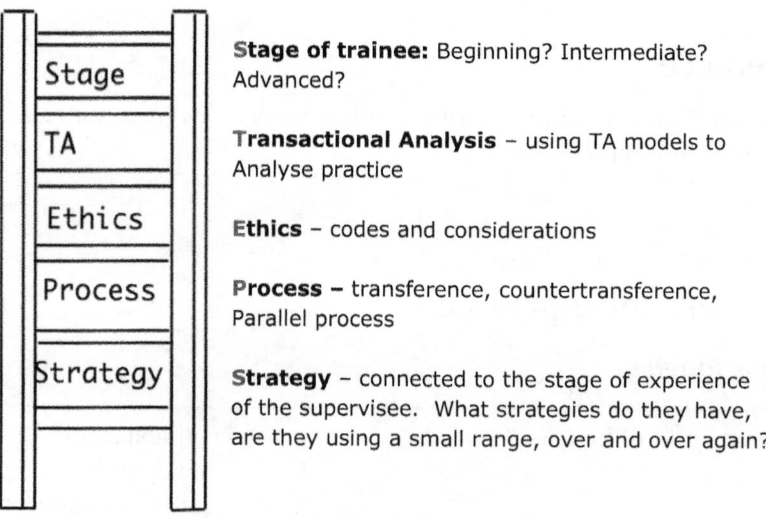

Stage
TA
Ethics
Process
Strategy
Stage of trainee: Beginning? Intermediate? Advanced?
Transactional Analysis - using TA models to Analyse practice
Ethics - codes and considerations
Process - transference, countertransference, Parallel process
Strategy - connected to the stage of experience of the supervisee. What strategies do they have, are they using a small range, over and over again?

Figure 6.8 The STEPS model

Step 3: As you engage in the supervision work, keep the model in mind to keep yourself on track. If you take notes (and have permission to do so) you might jot responses alongside the relevant part of the model to map progress.

Step 4: Engage in reflection in action – for example, questions for you to reflect upon in the moment could be:

- What is your attention being drawn to?
- What has yet to be explored?
- Where is your sense of what needs to be attended to?
- What is going on for you as the supervisor?
- What else needs to be contracted for to ensure a comprehensive approach?

Step 5: Consider – has the contract been met? If not, surface this with the supervisee. Review your options, for example contract for additional time either within the session or to bring the subject back another time.

How to work with the technique

The STEPS framework is a meta-model rather than a technique to be worked through 'step by step'. However, once familiar with it the practice of writing the word 'STEPS' might help to focus the supervisor's mind.

As supervisors, to be our most effective, we need to stay in the 'here-and-now', and invite our supervisee into that space with us, in order to explore the issue using all our combined capacities. A visual reminder (until both parties are so familiar with the model we do not need it any-more) will help with this process.

What else might need attention?

Over time with the same supervisee, a supervisor will notice patterns in their approach with clients. A Transactional Analysis supervisor will support the supervisee to see these patterns whether they are about Ego States, or Drivers, or their Rackets or Life Position that might be getting in their way, and once having recognised them, the supervisee can be supported to make the relevant changes.

A non-Transactional Analysis supervisor will of course also notice patterns and in the same way will seek to discover if the supervisee is aware of them. Once they have that awareness then the supervisor can once again help them to work through them and make developmental progress.

If you, as the supervisor, notice that you tend to emphasise the same part of the STEPS model across different supervisees – that would then need further exploration with your own supervisor.

A word of caution

Always work to make sure you have good contact with the supervisee – do not let the model distract you. Be prepared to start with it in mind and also to let it go if something else becomes more useful.

What other uses are there for this technique?

It is useful for the supervisor as a means of self-supervision. What might you have missed? How present in the process were you? What might you look out for during the next supervision session with this practitioner?

Coaches could also make use of this model. The nature of contract is different, and this will need to be taken into consideration. By keeping STEPS in mind, it may help the coach, to 'listen out for' aspects which might be blocking the client's progress, or where perhaps they might be managing boundaries better.

Further reading

Newton, T. (2012) The Supervision Triangle: An Integrating Model. *Transactional Analysis Journal*, 42(2), pp. 103–109.

~ ~ ~ ~ ~

74. Using time structuring to understand intimacy in relationships

David Crowe and Michelle Lucas

Where can this be used?				Typical level of supervisee experience required	

When is this used?

Unless the supervisee is already familiar with Transactional Analysis (TA), this is typically an educative piece from the supervisor. It can be referred to where the coaching client is experiencing difficulties in their relationships and can help the client reflect on how they typically spend their time. Additionally, it can be a useful framework to explore where the supervisee experiences a difficulty in connecting with their client.

What is the enquiry?

Time structuring is a theory developed by Eric Berne (Berne, 1961) who suggested that human beings need to structure time as a process:

- Withdrawal (spending time emotionally withdrawn in the presence of others or staying out of contact with others).
- Rituals (structured ways of acting that involve acting in a pre-programmed way).
- Pastimes (polite 'safe' conversation between people on socially acceptable topics).
- Activities (doing things with others, as opposed to just being with others).
- Psychological games (interaction with others that involved a hidden agenda and bad feelings for those involved).
- Intimacy (authentic encounters with others with trust, openness and honesty including working through our emotional responses to them).

The order is important. The emotional intensity in our relationships increases step-by-step as we move from withdrawal to intimacy.

Step 1: Seek permission to share the model, working appropriately with the supervisee's knowledge of TA.

Step 2: Help the supervisee elicit the behaviours they have noticed in their client and where this might fit into the model. Check out their understanding of the model as you do so. Useful questions might be:

- What did you notice them doing?
- What is your sense of where they get stuck, according to this model?
- Help me understand how you linked their behaviour to the framework ...
- Is this behaviour a regular pattern?
- Do you see the behaviour in the supervision relationship? What might be causing any differences in their response?

Step 3: Widen the discussion to explore this model in the context of the supervision question.

Step 4: Check out how useful the supervisee has found exploring the framework. Continue or change tack appropriately.

How to work with the enquiry ...

The supervisee might openly state their difficulty understanding how their client relates to those around them (or to the coach). Or the supervisor may notice unhelpful patterns (often experienced as avoidance or neediness) in the relational dynamic under discussion.

When sharing the theory with the supervisee, check for understanding and use practical examples to bring the theory to life. Wherever the exploration starts there is the distinct possibility that the relational dynamic will be mirrored elsewhere (i.e. a parallel process, see pp. 242–245). So if the supervisee brings the issue within the client's relational system, e.g. other organisational stakeholders, it is highly likely that the same relational dynamic will be repeated between the client and the coach. The opposite is also probable – difficulties in the coach–client relationship may mirror difficulties in other client relationships. Ensure the exploration is broad enough to identify what seem to be patterns of behaviour and what could be explained as one-offs.

The exploration elicits discussion – so keep the original supervision question in mind as you work.

What else might need attention?

The nature of the discussion is likely to be a deep one and through the exploration issues of Attachment (see pp. 110–113.) may well surface. Re-contract before continuing or signpost that alternative professional help might be more appropriate for either the supervisee or their client.

A word of caution

Contract openly for this more educative intervention, revert to a more collegiate space once input has been given. Remember that we are using the model to help understand apparently confusing behaviour. Be prepared to let go of it, if it begins to divert attention from the supervision question in hand.

What other uses are there for this technique?

In a group setting, it can be helpful to check out where each member would locate the behaviour in the model. Relational depth is a very individual matter (and offerings may reflect where that participant is in terms of the group process) however a diversity of input on how withdrawal to intimacy behaviours are experienced can be illuminating; not just for the scenario under discussion but for the connectedness of the supervision group.

Reference

Berne, E. (1961) *Transactional Analysis in Psychotherapy.* New York: Grove Press.

Further reading

Crowe Associates. (2019). *Time Structuring.* [online] Available at: www.crowe-associates.co.uk/psychotherapy/time-structuring/ [Accessed 26 September 2019].

Chapter 7

A Solution-Focused approach to coaching supervision

Evan George and Denise Yusuf

How is this philosophy described?

The Solution-Focused (SF) approach is a conversation-based model. The supervisor asks 'invitational' rather than 'forensic' questions. The purpose is not to aid the supervisor's understanding, rather the intention is for the supervisee to hear their own answers. The criterion for determining the usefulness of a question is merely whether the answer makes a difference. The supervisor has to trust and to believe in their supervisee and has to be able to put aside their own content expertise. As Insoo Kim Berg, the co-founder of the SF approach, would say 'we aspire to leave no footprints in the [supervisee's] life.'

The Solution-Focused approach was initially developed by Steve de Shazer, Insoo Kim Berg and their colleagues working at the Brief Family Therapy Center in Milwaukee. The approach emerged from two particular observations of practice. The first observation might appear obvious, and yet the approach that developed from it has had a considerable impact in the worlds of therapy, counselling, leadership, education, social care, in the corporate sector and, of course, in coaching (Berg and Szabo, 2005; Iveson et al., 2012). Steve de Shazer, the key theoretical founder of the SF approach, noticed that clients almost invariably indicated 'exceptions' to the rule of the problem, times when the problem either did not happen at all or impacted the client less. Sometimes clients spontaneously mentioned these exception times; sometimes the exceptions only came to light as a result of the worker's questioning. These exceptions could have been thought to be of little significance, but de Shazer saw meaning in them, framing these exceptions as moments when the client already had a small piece of the solved state. The change process, in de Shazer's early formulation of his approach encouraged exploration of how the client could do more of what was working at these 'exception' times, a radical shift in the context of the thinking about personal change at the time.

The second seminal observation was derived from a study of recordings of successful work with clients, with de Shazer and his team posing themselves the question 'What do workers and clients seem to do together when the outcome of the work is good?'. The conclusion he reached, was that clients are more likely to report change when the worker asks clients questions that invite those clients into 'solution talk' rather than 'problem talk'. This conclusion was undoubtedly challenging for the therapy world although perhaps a little more congenial to the world of coaching.

The core process lying at the heart of the approach is conversational. Miller and de Shazer write 'The solution-focused language game ... is designed to persuade clients that change is not only possible, but that it is already happening. It is, in other words, a rhetorical process designed to talk clients into solutions to their problems' (Miller and de Shazer, 1998, p. 372).

What are the underpinning principles and beliefs of this philosophy?

In de Shazer's writings (de Shazer, 1994) he makes reference to the work of Ludwig Wittgenstein and, in particular, to his thinking about 'language games' (Wittgenstein, 1953). De Shazer (1991) also references the work of the post-modern and social constructionist thinkers, whereby the metaphors of 'narrative' and 'conversation' become key to his description of the Solution-Focused process. Walter and Peller (2000) summarise this development stating,

> *conversation as author allows us to think that a new story can emerge between the client and us. Rather than searching for the real meaning within some structural interpretation of what the client is telling us, we assume that between the client and us is the possibility of a new story.*

As de Shazer comments, 'the therapist never actually deals with 'problems,' rather they deal with their clients' reports or depictions of the 'problems' (de Shazer, 1988). Solution-Focused practitioners are dealing with people's reports, how they describe their situations and collaboratively constructing, through conversation, what can be referred to as 'progressive narratives' (de Shazer, 1991). The rationale for so doing is simple and is based on de Shazer's observation that progressive narratives are more likely then complaint-centred narratives 'to produce transformations and discontinuities' (de Shazer, 1991).

In de Shazer's writings he defined four key characteristics of progressive narratives, they

1 Focus on the desired future.
2 Elicit whatever the client is doing that fits with that future.
3 Highlight change and progress.
4 Are strength-based, inviting people into resource focused stories of self.

In addition, SF practitioners have observed that the likelihood of change is positively correlated with our clients' expectations of change. All the elements of SF conversations can be seen to enhance the client's idea that a good outcome is not just possible, indeed not just probable, rather it is already beginning to happen. Solution-Focused practitioners choose to believe that change is constant and inevitable.

This approach contains no theory of problem, either of problem causation or of problem maintenance. It is merely a description of a very specific way of interacting and talking with clients, which appears to be associated with clients reporting positive changes in their lives.

What is the role of the coach supervisor in the context of this philosophy?

The role of the SF supervisor is to create a relational context within which SF questions are answerable. The purpose is for the supervisee to develop a changed 'narrative,' a set of different ideas that allow for the possibility of change. The supervisor is not assumed to know anything about what the supervisee should change, or indeed to have any useful ideas about the situation. Supervisees are merely invited to re-describe such that they find an alternate pathway through a restructuring of what they notice and hence the meanings that develop. The work is structured in three core areas of focus:

1 **Future.**

Since SF is an entirely non-normative approach at the beginning of every piece of work, the coach supervisor will enquire of the client their best hopes for the work (George et al., 1999). In coaching supervision this question is simply formulated as 'How will you know that discussing this piece of work has been useful?' Following from the supervisee's response, the SF supervisor might then invite the supervisee to describe in detail how they could know that the piece of work is going well, what they will notice, how the supervisee will respond to the client differently and how the client will notice the difference. The supervisor might ask the supervisee to describe, in relation to a challenging piece of work, 'How would you know that you are "at your best" when you are next with the client?' Solution-Focused practitioners repeatedly observe that describing the preferred future in detail is associated with an enhanced likelihood of change. Frequently during the course of the description, supervisees report that they now 'understand' what they should do. Observation of effective practice has led to the conclusion that preferred future descriptions are most effective when framed in positive rather than negative terms, what will be happening rather than what will not be happening. Similarly, when descriptions are framed in terms of action rather than feeling, i.e. what the supervisee will notice themselves 'doing'. Asking supervisees to identify what might be the smallest possible indicators of progress, a range of possibilities, seems to make progress, post-supervision, more visible and likely to be noticed. These preferred future descriptions are most effective when they are framed and held in the language of possibility ('What might you notice? Maybe? Perhaps?'), which engages the imagination and creativity allowing the supervisee to describe their way out of the current stuckness. Conversely the language of certainty, e.g. 'What do you need to do?' or 'What will tell you?', tends to reconnect the supervisee with their current experience of 'I don't know what to do'.

2 **Present and past.**
Based on the assumption that there are always instances when the preferred future has already occurred, the SF supervisor will invite the supervisee to bring to mind those times when the work has seemed to be progressing more effectively, or when the supervisee was more able to be optimistic or hopeful about the client and the outcome. The SF supervisor will invite the supervisee to identify what might have been different at these times. Projecting the conversation into the future the SF supervisor invites the supervisee to describe what difference it might make if they were to do more of those things that they did at these moments. For supervisees who find it difficult to identify anything that is working, the supervisor will broaden the focus. By enquiring about similar pieces of work and exploring what they may have done on those occasions that 'worked' and which might therefore be useful in the current 'stuck' situation. These questions invite the supervisee to identify alternative pathways from their current 'not-working' range of interventions.

3 **Change.**

The Solution-Focused supervisor is constantly progress sensitive. This focus on progress and change is manifested in the future-oriented questions and in the smallest signs of change questions but also in the present and past questions. Inviting supervisees to compare the current situation with the way things were at the beginning of a piece of work often results in supervisees acknowledging that there has been progress. Such progress is often at risk of becoming invisible when the work appears to be stuck or is stalling. The SF supervisor can then enquire what the supervisee has done that has been useful in arriving at the current position and, of those things that have worked, what it might be useful to do more of in the on-going work. Solution-Focused scale questions (see pp. 260–263.) are of particular use in highlighting progress already made.

How would you prepare yourself to work congruently with this approach?

The Solution-Focused approach is undoubtedly simple, if not easy, yet the approach requires of the supervisor highly developed and very specific conversational skills. Solution-Focused practice is associated with a number of practical assumptions that are required for supervisors, to implement the approach.

1 There are always exceptions to the rule of the problem or instances of the preferred future (Ratner et al., 2012) already in place. It is the role of the SF supervisor to ask questions in such a way that these become visible and meaningful.
2 The supervisee already has the requisite knowledge, resources and capacities necessary to find a way forward. The task of the SF supervisor is to support the supervisee in recognising that they do indeed know what to do.
3 The supervisee's own ideas are likely to fit better than the supervisor's ideas.
4 It is important for the SF supervisor to let go of their own ideas about the way forward in such a way that she can better the support the supervisee to discover their own.
5 There is no need to explore problem causation or maintenance for change and progress to occur.

When operating with these principles, it frees the supervisor to bring to the fore their process expertise, their capacity to ask useful questions.

How might this way of working be particularly useful to the supervisee?

Solution-Focused coaching supervision is typically experienced by both parties as hard work. There are no easy answers or telling the supervisee what to do, equally it is experienced as empowering, enabling supervisees to find their own best ways. The process is content free and so can be used with supervisees working with a range of different models and theoretical persuasions (Thomas, 2013). Solution Focus can be used equally in relation to case consultation, and to professional development, often both are integrated seamlessly into the same conversation. At the end of a SF conversation we can hope that the supervisee can walk away with the idea 'I came up with my own idea – I did know how to do this!'.

Anything else you need to consider before using the techniques that follow?

Supervisors new to the Solution-Focused approach can risk confusing the approach with simply being positive, thereby trivialising it. This in turn can lead them to actively block expressions of difficulty and distress, in a misguided manner assuming that negative expressions do not fit with the model. The experienced SF supervisor will always accept, validate and acknowledge such expressions of difficulty, utilising the acknowledgment as a platform for further enquiry, for example. 'It sounds like this piece of work has been a real struggle for you and so how will you know that the two of you are just beginning to find a way forward?' Denying supervisee's feelings and experiences, hardly surprisingly, is not a useful basis for collaborative conversations.

References

Berg, I.K. and Szabo, P. (2005) *Brief Coaching for Lasting Solutions*. New York: Norton.
de Shazer, S. (1988) *Clues: Investigating Solutions in Brief Therapy*. New York: Norton.
de Shazer, S. (1991) *Putting Difference to Work*. New York: Norton.
de Shazer, S. (1994) *Words Were Originally Magic*. New York: Norton.
Miller, G. and de Shazer, S. (1998) Have you heard the latest rumor about...? Solution focused therapy as rumor. *Family Process*, 37, pp. 363–377.
George, E., Iveson, C. and Ratner, H. (1999) *Problem to Solution: Brief Therapy with Individuals and Families*. 2nd ed. London: BT Press.
Iveson, C., George, E. and Ratner, H. (2012) *Brief Coaching: A Solution Focused Approach*. London: Routledge.
Ratner, H., George, E. and Iveson, C. (2012) *Solution Focused Brief Therapy: 100 Key Points and Techniques*. London: Routledge.

Thomas, F. (2013) *Solution-Focused Supervision: A Resource-Oriented Approach to Developing Clinical Expertise.* New York: Springer.
Walter, J. and Peller, J. (2000) *Recreating Brief Therapy. Preferences & Possibilities.* New York: Norton.
Wittgenstein, L. (1953) *Philosophical Investigations.* Oxford: Blackwell.

~ ~ ~ ~ ~

75. Sit in three chairs

Fredrike Bannink

Where can this be used?				Typical level of supervisee experience required	

When is this used?

What is nice about this creative technique is that supervisees can both look forward and backwards in reflecting on their life and work. It is useful when looking at their understanding of where they are in their journey. This could relate to their development as a coach or where they were, are, or will be in the future in respect of an issue at hand.

What is the technique?

Using three chairs to represent the past, the present and the future, the supervisee is encouraged to explore an issue, considering three different moments in time.

Step 1: Create a focus for the topic being brought to supervision.

Step 2: Set out three empty chairs to represent the past, the present and the future. Invite the supervisee to clarify the time frame they are working with.

Step 3: Explore with the supervisee which of the empty chairs they would like to sit in first.

Step 4: Once the supervisee is sitting on one of the chairs start exploring through questions like:

- What's good about being in this space?
- What is making you happy or satisfied?
- How do you manage to achieve that?
- What are your best hopes?
- What are you doing that will enable that?
- What will be the next (small) step or sign of progress?

Step 5: Once all three chairs have been visited, check if the supervisee thinks it would be helpful to visit any of them again.

Step 6: Return to the original focus of the supervision and invite the supervisee to tell you what they think has been useful.

How to work with the technique ...

Allow the supervisee to dictate pace and sequencing of the exploration. While logically you might expect supervisees to work through the time moments in chronological order, often the supervisee will start in 'the present' and it is of interest to notice which direction they then choose to move in. This might provide useful information for further reflection – are they most concerned with understanding what caused the issue (looking backwards) or more concerned with how they can move forward?

When considering the time frame being explored, invite the supervisee to decide what period is best. For example, if it is about a developmental journey, they might want to span one year previously and one year into the future. Time frames can range from one week, one month, to even several years.

What else might need attention?

When sitting in the past chair it is possible that unfinished business emerges. In a Solution-Focused approach, rather than diving into this, it is helpful to move to the future chair before exploring further. For example, you might pose questions like, 'Two years from now, when this issue might be resolved, what positive differences will you notice?' 'What will you be doing differently?'

A word of caution

Never use this technique as individual supervision dialogue while being observed by the remaining group members (Bannink, 2012).

What other uses are there for this technique?

The technique is very flexible as the concept of the passage of time can be applied to many situations. Once familiar with the technique, a coach could use it with their clients.

With some variation it could be used with group supervision or team coaching; here you might invite people to work in a co-ordinated fashion – each visiting the past, present and future of the team. Be careful not to answer questions yourself, ask group members to talk answer, react and help each other. Stimulate the growth of relationships in the group and find strengths, competences and resilience factors of all group members.

Reference

Bannink, F.P. (2012) *Practicing Positive CBT*. Oxford: Wiley.

Further reading

Bannink, F.P. (2015) *Handbook of Positive Supervision*. Boston: Hogrefe Publishing.

~ ~ ~ ~ ~

76. Solution-Focused scaling questions

Evan George and Denise Yusuf

Where can this be used?				Typical level of supervisee experience required	
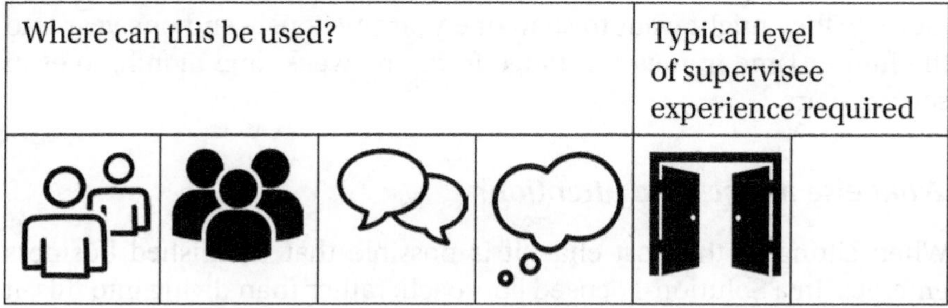					

When is this used?

When supervisees identify work as stalled and failing to progress, the progress already made can be obscured, making it harder for supervisees to recall what they have done that has been useful. Solution-Focused (SF) Scaling Questions can highlight the progress already achieved, providing a framework within which that progress can be accessed and leveraged.

This approach offers a flexible conversational framework which can serve to highlight and to clarify the key elements of the change process, such as:

- Coach and client resources.
- Effective strategies.
- Progress made.
- Indicators of further progress.

What is the technique?

The most generic formulation of the question, used in supervision is 'On a scale of 0 to 10 with 0 representing how things were when you started working with this client and 10 representing confident and successful closure where would you put things now?'

Step 1: Ensure that the scale is anchored, and that the points 0 and 10 have been clearly defined.

Step 2: Elicit the supervisee's view on how far the work has reached.

Step 3: Consider using any or all of the following frequently used subsidiary questions:

- What tells you that you have reached that point?
- What have you done that has been helpful in reaching that point?
- What have you noticed about your own capacities in reaching that point on the scale?
- How will you know that the work has moved just one point up on the scale?

Note: The client's perspective is also routinely incorporated by re-framing the above questions - for example question one would become 'Where would your client say that the work has reached?'

Step 4: In each of these areas of focus, continue to elicit greater detail for example, 'So what else have you noticed that puts things at 6 and not back at 0?' It is in the supportive persistence that supervisees are likely to generate and to articulate new thoughts about their work.

Step 5: At the end of supervision invite the supervisee to pay particular attention to tiny evidences of change in forthcoming sessions and to what they are doing that is associated with this progress.

How to work with the technique ...

Choice of language is significant, particularly in the framing of the 'one point up' question. Choosing the more 'strategic' framing 'So *what do you need to do* to move the work up by just one point?' consistently proves less effective (Ratner et al., 2012, pp. 125–126) than an alternative 'evidential' framing of the question. The strategic framing risks reminding the supervisee that they do not know what to do, whereas the evidential framing '*How will you know* that the work has moved ....' has an embedded suggestion that the supervisee is capable of knowing and that the work will move up, thereby tending to engage the supervisee's imagination and creativity. Typically, this will open up a range of new potential options for action, allowing the supervisee to choose the most appropriate of those possibilities in the moment.

Supervisors new to using the SF Scaling Questions are often tempted to quickly move towards a description of 'one point up' on the scale. Experienced practitioners will spend twice as long 'unpacking' where the work has already reached before describing how the supervisee will know that the work has progressed by a further point.

Word of caution

The SF approach chooses to assume that both clients and supervisees are at all times giving of their best to make the conversation useful. Therefore, if the supervisee is struggling to answer the supervisor's questions, or struggling to provide detail, then the SF supervisor's assumption is that they are asking the wrong question, or moving at the wrong pace, or have not made the purpose of the questions sufficiently clear. If what we are doing does not seem to be working *the onus is on the supervisor to do something different.*

What other uses are there for this technique?

Scale questions can be straightforwardly re-framed to focus on, for example, the supervisee's confidence in the likelihood of change or the supervisee's professional development. Once familiar with the approach it can equally be applied in one to one coaching and in team coaching. Teams can, for example, be asked to scale 'How effectively are we communicating?' or 'How well we support each other at times when things are tough?'

References

Ratner, H., George, E. and Iveson, C. (2012) *Solution Focused Brief Therapy: 100 Key Points and Techniques*. London: Routledge.

Further reading

Iveson, C., George, E. and Ratner, H. (2012) *Brief Coaching: A Solution Focused Approach*. London: Routledge.

Meier, D. (2005) *Team Coaching with the Solution Circle: A Practical Guide to Solutions Focused Team Development*. Cheltenham: SolutionsBooks.

Thomas, F. (2013) *Solution-Focused Supervision: A Resource-Oriented Approach to Developing Clinical Expertise*. New York: Springer.

~ ~ ~ ~ ~

77. Sparkling Moments: instances and exceptions

Evan George and Denise Yusuf

Where can this be used?				Typical level of supervisee experience required	

When is this used?

Used when the supervisee feels stuck and is asking the supervisor for ideas about what to do. This is a way of liberating the supervisee to generate their own useful ideas even when they are complaining of feeling stuck and asking for help.

What is the technique?

This technique assumes that even in the most difficult situations there will be some variability, there will be times when the work is going a little better, or the supervisee is feeling a little more hopeful. Sparkling Moments assumes that at these times the supervisee is likely to be doing something different and that doing more of this difference is likely to prove useful.

Step 1: Acknowledge the supervisee's experience of stuckness, for example '... it sounds like things are pretty tough right now and that you are not clear about the way forward.'

Step 2: Elicit permission to ask some questions, 'Would it be OK for me to ask some questions to see if we can find any clues as to what might be useful in moving forward?'

Step 3: Ask about the Sparkling Moments. 'Tell me about the times when you feel a little bit more hopeful' or 'Tell me about the times when he does seem to cooperate a bit better' or 'Tell me about the times that you have seen a little progress.'

Step 4 (a): If the supervisee can bring to mind more hopeful times or times when the work is going better ask the supervisee what they are doing at these times that is working, even a little.

Step 4 (b): If the supervisee cannot identify times when there is a little more hope or co-operation or progress, widen the field to other pieces of work where the supervisee has felt similarly and when they have nonetheless found a way forward.

Step 5: Ask the supervisee to identify in as much detail as possible what they were doing at these Sparkling Moments, either in the present piece of work or in these other similar pieces of work. Say, for instance, 'Tell me 5 (10) things that you were doing at these times that may have been useful.'

Step 6: Invite the supervisee to identify which of the things that they were doing at these 'better' times it might be useful to repeat and increase.

Step 7: Once the supervisee has chosen, suggest to the supervisee that they experiment with amplifying this aspect of their work.

Step 8: Ask the supervisee to watch out for evidence that what they are doing is working.

How to work with the technique ...

The Solution-Focused approach takes the view that supervisees are more likely to make effective use of the ideas that they themselves have generated rather than ideas provided by the supervisor. When working with this technique, this belief is a central component to its effectiveness. Without it the supervisor will be drawn to 'rescue' and either offer their solutions or engage in joint problem solving. A genuinely Solution-Focused mindset will create a generative energy in the supervision space. Should the stuckness continue, the supervisor's role is to broaden the enquiry, to help the supervisee think more laterally until some Sparkling Moments are found in different but nonetheless transferable situations.

What else might need attention?

If the supervisee is unable to identify any Sparkling Moments in the work or in their broader experience, the supervisor can use a SF Scaling

Question (see pp. 260–263), focusing on the supervisee's confidence in the possibility of change. Alternatively, the supervisor might ask the supervisee 'So in your work with this client what can you say for certain does not work and is not worth repeating?' Once this is known, then anything else might be worth trying.

A word of caution

Before asking about Sparkling Moments it is important to acknowledge the supervisee's feelings of stuckness, that they feel that they really do not know what to do. Failing to acknowledge the stuckness reduces the supervisee's capacity to scan for and to identify the Sparkling Moments.

What other uses are there for this technique?

This technique works well in personal coaching and in group coaching.

Further reading

Iveson, C., George, E. and Ratner, H. (2012) *Brief Coaching: A Solution Focused Approach*. London: Routledge.

Ratner, H., George, E. and Iveson, C. (2012) *Solution Focused Brief Therapy: 100 Key Points and Techniques*. London: Routledge.

~ ~ ~ ~ ~

78. Stopping and starting

Carmelina Lawton Smith and Evan George

Where can this be used?				Typical level of supervisee experience required	

When is this used?

This technique may be well known to some and can be applied in the supervision context. It is best used as a follow-up stage after a period of exploration with a supervisee about a particular situation, or pattern of behaviour in their coaching. It enables the supervisee to clear the ground and then to move forward into actions that they may want to test out.

What is the technique?

The Solution-Focused approach (Berg and Miller, 1992) was initially founded on three simple rules:

1 If it is not broken don't fix it.
2 If it works do more of it.
3 If it doesn't work do something different.

The third rule seems obvious and yet time and time again we find ourselves repeating interventions that have shown no evidence of utility, merely because they seem the obvious thing to do. As frustration increases and hope fades, any tiny evidence of what does work can be missed. In such circumstances there is a risk that the supervisee might conclude 'nothing works,' which in turn reduces or indeed eliminates creativity.

Step 1: List with the supervisee what they are currently doing that is not useful, does not make a difference.

Step 2: List with the supervisee what they have done in the current piece of work or have done in their coaching more generally that has seemed useful and which might be worth increasing either in frequency or in intensity or indeed in both.

Step 3: List with the supervisee five interventions that they have considered trying but for whatever reason have excluded and thus have not tried.

Step 4: Having agreed that what is not working and which is not worth repeating, examine the list of interventions that have been tried and which have been somewhat useful and the list of interventions considered but rejected.

Step 5: Invite the supervisee to select which of these interventions is most likely to be worth adopting or increasing. If the supervisee is presenting a specific piece of coaching work then it can be useful to explore the question 'Which of these interventions do you think that the client might most appreciate and most value?'

Step 6: Once the supervisee has selected one or, at most, two of these interventions/actions/behaviours invite the supervisee to describe, in detail, how they will know that they are at their very best when putting their selection into practice and how they could know that the stopping and starting was making a useful difference.

How to work with the technique ...

When using this idea remember that identifying what is not working and is not worth repeating serves to clear the ground for the new possibilities and should be negotiated with the supervisee first. When scanning with supervisees what has been or is useful this can require a careful focus on, for example, sessions that have been even a little better or more hopeful, or indeed sessions that have seemed even a little less 'stuck' or 'confrontational'. The differences to be explored can be slight and small when searching for useful possibilities.

A word of caution

When describing what is not working, there is inevitably a risk that that the supervisee could experience the conversation as critical of them and of their practice. Bearing in mind the idea that supervisees typically do what they do 'for their own good reason' and sometimes actively exploring their 'good reason' for acting the way that they have, can help supervisees to let go. Further, it seems to be the case that supervisees are less defensive and more able to stop behaviours that have been positively connoted. So, for example ask 'So what have you learnt from trying (...) that will be useful to you in moving forward?' or 'So what have you learnt from (...) not working out as well as you had hoped?'.

What other uses are there for this technique?

This can be modelled for use with clients when discussing actions to take forward. Some versions of this include 'What do you want to *continue* doing?' which can be added where appropriate, leading to five conversational possibilities: stop, start, continue, less of and more of.

Reference

Berg, I.K. and Miller, S.D. (1992) *Working with the Problem-drinker: A Solution-Focused Approach*. New York: Norton.

~ ~ ~ ~ ~

79. The tomorrow question

Michelle Lucas

Where can this be used?				Typical level of supervisee experience required	

When is this used?

This is useful when a supervisee is finding it particularly difficult to connect with their client and/or is feeling very 'stuck.' The supervisee might be finding it difficult to come up with ideas about what they can do or believe they have 'tried everything' without success.

What is the technique?

Based in the Solution-Focused approach, a question is offered that serves to leapfrog the current dynamic and open up new areas of exploration to create a new way forward.

Step 1: Seek permission to experiment with a more future focused exploration.

Step 2: Discuss what would be a good outcome for the supervisee by asking, for example 'What differences would you like to see in your working relationship with this client as a result of this supervision?'

Step 3: Help the supervisee craft a few words that capture the essence of this discussion, as you will use this in Step 4, e.g. [good sense of connection with this client].

Step 4: Support the supervisee to recall how resourceful they are ... picking up on the output of Step 3 invite the supervisee to talk about other occasions (either with this client or any other) when their aspired future state was present.

Step 5: The supervisor asks

> *If you woke up tomorrow and discovered that something had happened which resolved all the difficulties you are experiencing ... that suddenly*

your [connection with this client] was exactly what you had hoped for .... What would be the first difference that you would notice?

Step 6: Continue the exploration in an iterative fashion, considering how each difference noticed in one party prompts a noticing of difference in the other. For example:

- What might be the first difference that you notice in you?
- And if your client were to notice that, how do you think they would respond?
- So, when you then respond to your client, what other differences do you notice in you?

Step 7: Support the supervisee to connect with their aspired future state. For example: Following this conversation, imagine that you find yourself doing something different, however small, when you next sit with the client ... what might it be? What else? And what else?

Step 8: Consider if it would be helpful to elaborate this by looking at how they will know if they have moved one point better (see Solution-Focused Scaling Questions, pp. 260–263).

Step 9: The supervisor offers some words of appreciation, perhaps reflecting back those resources the supervisee articulated and which resonated for the supervisor. Where the supervisee has noted some improvement, the supervisor might reinforce what the supervisee had done to get to the current point. Additionally, offer appreciation regarding how the supervisee has engaged with this process.

Step 10: To close out the work check-in with the supervisee to see what they now need from the supervision.

How to work with the technique ...

Once you have established a form of words that capture the desired outcome for the supervisee, it is important to use their words just as they are even if they feel awkward to the supervisor. Step 6 really helps the client to see something different and then to focus on how they would be different with the client. It may be helpful to continue this exploration - for example, if the supervisee says they will feel more confident, a follow-up question like 'What will that look like?' or 'How will you know?', will typically elicit still further information. In Step 7 the supervisee may question what you mean by 'now' as often something will have already shifted within the session, compared to where they started. Interestingly, the questions about positive difference often prompt a shift in energy that yields a sense of resolution, the supervisee relaxes and is less occupied with what is causing the problem or what they might do next.

A word of caution

This technique was adapted from de Shazer's work, who invited the client to consider how it would be if a 'miracle' had happened. While intended as a metaphor, the word 'miracle' can trigger more emotive reactions. Therefore, while alternative phrases might be useful, be careful to use neutral language.

What other uses are there for this technique?

Once familiar with the technique, this may be of use with coaching clients.

Further reading

Connie, E. (2012) Solution building with couples: A solution focused approach – 'The most amazing thing I have ever heard a client say'. *Context*. June 2012, pp. 6–9.

de Shazer, S. (1988) *Clues: Investigating Solutions in Brief Therapy*. New York: Norton.

Ratner, H., George, E. and Iveson, C. (2012) *Solution Focused Brief Therapy: 100 Key Points and Techniques*. London: Routledge.

~ ~ ~ ~ ~

80. Transferring competence

Fredrike Bannink

Where can this be used?				Typical level of supervisee experience required	

When is this used?

This helps supervisees to find their existing competences, so that they can be leveraged for the current supervision topic or a future desired state. The enquiry can be used in many configurations and is most helpful when intending to create a positive atmosphere while simultaneously capturing existing competence.

What is the enquiry?

This technique is based on the work of Lamarre and Gregoire (1999) who described the notion of *competence transference*. The idea being that when you become stuck in one domain of your life it is probable that the qualities and skills you utilise in other domains (work, family, hobbies, sports, talents) could be of use to you. They describe how a client suffering from a panic disorder learned how to relax by applying his knowledge of deep-sea diving whenever he experienced anxiety.

Facilitate a semi-structured discussion along the following lines:

Step 1: Ask permission to experiment with some tangential discussion.

Step 2: Identify with them what other areas of their life they are successful at – useful areas to explore are typically work, family, hobbies, sports or special talents.

Step 3: Engage in a positive and exploratory discussion using questions like:

- 'What competences do you have?' 'How do/did you use those?' 'How do/did you succeed in doing that?'
- 'What would those around you in those moments describe as your competences?'

Step 4: Invite the supervisee to transfer one of those competences towards the issue at hand. This can be done explicitly, 'How might you use this competence to manage the topic we were talking about?' or it can be done in a more positive way, 'How can you bring this competence to bear in order to reach your goal?' Or it could be done in a more subtle way, 'If they could speak, what advice would your competence offer you for this issue?'

Step 5: Ask them to notice when and where else they have been able to leverage this level of resourcefulness. Talking about previous successes can help build self-confidence and remind them that their competences are a consistent part of them.

Step 6: Encourage the supervisee to consider what small next step they might take to move themselves forward on the problem or issue at hand.

How to work with the enquiry ...

Experiment rather than simply dig deeper or try harder, this in itself can liberate the energy in the discussion. If you know the supervisee well, you might invite the supervisee to think about areas of their life that you have already heard from them as success stories. Steps 4 and 5 serve to support the supervisee to transfer their competence from one domain to another.

Solution-Focused interviewing (Bannink, 2010) capitalises on the idea that all individuals have competences, despite life's struggles, that can be marshalled to improve the quality of their lives.

What else might need attention?

Sometimes supervisees feel embarrassed to talk about their strengths and successes. Or they never really have given it any thought. If the supervisee cannot - or dare not - come up with their competences, ask them what those around them would say their competences are. 'Suppose we were to ask your best friend what you are good at, what would they say?' Asking questions from other perspectives, such as the perspective of their best friend, makes it easier to name their own competences.

A word of caution

Remember, context may alter what behaviour is appropriate, so ensure you check that the behaviour being transferred is appropriate to the new context. Remember also that what works with one person may not always work for the next.

What other uses are there for this enquiry?

The enquiry can be used as an energiser and builds self-confidence and self-efficacy, perhaps pair work within a group. In this case begin by inviting partners to share what areas of their life they really shine in. It would conclude by inviting the pairs to consider when these competences have shown up in their work and how they might use them in a personal issue at hand.

The enquiry can be similarly applied to work with individual and team coaching clients.

References

Bannink, F.P. (2010) *1001 Solution-focused Questions. Handbook for Solution-focused Interviewing*. New York: Norton.

Lamarre, J. and Gregoire, A. (1999) Competence transfer in solution-focused therapy: Harnessing a natural resource. *Journal of Systemic Therapies*, 18(1), pp. 43–57.

Further reading

Bannink, F.P. (2015) *Handbook of Positive Supervision*. Boston: Hogrefe Publishing.

Chapter 8

A systemic approach to supervision

Maren Donata Urschel

How is this philosophy described?

All human beings are part of multiple systems. Multiple systems create multiple belongings. Belonging is one of the deepest human needs. Our first and most formative belonging in our lives is the family system we are born into. Without that belonging we would not survive. Other belongings include current and past work relationships, our culture of origin and education systems.

There are hidden rules of belonging in every system. These generate behavioural patterns, loyalties and entanglements – often on an unconscious level. These are invisible dynamics that deeply affect our choices, the way in which we relate to other people and what we are able to attain in life and at work.

Systemic supervision elicits and acknowledges invisible dynamics in systems. It illuminates hidden patterns, loyalties and entanglements that keep a system stuck and in its habit. As a result, paths towards restoring energy and flow in the system emerge. Systemic supervision allows both coach supervisor and supervisee to elegantly step back and move beyond stories, judgments and the need to be the expert.

Many supervision approaches use our habitual and often most practised way of knowing, which is through our conscious mind. Systemic supervision is based on an understanding that there are different ways of knowing and of accessing information. While our conscious mind could never simultaneously store the complexity of all those current and past relationships and belongings, our body and unconscious mind can.

This is what is called our 'felt sense' of our relationship systems. It manifests in an inner image of everything and everybody we have been or are in relationship with. A systemic 'constellation' is an external expression of the supervisee's inner image of their supervision issue. By placing the most resonant representatives for people and events within an agreed boundary, a three-dimensional spatial relationship map emerges. The map shows the supervisee in relation to other people or elements in the system. This enables supervisor and supervisee to access the so-called 'field of information,' which connects all elements within relationship systems. Gradually, a fresh image of the supervisee's issue emerges that leads to new insights and a movement towards health and flow in the system.

Systemic constellations are often described as an applied philosophy. It is a way of being and doing that manifests through the supervisor's Stance and the application of the systemic Organising Principles.

What are the underpinning principles and beliefs of this philosophy?

The application of the systemic Organising Principles underpins all systemic supervision. They are observed truths that translate across cultures, generations and languages. They serve as a diagnostic tool to elicit which parts of systems are in and out of balance.

Bert Hellinger originally articulated them in the context of social systems to support the flow of life and love in family systems. The systemic Organising Principles have been widely applied to the organisational context. Applied to systemic supervision, they serve to restore energy, flow and clarity for the supervisee and the system they are working in – see 'systemically oriented questions' technique. They are called *Time*, *Place* and *Exchange*. Examples of how they manifest in systemic supervision follow below.

- **Time** – who or what came first has precedence over what follows. A coach was working with a leader who was unable to exert any influence. Systemic supervision showed that the leader had joined the organisation without acknowledging who or what was there before them. By holding an inner respect for those who joined first, the leader was able to step into their full authority.
- **Place** – everybody and everything in a system needs a safe and respected place. A coach was working with a capable leader who struggled to get their team's commitment. Looking at who had occupied the role before them revealed that one of their predecessors had left for unexplained reasons. Their contribution had never been acknowledged. As a consequence, the team's energy was with the predecessor not with the current leader. By acknowledging the

predecessor's contribution to the company, the new leader was able to fully occupy their role and get the team's commitment.

- **Exchange** – all systems strive for a balance between giving and taking. A supervisee felt drained by their work. Looking at the balance of exchange across the supervisee's work/life revealed that they over-gave in their work, secretly hoping to receive something back, thereby resolving un-met needs from their childhood. Acknowledging that, respectfully disentangled the supervisee from a hidden pattern that deeply affected how they related to their clients. As a result, the supervisee was able to move their energy from being over-helpful to being useful to the client and the wider system.

Acknowledging what is, is the beginning of any systemic intervention in supervision. It enables both supervisor and supervisee to stand in the difficulty without the need to judge, interpret or interfere. As a result, the underlying systemic truth emerges and the system returns to balance – see 'mapping what is' technique.

What is the role of the coach supervisor in the context of this philosophy?

In addition to *Acknowledgment* and the *Organising Principles*, the *Stance* of the supervisor is a cornerstone of systemic supervision. Systemic supervisors:

- **Work in service of the system** – in systemic supervision the focus of attention is on the entire system, rather than on the individual client. Supervisors fully work in service of the system when they let go of the need to know or be an expert and trust the information it reveals. That way an ego-free process emerges that lets the system speak and shows where it needs re-alignment.
- **Model compassionate distance** – a respectful combination of compassion and distance enables the supervisor to be present to the truth of what is without getting entangled in the client's system. To support this distance, the supervisee sets up a spatial relationship map of their issue with representatives (in a group supervision setting) or objects (in an individual setting).
- **Elicit somatic knowledge** – the 'field of information,' supported by the supervisor's *Stance* and knowledge of the *Organising Principles* holds all information needed to enable the system to return to

balance. Supervisor and supervisee access the field of information by eliciting the somatic knowledge – the 'felt sense' – of everybody involved. To access the 'felt sense', the supervisor invites everybody to tune into their bodily sensations rather than into what they think they feel. Somatic knowledge arises in a systemic constellation based on how representatives/objects are placed.

- **Give everything a place** – any exclusion draws energy out of relationship systems. By acknowledging what is true from different parts of the system and giving everything a place, the system settles.
- **Create safe boundaries** – to keep the work focused and safe it is important to contain the supervisee's issue by setting boundaries. This can be done as follows:
  1 Put a time limit to the constellation exercise.
  2 Work, quite literally, within a clearly defined boundary (e.g. a sheet of paper, a table-top or the space within a circle of chairs).
- **Take one small step at a time** – shifts in the system are always preceded by inner shifts in the client. Inner shifts take time to emerge and integrate because they need to be embodied. Embodied work cannot be shortcut by 'jumping' straight to solutions. Systemic supervisors encourage their supervisees to take and acknowledge one small step at a time – see 'a step towards better' technique.
- **Navigate complexity** – relationship systems are complex to navigate, particularly in organisations. The supervisee's key question (the part of the system they choose to look at) acts as a compass for navigating the vast complexity of relationship systems.

How would you prepare yourself to work congruently with this approach?

Systemic supervision is an applied philosophy. Coach supervisors who work congruently with this approach, fully trust the system and the information it reveals. This requires practice and experiential learning. Here is how to get started:

- **Look at your own systemic connections** – to be able to support the supervisee in standing in the difficulty of what is without the need to judge, consult or help, systemic supervisors need to look at their own systemic belongings and loyalties to:
  1 Resource themselves from their own systemic connections.
  2 Avoid entanglement with the supervisee's patterns and dynamics.

- **Build somatic capacity** – systemic supervision accesses the tacit knowledge that is stored in our guts and hearts, our 'felt sense' of relationship systems. Therefore, it is important to build capacity to work with and take in information through the body.
- **Experience the work** – any embodied process takes time to integrate and requires experiential learning over time. In addition to understanding the stance, principles and applications of systemic supervision, participating in constellations and experiencing system dynamics in action is a precondition for the safe use of this methodology.

How might this way of working be particularly useful to the supervisee?

Systemic supervision that uses an embodied process like constellations, enables supervisees to get a somatic, three-dimensional experience of their issue in the wider system. It can be applied to individuals, teams and entire systems in an individual and group supervision setting. Here are some examples of its benefits to the supervisee:

- **Illuminating systemic connections** – systemic supervision illuminates the supervisee's own entanglements, loyalties and belongings. This enables them to work in service of their client's system without trying to fix or change anything.
- **Building knowledge about systems** – the organising principles that limit and sustain systems come alive in every systemic supervision session. Applying them enables supervisees to use them in their work with their clients so that they also benefit.
- **Resourcing the supervisee** – systemic supervision leads to clarity for the supervisor and the supervisee on where and how in the system the supervisee can be most useful and resourced – see 'resourcing' technique.
- **Getting to the source** – systemic supervision enables supervisees to uncover repeating patterns and hidden dynamics behind the issues they present. For example, rather than addressing demotivation with motivation techniques, systemic supervision looks at demotivation in the context of the entire system, uncovers its source and uses the emerging systemic truth as the fundament for restoring flow and balance in the system.
- **Surfacing fresh information** – systemic supervision elicits and acknowledges invisible dynamics by surfacing and giving a voice to the unspoken and tacit knowledge in systems.

- **Liberating both supervisor and supervisee** – systemic supervision is free of judgment and stories. This liberates both supervisor and supervisee from needing to be the expert.

Anything else you need to consider before using the practices that follow?

Systemic supervision with constellations reveals fresh information that can be different from and sometimes contradictory to the information that arises by thinking or talking through an issue. This may be surprising or unsettling for supervisees. The most useful attitude towards systemic constellations is to treat everything as information without judgment or interpretation. Systemic constellations are an embodied experience. They are an event that changes something in the system. Their effect unfolds over time and they are best left to work in the body on a somatic level, rather than in the brain on a rational level.

Systemic supervision is a process that is bigger than the supervisor and the supervisee. It invites them both to put their ego aside and liberates them from needing to be the expert or from having to solve anything just by themselves. Systemic supervision is a joy to facilitate. It provides a new perspective, fresh information, access to resources, a way of expressing the previously unexpressible and clarity on hidden loyalties and entanglements. Above all it provides an experience of the interconnectedness between all human relationship systems and the dynamics that keep them in and out of balance.

Further reading

Whittington, J. (2020) *Systemic Coaching and Constellations*, 3rd ed. London: Kogan Page.
Hellinger, B. and Ten Hövel, G. (1999) *Acknowledging What Is – Conversations with Bert Hellinger*. Phoenix, AZ: Zeig Tucker & Co., Inc.
Horn, K.P. and Brick, R. (2009) *Invisible Dynamics*, 2nd ed. Heidelberg: Carl Auer.
Manné, J. (2009) *Family Constellations*. Berkeley, CA: North Atlantic Books.

Resources

www.coachingconstellations.com [Accessed 2 October 2019]

~~~~~
~~~~~

81. Mapping what is

Maren Donata Urschel

Where can this be used?				Typical level of supervisee experience required	

When is this used?

All systemic constellations start with mapping 'what is,' in line with *Acknowledging* what is, the beginning of any systemic intervention in supervision.

We all carry an inner image of everything and everybody we have been in relationship with. Mapping enables supervisees to create a three-dimensional, embodied representation of their inner image of a relationship dynamic. Mapping enables supervisees to access hidden or unconscious information about an issue in the context of the wider system.

What is the practice?

Mapping 'what is,' is an intervention in itself and it can often be enough. Being a somatic technique, it usually reveals different information in comparison to thinking through an issue.

You could introduce 'mapping what is' as follows:

> *Bring to mind a relationship system in which you feel challenged, stuck or sense some kind of difficulty. We are going to map out the most important people and elements in that system to enable you to access the benefits of a three-dimensional representation of your issue.*

The supervisor talks the supervisee(s) through the exercise as follows:

Step 1: Find a space with a boundary, for example, a blank sheet of paper on a table-top.

Step 2: Identify the most important people, elements or events relating to your issue. Keep them to as few as possible (maximum six). Select arrow-shaped post-its or other representative objects with a sense of direction to identify each of them. Make sure you include yourself.

Step 3: It might be useful to identify an orientation to map against. If useful, place a post-it/object representing an 'outcome' or a 'purpose' on the boundaried space ('the map').

Step 4: Tap into your intuition and somatic sense of the situation as it is right now, slowly place the objects representing (1) yourself and (2) the next most resonant person or element. Pay attention to the distance between them and the direction they are facing.

Step 5: Slowly add the remaining post-its/objects one by one. Trust your intuition and your body's sense of where each would be best placed. Make sure the map represents the 'what is' not what you would like it to be.

Step 6: Articulate in as few words as possible what you notice or want to acknowledge about the map created. For example, 'this is difficult,' 'I am too close,' 'I feel stuck,' etc. Resist the temptation of changing the map to 'resolve' or 'fix' anything.

Step 7: Supervisor and supervisee work with what emerges, supervisor asks 'systemically oriented questions' (see pp. 287–289) and supervises as appropriate.

Step 8: Find a way of internalising the map, e.g. by taking a photo.

Step 9: Respectfully dismantle the map.

How to work with the practice ...

It is important that supervisors do not get seduced into the supervisee's 'story.' Signs of that might include:

- Taking a personal position or stake in the supervisee's story.
- Judging the supervisee or any other person, element or event in the system represented.
- Feeling like being treated or addressed as someone from within the system by the supervisee, e.g. a previous boss they disliked.
- Focusing only on the individual rather than including the dynamics in the whole system.

When the supervisor becomes aware of any of the above, they might try the following:

- Encourage the supervisee to stay with the facts.
- Be present to the truth of what is.

- Treat everything as information.
- Focus on the dynamics held within the whole relationship system.
- Walk round the map with the supervisee (to avoid becoming caught up in their projections and identifications and to get a different perspective).
- Look at your own systemic connections to hold a safe space for the client without getting entangled.
- Agree to everything as it is (not the same as agreeing *with* everything).

What else might need attention?

In our experience, using people (rather than objects) as representatives in a system is best reserved for experienced practitioners, especially when it is appropriate to go beyond the initial map of what is and start to illuminate relationship dynamics and sources of resolution.

A word of caution.

The exercise works best without too much explanation upfront. Usually, once participants have started mapping, they become fully immersed into the process.

Mapping what is with representative objects on a table-top, even in this simple context, elicits a somatic response in the supervisee and the supervisor. Therefore, it can be very useful for supervisors to have the somatic experience of being a representative in a constellation workshop with other live representatives.

What other uses are there for this practice?

Once supervisees have experienced the exercise in supervision and tried it out in self-supervision they can use the exercise with their clients.

Further reading

Whittington, J. (2020) *Systemic Coaching and Constellations*, 3rd ed. London: Kogan Page.

Resources

Available at: www.coachingconstellations.com [Accessed 2 October 2019]

~ ~ ~ ~ ~

82. One step towards better

Maren Donata Urschel

Where can this be used?				Typical level of supervisee experience required	

When is this used?

Following on from 'Mapping what is' (see pp. 279–281) supervisors might invite supervisees to take one step towards 'better'. 'Better' in systemic work is not an evaluation or a judgement but rather a movement that sets off an inner shift and releases some of the tension or stuck-ness in the system.

What is the practice?

Taking a step towards 'better' enables supervisees to experiment with a possible next step and understand what the system requires of *them* to release some of the difficulty.

Once the supervisee has created a map of 'what is' and articulated some words of acknowledgment about their map (see Steps 1 to 6 in 'Mapping what is'), the supervisor talks the supervisee(s) through the exercise as follows:

Step 1 to Step 6: See 'Mapping what is' on pp. 279–281.

Step 7(a): Move the representative object/post-it of yourself one small step towards 'better'. 'Better' in the sense of releasing some of the tension or difficulty in the system. You can only move your own representative object. Tap into your gut feel or intuition about where that place might be. Take your time. Pay attention to distance and direction.

Step 7(b): Notice if any words come up that accompany this movement towards 'better'. If so, express them succinctly, for example, 'now I can see you', or 'I am taking a step back'.

Step 8: Articulate what the system requires of you to make a move towards better. For example, 'I need to be closer to my team so that I can really see them,' or 'I need to leave the system to serve it best.'

Step 9: Supervisor and supervisee work with what emerges using 'systemically oriented questions' (see p. 0).

Step 10: Find a way of internalising the map, e.g. take a photo.

Step 11: Respectfully dismantle the map.

How to work with the practice ...

Sometimes supervisees are tempted to move all representatives objects a 'step towards better' in a desire to resolve the issue. Inviting the supervisee to move only the representative object for themselves allows them to embody the inner shift *they* are capable of making to ease some of the difficulty in the system. This connects the supervisee with their inner capacity to effect change in one part of the system. Moving one part of the system, has an effect on all others, just like in a child's mobile.

Occasionally, supervisees struggle to come up with words that accompany the movement towards 'better.' It can be useful to invite them to make physical contact with their representative object by lightly touching it with their fingers, while tuning into what information emerges from that part of the system. This process can be replicated with all other representative objects. It naturally supports supervisees in accessing information from different parts of the system. That said, it is also information in itself if the supervisee does not come up with any words.

What else might need attention?

See 'Mapping what is' on pp. 279–281.

A word of caution

'Mapping what is' is an intervention in itself and it can often be enough. Therefore, it is important to let the supervisee decide whether to add 'a step towards better.' A simple question could be 'have you got enough (information)?' Once the supervisee has set up and internalised their map of 'what is' (and throughout any systemic work), empower the supervisee to integrate systemic information at their own pace.

Systemic work is embodied work, it takes time to integrate and requires an inner shift in the supervisee. There is no shortcut – swiftly moving to solutions in a desire to 'fix' an issue, often deprives the supervisee and the system of the possibility to experience and move through the sometimes subtle, yet important, stages of inner shift/change. Therefore, systemic supervisors encourage supervisees to take and acknowledge one small step towards 'better' at a time.

What other uses are there for this practice?

See 'Mapping what is' on pp. 279–281.

Further reading

Whittington, J. (2020) *Systemic Coaching and Constellations*, 3rd ed. London: Kogan Page.

Resources

Available at: www.coachingconstellations.com [Accessed 2 October 2019]

~ ~ ~ ~ ~

83. Resourcing

Maren Donata Urschel

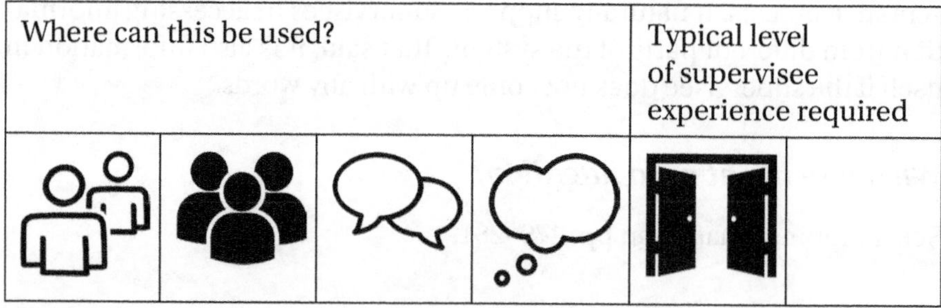

Where can this be used?				Typical level of supervisee experience required	

When is this used?

Mapping resources is useful for situations in which supervisors or supervisees feel a need to but struggle to identify and access resources to support them. Resources support and strengthen supervisors and supervisees in serving a relationship system in the most useful way. Resources can be people, concepts (e.g. systemic coaching), concretes (e.g. money) or abstracts (e.g. insight).

What is the practice?

This approach accesses resources through mapping enabling supervisors and supervisees to get out of their heads into a three-dimensional representation of how they can resource themselves in a particular situation.

The supervisor could introduce a resource mapping exercise to the supervisee as follows:

> *Think of a particularly challenging situation with one of your clients where you feel under-resourced. We are going to experiment with a different way of accessing and identifying resources that support you in your client relationship. Rather than thinking or talking about them, we are going to put them on a three-dimensional map representing yourself, your client and the most important resource(s).*

The supervisor talks the supervisee(s) through the exercise as follows:

Step 1: Find a clean, free space with a clear boundary, for example, a sheet of paper on a table-top.

Step 2: Identify three objects representing (1) yourself, (2) your client and (3) a resource (you may or may not know who or what the resource is at this stage).
Note: Make sure the objects have a really clear sense of direction. There are representative objects specifically designed for this purpose as well as arrow-shaped post-its. If you don't have either, you could simply use coffee cups where the handle represents the direction of attention.

Step 3: Tap into your intuition and somatic sense of the situation as it is right now, and place the objects representing (1) yourself and (2) your client within the boundaried space. Pay attention to the distance between them and the direction they are facing.

Step 4: Articulate in as few words as possible what you notice about the map you created.

Step 5: Without worrying about what the resource is and trusting your intuition and your body's sense of where it would be best placed, add the object representing the resource (3) to the map created.

Step 6: Notice whether any words come up you would want to 'say' to the resource to acknowledge it. For example, 'now I can see you', 'I had forgotten about you', 'thank you for showing up', etc. Adjust the position of the resource, if it feels appropriate.

Step 7: Add one further object (*if needed*), representing one additional resource. *Repeat Step 6.*

Step 8: Work with what emerges, supervise as appropriate.

Step 9: Find a way of internalising the map, e.g. by taking a photo.

Step 10: Respectfully dismantle the map.

How to work with the practice ...

This exercise enables supervisees to discover previously unseen or unknown resources in the systems in which they belong or have belonged. Therefore, it is possible that the supervisee does not know what exactly the resource is. It is important to focus on the embodied experience of being resourced rather than thinking about what the resource is. Often, the name of the resource emerges naturally - during or after the exercise.

If the supervisee gets distracted by identifying the resource, it can be useful to point out that both - knowing what the resource is and not knowing what the resource is - is information in itself. The supervisor might suggest to the supervisee to say something to the representative for the resource along the lines of 'thank you for showing up. I don't know who or what you are yet. Please give me time to find out'. This acknowledges the resource's existence and gives it a place.

What else might need attention?

Accessing new or long-forgotten resources might generate an emotional response in supervisees. It is most useful to treat any (emotional) response as information, acknowledge it and encourage the supervisee to let the resourcing map settle so that it can integrate and unfold.

A word of caution

See 'Mapping what is' on pp. 279–281.

What other uses are there for this practice?

Once supervisees have experienced the exercise in supervision and tried it out in self-supervision, they can use the exercise with their clients to resource them for a particular situation.

Further reading

Whittington, J. (2020) *Systemic Coaching and Constellations*, 3rd ed. London: Kogan Page.

Resources

Available at: www.coachingconstellations.com [Accessed 2 October 2019]

~ ~ ~ ~ ~

84. Systemically oriented questions

Maren Donata Urschel

Where can this be used?				Typical level of supervisee experience required

When is this used?

Systemically oriented questions based on the systemic *Organising Principles, Time, Place* and *Exchange* (see Philosophy, pages pp. 273–278) enable supervisor and supervisee to 'diagnose' and acknowledge which parts of a relationship system are in and out of balance. As a result, energy, flow and clarity for the supervisee and the system they are working in are restored.

What is the practice?

Systemically oriented questions enable a shift from a person-centred towards a system-centred perspective by moving beyond focusing solely on the supervisee towards taking the entire relationship system into account.

To illustrate the power of systemically oriented questions in a coaching context, here are some examples around each of the *Organising Principles*. These are the sort of questions that the supervisor might ask the supervisee in other systemic techniques, for example 'Mapping what is' (Step 7) – see pp. 280 and 'One step towards better' (Step 10) – see p. 283.

Time

- **Purpose:** asking questions about the order of time acknowledges contributions, people and events in the past to clear the present and future from entanglements and hidden loyalties.
- **Examples:** who served the longest in this system? Who was the last person to join? Who are the founders of this system? Is their original intention known and acknowledged? What were the key events

in the history of this company? How many people held this role before you took it up? To what extent has their contribution been acknowledged?

Place

- **Purpose**: asking questions about the extent to which everybody and everything has a safe and respected place in a system, keeps energy, flow and focus in the system that would otherwise be diverted.
- **Examples:** whose contribution to the company is excluded or has been forgotten about? Are difficult events in the company's history known and talked about? To what extent is the contribution of people who left the system acknowledged? Does everybody have the same right to a safe and respected place in the system? Are there roles that seem particularly difficult to fill?

Exchange

- **Purpose:** asking questions about the balance of exchange in a system highlights the extent to which there is a dynamic balance between giving and taking over time, a precondition for enabling all system elements to take full responsibility for themselves and their contributions.
- **Examples:** who in this system gives too much, who gives too little? Who earns the money to pay for the coaching assignment? What is your sense of what you give/receive and what your client gives/receives in the coaching assignment?

How to work with the practice ...

Systemically oriented questions naturally integrate into any supervision conversation. They are useful in untangling complexity and in exploring inertia, stuckness and conflict in relationship systems. Examples of when a supervisor might ask them follow below.

- A supervisee feels unusually drained by a client assignment without knowing why.
- A team displays challenging behaviour without any obvious cause.
- An organisation struggles to keep a leadership role filled despite each role holder's skills and experience.

- A pattern of withholding key information from decision makers – for no apparent reason – surfaces.
- An organisation avoids talking about the people who left the organisation and about what they contributed.

A word of caution

Systemically oriented questions often reveal fresh or hidden information about a relationship system. This might be surprising or even unsettling for the supervisee. It is most useful to treat any reaction in the supervisee as information, acknowledge it and encourage them to allow it to settle so that it can integrate and unfold.

What other uses are there for this practice?

Once supervisees have experienced systemically oriented questions in supervision they can safely use them with their clients to gently introduce them to the *Organising Principles* and to a more systemic perspective on their issue.

Further reading

Whittington, J. (2020) *Systemic Coaching and Constellations*, 3rd ed. London: Kogan Page.

Resources

Available at: www.coachingconstellations.com [Accessed 2 October 2019].

~ ~ ~ ~ ~

85. Using free movement

Damion Wonfor

Where can this be used?				Typical level of supervisee experience required	

When is this used?

This is useful to understand the relationship dynamic in a client system more fully. Perhaps stakeholders seem stuck in unhelpful patterns or there is a sense of divided loyalties, mixed messages or confusing political undercurrents.

What is the approach?

Based on systemic mapping principles, the supervisor engages group members in a process that may give insights into a new equilibrium in the system. Additionally, the group's somatic experience may hold information about relational dynamics.

Step 1: Begin the enquiry individually with the supervisee to articulate their supervision question.

Step 2: Once articulated, check with the supervisee what kind of energy they have, while also noticing yours, then question, challenge or affirm accordingly.

Step 3: Set up the map by inviting them to identify the stakeholders involved.

Step 4: The supervisee chooses a representative for each stakeholder, including someone to represent themselves. Where there are more stakeholders than group members, use pieces of paper. The supervisee moves each group member to a place that feels true, guiding them by gently putting their hands on their shoulder blades. They will map the representatives out considering the *distance between* their relationships and the *direction of travel* (if using pieces of paper, add an arrow to indicate the sense of direction as well as the representative name).

Step 5: Brief group members to settle into what they are representing, to immerse themselves in their somatic experience, quietening their cognitive understanding. Encourage them to trust that whatever is emerging (or not), is information.

Step 6: With the supervisee observing, visit each group member and ask a question to tap into their perception for example: 'What are you noticing as you stand here?' or 'How are you in relationship with the other representatives?'.

Step 7: Check back with the supervisee to understand what meaning is emerging for them.

Step 8: With the original supervision question in mind, invite the representatives to engage in 'free movement,' i.e. to find a space that feels true for them. Remind them to move slowly and to listen to their somatic sense. Repeat Steps 6 and 7 to see what new information is emerging.

Step 9: Return to the supervisee and enquire if the new map offers them any new insight. On occasion, they might find it useful to stand in the place occupied by the representative for themselves, tapping into their own somatic experience in that space.

Steps 10–14: Close out the exercise as outlined on p. 283.

How to work with the approach ...

The steps outlined above are a simplification of the work. The pace, structure and enquiry are crafted by the supervisor each time creating a bespoke supervision experience. As with the approach 'Working with the supervisee's dilemma' (pp. 297–299), the exercise can be done 'blind,' i.e. without knowing which group member is representing which stakeholder; the supervisor might also voice some narrative as they work with each representative.

Often, when group members engage in the free movement, they rush to find their new place. Remind representatives to slow down, to try some experimental moves and truly experience their own sense of 'rightness' about the space they have chosen. Sometimes, when moving away from a chosen space and then back again, it can help clarify what is most true for them.

Typically, representatives find their space at different paces, and when one element moves it triggers a desire to move in other elements. A kind of dance then emerges as each representative attempts to find the space that feels true for what they are representing and which also feels true in relation to all the other representatives. Gradually, the dance will slow down and the representatives will settle at a place which creates a new sense of equilibrium. Facilitating this requires careful observation,; allow additional time even when it appears that a new order has been found.

Sometimes, due to systemic dynamics the representatives may not be able to find their place. The supervisor will require a depth of systemic training to work with these forces.

A word of caution

See 'Working with the supervisee's dilemma' on pp. 297–299.

What other uses are there for this approach?

In individual supervision the supervisee could create the map with paper and then stand on each representative piece of paper in turn.

With experience and systemic training, the approach could be used with coaching clients.

Further reading

Stam, J. (2016) *Fields of Connection.* Nijmegen, Netherlands: Uitgeverij Het Noorderlicht.

Whittington, J. (2016) *Systemic Coaching & Constellations: The principles, practices and application for individuals, teams and groups*, 2nd ed. London : Kogan Page.

~ ~ ~ ~ ~

86. Working with the Seven-Eyed model

Michelle Lucas

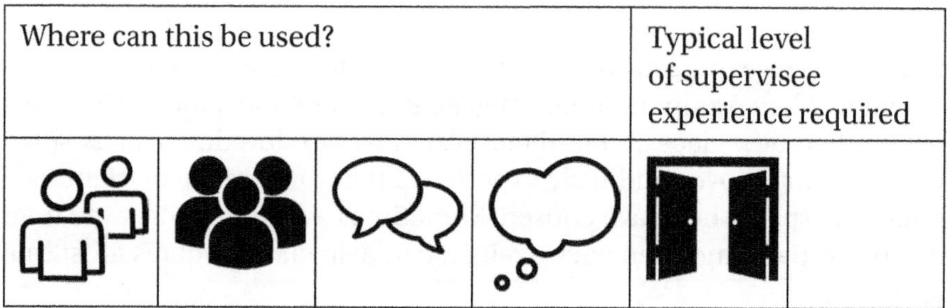

Where can this be used?				Typical level of supervisee experience required	

When is this used?

This technique is universally useful as it encourages a holistic approach. Typically, the supervisor holds it as a mental map, using it to clarify which perspectives are being attended to and which may have been overlooked.

What is the technique?

The technique rests on an understanding of Hawkins and Smith (2006) Seven-Eyed Model, which deliberately draws our attention to seven different perspectives from which any supervision issue can be explored – see Figure 8.1. Input from the group is structured to ensure each of the seven perspectives are considered.

Step 1: Where the group is unfamiliar with the model provide a short explanation.

Step 2: Set up so that each group member holds responsibility for questions from one particular 'eye'. The supervisor holds those eyes which have not been allocated.

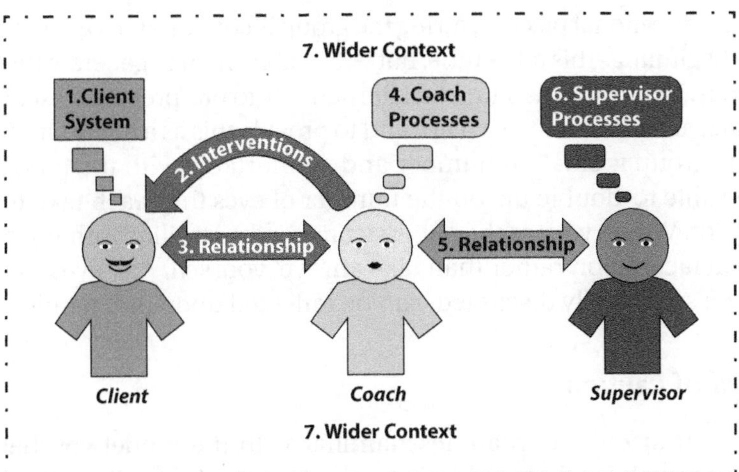

Figure 8.1 The Seven-Eyed Model by Lucas 2010, adapted from Hawkins and Smith (2006)

Step 3: Invite the supervisee to provide an overview of their client scenario.

Step 4: Check with the supervisee which 'eye' they would like to explore first. Alternatively, look to the group to see who has the strongest sense of wanting to start.

Step 5: Encourage a dialogue to unfold. Once the supervisee has responded to the first question, the discussion tends to move towards a different eye. The supervisor then signals this to the group, inviting the person holding the next eye to become more active in the conversation. This emergent approach continues until all of the eyes have been considered.

Step 6: Allow a couple of minutes for quiet reflection for everyone. Useful questions might be:

- Supervisee: Which 'eye' brought you the greatest insight?
- Group members: How easy or difficult did you find it to connect with your chosen 'eye' ... and why do you think that was?

Step 7: Return to the supervisee and enquire what their learning has been.

Step 8: Open the enquiry to the whole group to share their learning.

How to work with the technique ...

This is a complex model that many supervisees shy away from. It is best to work slowly and to afford it a significant amount of time. It may be prudent to do an educational piece ensuring the group is comfortable with the model before beginning. This takes time, but will enable them to generate their own questions. Where time is short, an alternative is to pre-prepare a list of questions that are relevant for each eye and to provide this as a handout.

If the group is small in number and comfortable with the model they may be able to 'double up' on the number of eyes they each take responsibility for. Where you, as the supervisor, are less familiar with the model, focus on facilitation rather than take an 'eye' yourself. Any eyes that have not been specifically discussed, can be reflected upon independently.

A word of caution

Where you or the group are less familiar with the model you have the option of working through each 'eye' sequentially. While this ensures comprehensiveness it can create a more stilted experience for the supervisee.

Give the supervisee sufficient time in Step 5 to digest the experience. Being on the receiving end of a series of questions all coming from different angles can knock the supervisee off balance. If not facilitated gracefully the supervisee can feel interrogated.

What other uses are there for this technique?

An alternative is to arrange chairs to reflect the model. Often, there are two chairs for eye four – one to represent the supervisee as coach (facing the client), placed back to back with the second to represent the supervisee in supervision. As a group member raises a question, they are asked to say where in the model they think the question comes from. The supervisor facilitates a sculpture whereby the group member moves to sit (or stand nearby) the chair representing the relevant eye in the model. This can be particularly powerful to illustrate areas of common interest or indeed common blind spots. In individual supervision (or individual reflection) the same kind of 'tracking' can be achieved by mapping the discussion on paper.

Although this model was developed for supervision, the seven eyes can easily be translated to client work. Here, Eye One becomes the stakeholder under discussion, Eye Four becomes the client, and Eye Six becomes the coach.

Reference

Hawkins, P. and Smith, N. (2006) *Coaching, Mentoring and Organisational Consultancy: Supervision and Development.* McGraw-Hill: Maidenhead. pp. 136–159.

~ ~ ~ ~ ~

87. Working with the shadow

Clare Norman

Where can this be used?				Typical level of supervisee experience required	

When is this used?

This enquiry would likely be used part way through a programme of supervision, or annually to keep sharp. It is typically offered as preparation for a supervision session, or to reflect on themes at the start of a supervision session. It is particularly useful where an existing relationship has plateaued or where the supervisor senses that the supervisee avoids (or excludes) certain themes.

What is the enquiry?

Our shadow can be something forbidden, taboo, or unwelcome ... and it can equally be our talents, ways of being, artistry, intellect, athleticism. A set of questions is offered prior to a supervision session, to highlight what they tend *not* to bring to supervision, either consciously or unconsciously. They may then make a conscious choice about what to bring to supervision this time.

Step 1: The supervisor offers questions such as:

- What is in me that I don't want to own?
- What makes me unique, compared to other coaches?
- What would I not want my clients to know?
- What is sabotaging my efforts?
- What haven't I brought to supervision?
- Therefore, what will I bring to supervision this time that is really challenging for me?

Step 2: The supervisee(s) reflects on the questions.

Step 3: The supervisor asks the supervisee to reflect on the experience of working with the questions. 'What was that like?' This gives an indication of how ready they are to explore in Step 4.

Step 4: The supervisor asks what insights the supervisee(s) has had, and what they would like to bring to supervision. This can be as light-touch or as deep as the supervisee(s) wishes to go. For example, you may go deep into exploring each question, and as a result of saying things out loud, the supervisee may get additional insights. Or you may simply get straight into the supervision question that has arisen.

How to work with the enquiry ...

Supervisees often bring issues that are front of mind to their supervision. This approach works best where the supervisee has time to prepare. As such, the questions might be provided as part of the joining instructions for a session. Step 2 can be illuminating as there is often significant impact for the supervisee simply through facing these questions. They tend to enable supervisees to go deeper, to discover some untapped potential for themselves and their clients.

In a group setting, the supervisor might ask each person in turn to share their perspectives to Steps 3 and 4. Where that feels overly challenging, start with a discussion in pairs, before sharing with the whole group. Or, the supervisor may choose to simply have them share with the group what this has prompted them to bring to supervision.

A word of caution

Be sure that you pay attention to the psychological contract so that there is enough trust and intimacy between you and your supervisee(s) and between supervisees to allow for the vulnerability that this exercise may expose. It can be tough to admit to some of these things – and perhaps this is why they have not already been brought to supervision. For some, recognising their strengths is difficult; for others, it is the things they dislike about themselves. Empower your supervisee(s) to choose how much they wish to disclose at this time – while also challenging them to stand at the edge of their comfort zone or just outside of it.

Be willing to explore your own shadows so you don't get caught in your own projections and transference; parallel process can then be used in service of the learning for the supervisee.

What other uses are there for this enquiry?

Look for patterns so that you can tailor these questions to create balance in their supervision. For example, where someone seems overly self-critical, add a question like 'What well-deserved praise is hard to hear?' or 'What passion would you like to explore, but something holds you back?'

The purpose here is to shine a light on aspects of themselves that they do not want to look at, but where it could be useful to their clients to do so.

With care this could also be used for some coaching clients. The coach would need to be highly skilled and the coaching client comfortable with their own vulnerability.

Acknowledgement

Prentice, K. (2013) Me and my shadow. In: Oxford Brookes University, *3rd International Supervision Conference*, 20 June 2013. Wheatley Campus.

~ ~ ~ ~ ~

88. Working with the supervisee's dilemma

Damion Wonfor

Where can this be used?				Typical level of supervisee experience required	

When is this used?

Useful when a supervisee seems stuck; perhaps because they are faced with a number of different options and their 'head and heart' are in conflict. The scenario may relate directly to client work, and it can also be used to explore decisions about their wider coaching practice or CPD.

What is the technique?

Based on systemic principles, the supervisee creates a map of the options they want to explore in answer to a specific question. Through tapping into the group's somatic experience, additional information can be sourced.

Step 1: Begin the enquiry individually with the supervisee. Help them articulate their supervision question.

Step 2: Once articulated, check with the supervisee what kind of energy they have, while also noticing yours, then question, challenge or affirm accordingly.

Step 3: Invite the supervisee to identify how many options they would like to explore (recommend no more than 5). Using a separate piece of paper for each option (labelled with a letter A, B, C ...) ask the supervisee to set up a map by laying out the paper in a way that feels true for them.

Step 4: Invite the supervisee to move each group member, guiding them by their shoulder blades until they reach a piece of paper, and to then stand on it. They now represent that option.

Step 5: Ask the supervisee to stand in a place that represents their relationship with each of the options.

Step 6: Brief the group members to settle into what they are representing, tuning into their somatic experience. Remind them that there is no right and no wrong, that there is no such thing as coincidences and trust that whatever is emerging (or not), is information.

Step 7: With the supervisee observing, the supervisor visits each group member asking 'What are you noticing as you stand here?' or 'How are you in relationship with the supervisee?'

Step 8: Check back with the supervisee to understand what meaning they are making of what has been offered and what they are noticing about their own embodied response.

Step 9: Repeat Steps 7 and 8 to see what new information is emerging.

Step 10: Return to the supervisee and enquire if their choices seem any clearer to them; check their own sense of congruence and rightness with each option. On occasion, they might find it helpful to 'step onto' their chosen option to tap into their own somatic experience.

Step 11: Invite the supervisee to reconfigure the pieces of paper from the strongest congruence with their question to the lowest sense of rightness. The supervisee then reveals to the other group members which option was represented by each letter. The Supervisor debriefs the supervisee's response.

Step 12: Invite the group members to write down a piece of wisdom that came from their experience which they will give to the supervisee before Step 14.

Step 13: De-brief the supervisee by checking in with them how they are now.

Step 14: Check in with the whole group about the need to de-role; take a comfort break such that they can approach the next part of the session cleanly.

How to work with the technique ...

The steps outlined above are a simplification of how this technique unfolds. The pace, structure and enquiry is crafted by the supervisor each time creating a bespoke supervision experience. For those supervisors experienced in systemic work, they might offer some narrative or the 'voice' of each element without any attachment, checking each time with the representative how true this feels for them and inviting the representative to adjust it as they speak it.

The options here are explored 'blind', i.e. the group members do not know what each option represents, which can help group members to trust their somatic experience. However, in Step 3 the supervisee could identify what each person represents.

A word of caution

With those new to systemic work, there can be a tendency to interpret the enquiry discussion in Steps 1 and 2. Re-direct contributions that feel overly rational towards a somatic enquiry, for example 'And what are you noticing in you right now?'

What other uses are there for this technique?

In individual supervision the supervisee could stand on each option in turn. With experience and systemic training the approach can be used with individual coaching clients.

Further reading

Stam, J. (2016) *Fields of Connection.* Nijmegen, Netherlands: Uitgeverij Het Noorderlicht.

Whittington, J. (2016) *Systemic Coaching & Constellations: The principles, practices and application for individuals, teams and groups,* 2nd ed. London: Kogan Page.

Chapter 9

A Thinking Environment approach to coaching supervision

Linda Aspey

How is this philosophy described?

The Thinking Environment is a way of being more than a way of doing. It offers people an easeful, non-judgemental environment that enables them to think for themselves, gaining clarity, generating new ideas, overcoming limiting assumptions that are blocking them, and making well considered decisions for optimal outcomes.

Developed throughout the 1980s by teacher, counsellor and philosopher Nancy Kline, the Thinking Environment arose from her quest for the most basic truth she could find. 'Eventually I settled on the observation that everything we *do* depends for its quality on the *thinking* we do first ... every action is only as good as the idea behind it.' 'It then followed that to improve action we had first to improve thinking' (Kline, 1999, pp. 15–16).

Over time, she identified ten behaviours or conditions that create a conducive environment for independent thinking, which she called the Ten Components of a Thinking Environment.

With the Ten Components as the foundation, she and others evolved applications for use in one-to-one and group work where good thinking is desired to achieve better outcomes. The most well known is the Thinking Partnership session, where one person asks the other, 'What would you like to think about, and what are your thoughts?' and then provides sustained, uninterrupted, fascinated Attention, only asking further questions when invited. In so doing, the thinker comes to their own insights and decisions in a way they often describe as liberating.

What are the underpinning beliefs and ideas of this philosophy?

There are several principles that inform this way of being, based on observation, testing and feedback of what works to get the best, high quality independent thinking. In practice, it is a blend of humanistic and cognitive approaches, most particularly on the far side of Carl Rogers' person-centred approach (Rogers, 1951) in his unshakeable belief that people are innately self-resourceful.

1 *The quality of everything we do depends on the quality of the thinking we do first.*

   Behind every good action is quality thinking, which probably involves a blend of cognition, accessing our feelings, somatic sensations and gaining insight.

2 *The quality of our Attention determines the quality of other people's thinking.*

   Kline discovered that our thinking is more heavily influenced by the way that we are treated by other people around us than it is by our IQ, age, background, gender and even experience. Most particularly, when given high quality Attention, we think for ourselves 'with rigour, imagination and grace' (Kline, 1999, p. 12).

   Listening to ignite rather than listening to respond is key; this requires being more drivingly interested in the supervisee's thoughts than what is going on (quite naturally) in the supervisor's head. This requires supreme focus and genuine interest, and only truly occurs with a deep-rooted belief and respect that the supervisee *can* think for themselves.

   To demonstrate Attention, the supervisor (and in groups, the whole group) keeps their eyes on the eyes of the supervisee, who can look wherever they wish while accessing their thoughts. The sustained nature of Attention is *generative.* Attention is, quite simply, an act of creation.

3 *Ten Components create the Thinking Environment.*

   These are the conditions that seem, individually and collectively, to provide optimal conditions for independent thinking. As a system they impact on each other; for example Attention – the first thing that Kline observed as having an impact – helps to generate Equality and Ease. Each of the Ten Components has a specific definition as described by (Kline, 2015, p. 31)

   i Giving your **Attention** with deep curiosity in what the person is saying and where they will go next will help them think better around you rather than if you interrupt them or listen simply to reply.

   ii Regarding the person thinking as your thinking **Equal**, regardless of hierarchy, will mean they think better around you.

iii Being at **Ease** yourself, free from urgency or the rush outside of you, will help others think better than if you are in a rush yourself.

iv If you genuinely **Appreciate** people five times more than you criticise them, they will think more imaginatively around you than if you focus on their faults.

v When you **Encourage** people, build with them their courage to go to the edge of their thinking, they will think better around you than if you compete with them.

vi If you offer accurate **Information** that is in service of their thinking and respect what they may be facing, they will think better than if you collude with their assumptions about what is true and what it is not true.

vii When you allow for them to express their **Feelings:** their tears, their anger, their frustration, they will think better around you rather than if you step over or seek to avoid their feelings.

viii If you are interested in the **Diversity** between you and others, the differences between you, they will think better around you than if you prefer others to think and be just like you.

ix If you can ask people an **Incisive Question** to cut through what is a limiting assumption and replace it with one that is more liberating, they will tap into their natural creative, resourceful self where breakthroughs and fresh ideas are born.

x When you prepare the **Place** for thinking together that says 'you matter' they will think better around you, than if you allow the place to feel intimidating and peppered with interruptions.

4 *To know that you will not be interrupted allows you truly to think for yourself.*

If we are expecting to be interrupted (which is normal and frequent in most settings) we will not relax or be as productive in our thinking as when *promised* that we won't be interrupted. This is rare and the promise is powerful.

5 *The mind thinks best in the presence of a question*

Over the years, Kline searched for the most effective and non-directive question for generating independent thinking, arriving at, 'What do you want to think about, and what are your thoughts?' If desired, in supervision this can be phrased as, 'What from your coaching practice would you like to think about today, and what are your thoughts?'

A question triggers thinking, which is usually verbalised. Yet if there are periods of silence, even if sustained, the supervisor does not speak but maintains Attention. When ready for another question, the supervisee asks for one. The supervisor waits to be invited, and then asks, 'What more do you think, or feel, or want to say?' Surprisingly, repeating this question (on each invitation) is experienced as very powerful to the supervisee. Only when there is no more to think or say does it lose its generative power.

6 *The mind that contains the problem usually contains the solution.*

If the human mind has the capacity to ask a question, it has the capacity to answer it too, so the Thinking Environment supervisor's role is to encourage the supervisee to answer their own questions. This will test the supervisor's ability to listen to ignite when they're strongly, perhaps innately, drawn to formulating a solution or opinion themselves.

Perhaps, when a question moves from silent thinking into being articulated, the thinker has already started answering it (Aspey, 2017). So, the supervisor's first response to a supervisee's question is, 'What do you think?' or 'What are your first thoughts on that?' This may seem no different to other forms of non-directive supervision, however, it is different because here it's the *default* position of the supervisor.

7 *Assumptions play a starring role in our lives.*

Assumptions appear to be key to our daily living, from assuming the floor will hold our weight when we get out of bed in the morning, through to assumptions about ourselves, others or situations. We are rarely aware of them all; they probably arise from experiences and then shape our decisions and lives. However, when assumptions are untrue but being lived as true, they can block productive thinking, which can cause the supervisee to stop thinking for themselves. So at an appropriate time in the session, the supervisor can help the supervisee to explore and test the assumption and find something that is true and liberating instead. Helping people to uncover, prioritise and overcome untrue, limiting assumptions requires skill and practice and is taught in detail on some of the Time to Think courses.

8 *The human mind seems to think in waves and pauses.*

This is the most recent of discoveries (2019) by Kline and is still in the testing phase. After a wave of verbalised thought there comes a pause, inside which something happens that produces another wave. Kline thinks that underlying this process and in the pause is a series of innate questions or 'considerations,' that end in a breakthrough question, producing more waves of independent thinking.

These considerations, while not voiced, appear to be along the lines of: 'Do I still want to continue thinking independently? What have I just done? What next outcome do I want? What do I need to accomplish that? And what question will meet that need?' The pause is therefore as important as the wave – one occurs as a natural result of the other.

At this point the session can continue as before or take on a different direction. For example, the supervisee may want to achieve something more which might mean uncovering assumptions, or to take notes, or to seek input from the supervisor. All of this is driven by the supervisee, not the supervisor.

What is the role of the coach supervisor in the context of this philosophy?

In the Thinking Environment the focus is on the thinking, insight and action emanating almost completely from the supervisee; it's useful for the supervisor to hold this in mind throughout: 'How far can the supervisee go in their own thinking before they need mine?'

Naturally, the supervisor has a duty to ensure the welfare and safety of the supervisee's client and the supervisee; sometimes there's a need to educate the supervisee or perhaps share a concern. However, in a Thinking Environment,

> *Firstly they must provide time and space for the supervisee to discover that for themselves. It's rarely a red flag issue; it's just that they [supervisors] have been conditioned to think they know more or know better than the supervisee and that it's their job to set them straight.*
>
> (Aspey, 2016)

During the contracting, time is allocated for the supervisee to seek input from the supervisor, and vice versa. Typically, this might be along the lines of 'What question (s) do you have for me?' or 'What observation, question or input do you have for me that we have not covered?' (see Adshead-Grant et al., 2018).

How would you prepare yourself to work congruently with this approach?

The supervisor needs to not only know, but to feel it is true, that they add more value through their Attention than they do through their input. The supervisor needs to be driven by a desire to get out of the supervisee's way so the supervisee can make their own progress. It's useful to consider what roles, power, expertise, ego, or behaviours need to be relinquished to be of service to the supervisee. Focusing on *being* (rather than doing) a Thinking Environment is key. Noticing what triggers us to move from fascinated listener to interrupting problem-solver is essential, as is taking these questions to our own supervision.

How might this way of working be particularly useful to the supervisee?

In choosing to engage in supervision in a Thinking Environment, they make a commitment to think for themselves, and the supervisor makes a commitment to provide the very best quality conditions for that to happen. Everything else flows from that. Contracting is therefore key.

Anything else you need to consider before working with the approaches that follow?

The Thinking Environment has several techniques that are called 'Applications,' categorised as 'Building-block,' 'Full' and 'Bespoke.' The 'Building-block' Applications are Thinking Pairs, Dialogue, Rounds and Open Discussion; and can be used to build other 'Full' Applications including the Thinking Partnership, Time to Think Council, Presentations. Some of the 'Bespoke' Applications are Facilitation, Coaching and Supervision, Mentoring, Mediation and 'The Diversity Process,' which are explained in Time to Think Course manuals.

This apparently simple approach can be challenging for supervisees who have experienced more of a dialogical style of supervision. It might surface a dependence on them to be guided, led or taught or to have their thinking verbally challenged by an 'expert.' Thinking Environment newcomers might expect to feel a little adrift before they are able to ease into the luxury of truly exploring their own thinking, uncontaminated by influence, infantilisation or interruption.

References

Adshead-Grant, J., Hathaway, A., Aspey, L., and Turner, E. (2018) Supervision in the Thinking Environment. In: E. Turner and S. Palmer. Eds. *The Heart of Coaching Supervision – Working with Refection and Self-Care*. Abingdon: Routledge, Ch. 8, pp. 147–168.

Aspey, L. (2016) Coaching supervision: Who is the expert in the room? *LinkedIn* [pulse] 14 December. Available at: <www.linkedin.com/pulse/coaching-supervision-who-expert-room-linda-aspey/> [Accessed 05 August 2019].

Aspey, L. (2017) In articulating the question, you're starting to formulate the answer. *LinkedIn* [pulse] 5 October. Available at: <www.linkedin.com/pulse/

articulating-question-you-have-already-started-formulate-linda-aspey/> [Accessed 05 August 2019].

Kline, N. (1999) *Time to Think: Listening to Ignite the Human Mind.* London: Cassell Illustrated.

Kline, N. (2015) *More Time to Think: The Power of Independent Thinking* (2nd ed.). London: Cassell Illustrated.

Kline, N. (2019) *The Thinking Partnership Course: A Companion.* Oxfordshire: Time to Think Ltd.

Rogers, C. (1951) *Client-Centred Therapy.* Trowbridge: Constable and Constable.

Further reading

Aspey, L. (2016) Attention, the generator and the gift. *LinkedIn.* [pulse] 3 March. Available at: <www.linkedin.com/pulse/attention-generator-gift-linda-aspey/> [Accessed 5 August 2019].

Resources

Kline, N. (2008 onwards) 'Time to Think' training course and teaching materials. Available at: <www.timetothink.com/learn/first-courses/≥ [Accessed 2 September 19].

Nancy Kline's website: www.timetothink.com [Accessed 2 September 19].

~ ~ ~ ~ ~

89. Dialogue

Linda Aspey

Where can this be used?				Typical level of supervisee experience required	

When is this used?

This can be useful when a supervisee would like to exchange thinking with another peer on a common topic; and could also occur after a Thinking Pair.

Alternatively, this approach can be prompted by a supervisor/supervisee when using the Thinking Environment approach to supervision and they recognise/request an opportunity for sharing information

What is Dialogue?

Dialogue is, like Thinking Pairs, one of the 'building-blocks' of the Thinking Environment, where two people support each other to generate independent thinking. The key differences here are that they each address the same question, and they share the whole time, for example, ten minutes, taking turns to go back and forth every couple of minutes as opposed to each taking a chunk of half of the time (e.g. five minutes each way). In supervision it can be used thus:

Step 1: The contract.

Agree the question for consideration, phrased succinctly and inviting broad and deep thinking rather than going straight to solutions, for example 'What are your thoughts about ...?' rather than 'How can we ...?'

Together agree who will go first, and what the signal will be when the person speaking has finished so the other can have a turn. Typically, this will be by asking, 'What do *you* think?' or 'What are *your* thoughts?' They agree not to interrupt and to be succinct when it is their turn to speak. Sharing the time equally is key.

Step 2: The exercise.

The Listener asks 'What do you think about ... [insert the agreed question]?' The Thinker responds, safe in the knowledge that they may think on this question with a guarantee of not being interrupted. Meanwhile, the Listener listens with ease, fascinated Attention, with encouragement, and without interruption. The Thinker honours the other by being succinct and self manages so they don't take all the time. They then invite the Listener to have a turn asking, 'And what do *you* think?' or something similar. Being responsive to both oneself and the other, the pair establish a rhythm of thinking and listening, tuning into each other such that each person has a broadly equal share of the time over the period.

Step 3: The close.

When the agreed duration has elapsed, each person offers some words of Appreciation of a *quality* or strength observed in the other.

Note: Appreciation is not a comment on the content of their narrative or their actions.

How to work with Dialogue …

A professional or peer supervisor using this technique needs to adopt a genuine sense of enquiry as they engage in Dialogue. Both Thinker and Listener may hold different ideas or positions on the topic being given Attention. While this building block invites each person to share information that might not be known to the other, the intention is not to influence the other. Rather, it is an invitation to offer additional input and allow the other person to take or leave whatever they feel is in service of their thinking. The Listener listens with fascinated Attention to see how the Thinker's thoughts unfold, aiming to be more drivingly interested in what is real and true for the other person than they are in being right, or alternatively, frightened of being proved wrong. If, during their turn, the Thinker responds to the other's views from a defensive position, the Thinking Environment will be lost.

Dialogue can be used to bring the component of Information into a supervision session, enabling the supervisor to fulfil their normative role. Sometimes a practice or ethical concern comes up, and the supervisee or supervisor can suggest a Dialogue. The supervisor could use this approach to educate, provided they keep their input short and only for the purpose of generating more independent thinking in the supervisee.

A word of caution

See Thinking Pairs on pp. 311–314.

What other uses are there for Dialogue?

See Thinking Pairs on pp. 311–314.

Further reading

Kline, N. (1999) *Time to Think: Listening to Ignite the Human Mind.* London: Cassell Illustrated.

Kline, N. (2015) *More Time to Think: The Power of Independent Thinking* (2nd ed.) London: Cassell Illustrated. (See chapter entitled 'How's it going? Coach supervision in a Thinking Environment', pp. 191–192).

~ ~ ~ ~ ~

90. Rounds

Linda Aspey

Where can this be used?				Typical level of supervisee experience required	

When is this used?

Rounds enable all group members to contribute and be heard. They are useful as a check in, or as a way of sharing all views on a question, or generating new ideas. They help to ensure equality is honoured and create a level playing field in a diverse (communication styles, hierarchy, experience) group. When used at the end of a session it can offer everyone a sense of completeness and closure.

What are Rounds?

Rounds are one of the building-blocks of the Thinking Environment, underpinned by the Ten Components. Like the other applications, they start with a question to stimulate thinking, which will vary according to the purpose of the Round.

A significant benefit is that everyone knows they will have a turn to speak if they wish to. This can be particularly useful for those who may feel less able to speak in a free-flowing discussion. Equality creates courage. Turn-taking frees up the group member's energy for listening, and rather than jostle for position and airtime, or rehearsing what they will say, they can genuinely pay Attention to others.

Step 1: The contract.

Having agreed the question, the supervisor/facilitator briefly outlines the best way to benefit from the Round, as follows:

Each person can have a turn if they wish, or they can skip. All group members are asked to give their complete Attention, to look at the speaker, and to not interrupt, verbally or physically (staying still and easeful). In return, the speaker needs to be succinct so that everyone can have a turn, encouraging Equality.

Reassure group members that it is common for minds to wander at first, and upon noticing this simply refocus Attention back to the speaker. Reinforce the importance of Diversity and that all views are welcomed, even radical or unpopular ones. Difference is useful.

Step 2: The exercise.

The supervisor/facilitator states the direction of the Round (clockwise or anti-clockwise), reminds them of the question and invites anyone to start.

The first supervisee responds, safe in the knowledge that they can speak openly and without interruption. Meanwhile the others listen with Ease, fascinated Attention, with Encouragement, and without interruption. Each person takes a turn and has the opportunity to respond to the question posed, each receiving full Attention from the others.

Depending on the question, the supervisor/facilitator may suggest another Round, perhaps asking 'What's your freshest thinking?'. With each new Round the direction reverses.

Step 3: The close.

Where Rounds are part of closing a meeting, the questions can invite reflection or appreciation, for example 'What have you learned or re-learned today?' or 'What have you most appreciated about this group today?' Once the Round(s) are complete the group can move on.

How to work with Rounds ...

Questions for Rounds can be suggested and circulated before the session by the supervisor/facilitator, or a member of the group, or within the session by anyone. Thinking Pairs (see pp. 311–314) or Dialogue (see pp. 306–308) can be used to give people thinking time on questions before the group session (which is often appreciated by those who do not enjoy being 'put on the spot') and then they can share their thinking in the Round. Typically, the supervisor will start and end sessions with a Round so that each person has the opportunity to speak and to finish, giving a sense of completeness. Questions are best phrased succinctly and inviting of people to share their thoughts rather than solutions, for example, 'What are your thoughts about X?' rather than 'What can we do about ...?' Supervisees can also use Rounds to harvest new ideas, concerns, experiences and then bring this into the supervision work.

What else might need attention?

Groups new to this approach may struggle to contain the impulse to respond to others or disrupt the order of the Round. A gentle reminder from the supervisor/facilitator can be useful; people are often so used to interrupting or 'getting ready to fire' they may not realise they are doing so. With practice they will become more easeful.

A word of caution

Supervisors/facilitators are often afforded a form of 'role power'. It is not unusual for people to address their answers towards you and not the whole group. If this happens, gently remind all members to address everyone, thereby creating Equality.

What other uses are there for Rounds?

The structure of the Round is a useful way of creating an inclusive way of sharing information. It could be useful to hear the groups thoughts on a client case brought to supervision. It could equally be useful to coaching clients as they chair a business meeting.

Further reading

Kline, N. (1999) *Time to Think: Listening to Ignite the Human Mind.* London: Cassell Illustrated.

~ ~ ~ ~ ~

91. Thinking Pairs

Linda Aspey

Where can this be used?				Typical level of supervisee experience required	

When is this used?

This can be useful when deciding what a supervisee wishes to focus on in the session, or to deeply explore each person's own thoughts on an issue before the whole group considers it, or as protected time for brief reflective practice with a peer supervisor.

What is the Thinking Pair?

Thinking Pairs are one of the Building-block applications of the Thinking Environment. It is based on the Thinking Partnership session, one of the full Applications of the Thinking Environment, where two people offer each other sustained listening to generate independent thinking. Where a Thinking Partnership session typically lasts 30–90 minutes, a Thinking Pair will use less time. In supervision it can be used as follows:

Step 1: The contract.

Either agree that each person will think about their own material or agree a shared question that both will consider in turn. If a whole group is working in pairs, perhaps with the intention of sharing thoughts afterwards, agree a common question.

Agree the duration of the Thinking Pairs – typically five to ten minutes each and who will be the first to think. Commit to an absence of interruption, and that the Listener will only speak if the Thinker invites them by saying 'I'm done' or requests a question.

Step 2: The exercise.

The Listener asks, 'What would you like to think about today, and what are your thoughts?' Or if a group-in-pairs exercise, the question they have agreed, e.g. 'What do you think might be common ground arising from our work?'

The Thinker responds, safe in the promise that they will not be interrupted, the Listener listens with Ease, fascinated Attention and Encouragement. Should the Thinker invite a question, the Listener offers 'What more do you think, or feel, or want to say?'

When the agreed time has elapsed, they swap roles and repeat the exercise so the other has their turn.

Step 3: The close.

Each person offers a brief Appreciation of a *quality* or strength observed in the other. Note this is not a comment on narrative content or actions.

How to work with the Thinking Pair ...

In most conversations we interpret pauses and silences as an opportunity or subtle invitation for a question or comment. People seem to think in waves (often out loud) and pauses (often silent) and both are of equal value. In this approach, a pause is not a prompt to contribute rather an invitation to stay Easeful.

If the Thinker says they are completely finished before the agreed time and the 'What more' question does not generate more, both can sit comfortably in case more thinking may come. Alternatively, the Thinker may finish and invite the other to become the Thinker.

What else might need attention?

The purpose here is to generate independent thinking, which means the process is highly emergent. In the context of supervision, it may be helpful to think more strategically about client work and to introduce some structure.

For example, using Clutterbuck, Whitaker and Lucas (2016) distinctions of long-term approaches to supervision, then the question posed could take a particular direction:

1 Whole case load: 'What from your coaching practice would you like to think about today, and what are your thoughts?'
2 Supervisee-led: '... which clients do you most want to think about today ...?'
3 Developmentally led: '... given your current development needs who or what would be most helpful to think about today ...?'
4 System led: '... what do you think your client organisations would invite you to think about today ...?'

A word of caution

As in all forms of conversation, any narrative can trigger the Listener and make it challenging for them to stay interested in the Thinker's thoughts. It helps to relax and remember that that they will have a turn, they can then return to being fascinated by how the Thinker's thinking is unfolding.

What other uses are there for the Thinking Pair?

It can be used in a variety of situations and contexts for example team meetings, facilitated events, and mentoring, where quality independent thinking is the goal. Coaching clients can find a Thinking Partner outside of the coaching sessions. Thinking Pairs are not suggested as a way of working between Coach and Client as it can elicit content that is beyond the coaching boundary, but a Dialogue (see pp. 306–308) could be used instead.

Reference

Clutterbuck, D., Whitaker, C. and Lucas, M. (2016) *Coaching Supervision: A Practical Guide for Supervisees*. Maidenhead: Routledge, pp. 158–161.

Further reading

Kline, N. (1999) *Time to Think: Listening to Ignite the Human Mind*. London: Cassell Illustrated.

Kline, N. (2015) *More Time to Think: The Power of Independent Thinking* (2nd ed.). London: Cassell Illustrated. (See chapter: 'How's it going? Coach supervision in a Thinking Environment,' pp. 191–192).

Chapter 10

A transpersonal approach to coaching supervision

Hetty Einzig

How is this philosophy described?

Modern transpersonal psychology came to prominence in the 1970s. A generic term, all transpersonal psychologies integrate wisdom from ancient spiritual traditions with modern Western psychology. The aim was to reclaim spiritual principles from their religious domain and through scientific and contemporary language make them accessible in a secular society. Transpersonal psychology addresses the full range of human development 'from our deepest wounds and needs ... to the most transcendent capacities of our consciousness' (Caplan, 2009, p. 231). Its focus is on growth rather than pathology. In this it distinguished itself from psychoanalysis, behaviourism and humanistic psychology, leading to Abraham Maslow defining it as the 'fourth force' in psychology.

Along with Maslow, Carl Jung and Roberto Assagioli are the key figures who shaped the transpersonal school of thought; it goes beyond the personal to include the collective, the social and the universal and beyond the psyche to include the spiritual and what Maslow termed 'peak experiences' - hence *trans*-personal.

Assagioli (1888–1975) saw Freud's psychoanalytic model as partial, giving scant attention to the dimensions of joy, will, creativity and wisdom. Like Maslow, Assagioli wished to enable the best in humans rather than diagnose their worst. He therefore developed his own model, which in contrast to psycho*analysis* he called psycho*synthesis*. Psychosynthesis philosophy is systemic, holistic and emphasises interdependence. A central current of spirituality informs a socio-political awareness and moral commitment.

John Whitmore, who trained with Assagioli, adapted psychosynthesis concepts for coaching. For example, 'service' was at the heart of Whitmore's development of the GROW model: he emphasised the dream goal or aspiration beyond the self in 'G' (for Goal) and the concept of Will derives directly from psychosynthesis. In the 1990s, Einzig and Whitmore developed a model of transpersonal coaching based on psychosynthesis principles and techniques. It was felt that the term 'transpersonal' was more appropriate than 'psychosynthesis' for the coaching field. Transpersonal coaching and supervision incorporate the major contribution made by Assagioli, and continue to evolve in response to changing needs and changing times.

The transpersonal approach to supervision is rooted in these foundations: an inbuilt tendency towards healthy growth and fulfilment that is interdependent with our spiritual need for meaning and purpose and for service, with the well-being of others and with our cultural and historical context – including the social and environmental.

What are the underpinning principles and beliefs of this philosophy?

As the name suggests, a fundamental principle of psychosynthesis is the intention to synthesise, to connect and heal fragmentation. We can refer to Assagioli's model of the human psyche (see Figure 10.1), to help us to understand the concept of interdependence and synthesis.

This 'egg' model (Figure 10.1) illustrates a number of elements that inform the transpersonal approach. Each of those elements are clarified below.

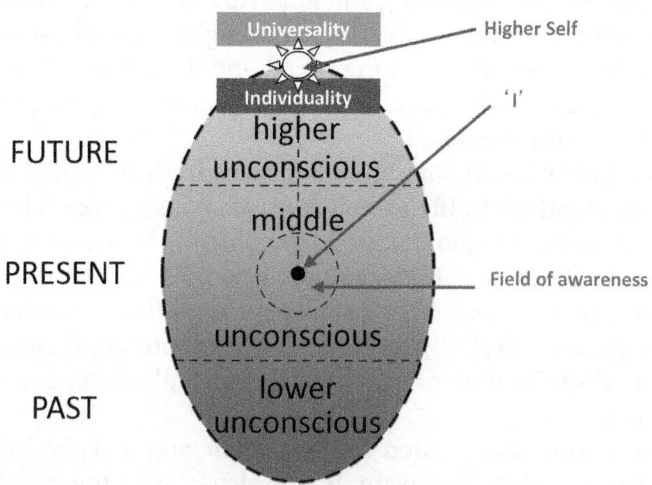

Figure 10.1 An interpretation of Assagioli's psychosynthesis model of the human psyche

Clarification of psychosynthesis terms:

- Lower Unconscious: a repository of memories, assumptions or fixed beliefs that may block our energy.
- Middle Unconscious: behaviours, beliefs, thoughts and feelings that are just out of sight but available to us with reflection and prompting.
- Higher Unconscious: our aspirations, wisdom, hidden strengths and creativity.
- Collective unconscious: cultural norms, behaviours and beliefs shared by our society – the realm of the 'zeitgeist.'
- Field of Awareness: what we are aware of about ourselves – active thoughts and feelings.
- The 'I': two energies, Love and Will are in constant and dynamic relationship within our personality with our 'I' at the centre as a still centre of pure consciousness, essential and enduring (see below).
- Higher Self: the best of ourselves, spiritual and ethical qualities such as wisdom, altruism, heroism, the aesthetic, our yearning to make a difference, to serve. These qualities are universal, shared throughout humanity. This acts like a magnet drawing us towards the actualisation of our 'best self' in service to the world and its future. We become most aware of the Higher Self in moments of profound or transcendent experiences, e.g. Feeling at one with the world, feelings of joy, of rightness, alignment and connection, and deep compassion.
- Individuality: that which belongs to and is an expression of the individual.
- Universality: qualities universally shared such as wisdom, love, compassion, courage.

Growth is seen as an expansion and shifting of consciousness. Most coaching supervision works within the middle unconscious seeking to expand the field of awareness. Transpersonal work seeks to integrate the three levels of the unconscious; to raise awareness of the interdependence between Individuality and Universality, and to help the supervisee strengthen and utilise their Higher Self. The Higher Unconscious is a source of inspiration, intuition and illumination. It is within us all and can be actively worked with, strengthened and drawn upon to empower the individual to 'self-actualise' (e.g. using the Wise Being visualisation – see pp. 341–344).

In the figure, the dotted lines indicate that past, present and future interact within the individual who influences and is influenced by society, environment, culture and the global zeitgeist. The transpersonal emphasises the interdependence of all these elements and seeks synthesis as a counter to our tendency for splitting and projection, e.g. this is me, that is not me, I am good, that is bad etc. The transpersonal emphasises oneness over duality.

A central belief of psychosynthesis is that while we *have* a personality (complex and multiple) we are, at our core, an essential spirit that endures and is oriented towards good (infused by our Higher Self). We have at our core two fundamental and complementary forces, or energies. Borrowing from psychosynthesis terminology, in transpersonal supervision we articulate those two forces as '*Love* and *Will*.' This dynamic exists in all wisdom traditions, expressed, for example, as darkness and light or Yin and Yang.

1 *Love* denotes our capacity for being, receiving, supporting, offering compassion, and is expressed through empathy and care. It is this that enables a supervisor to provide containment and 'safe space.'
2 *Will* denotes the drive to assert our individuality, to express, develop, change, act and achieve. It is this that enables a supervisor to challenge and enable risk taking.

These forces and the dynamic between them play out differently in every person and there are distortions for each energy (e.g. submission is a distortion of Love energy; aggression a distortion of Will energy). The ultimate aim is to achieve a balance between the two with an ability to flow between being and doing, reflection and action, as occasion demands.

What is the role of the coach supervisor in the context of this philosophy?

Supervision offers a container for thinking, a space for reflection. Like their clients, coaches need a place to step back, reflect and make sense. Supervision helps to contain the anxieties aroused by the dilemmas, conflicts and decisions of client work. Several levels of emotion and several points of view are present.

Transpersonal supervision serves to strengthen the coach's capacity to observe these dynamics at many levels and develop a meta-narrative: of the interdependence of these different aspects, of the themes, links, patterns within the issues presented and of the deeper meaning that might be emerging and the higher purpose which both coach and client might be serving.

Emergence is a key feature of the transpersonal perspective, inviting the question 'What is seeking to be born here, to emerge, to grow?' Meaning-making provides the supervisee with a sense of purpose when their client work gets tough or seems to run into the sand.

Within the transpersonal approach, supervision can be seen as a 'transitional space' – both 'contained enough' to *allow* risk taking and 'challenging enough' to *stimulate* risk taking. The idea is similar to Winnicott's concept of the 'good enough mother': the aim is not to be perfect, nor to keep child or client totally safe, but to 'hold' a space that allows exploration and growth.

From a transpersonal perspective the role of supervisor is as follows:

Formative:

1 To enable and foster self-development and the realisation of potential of the supervisee.
2 To support the supervisee to thrive and to create contexts in which they can flourish.
3 To help supervisees author their own story in connection and in collaboration with others.
4 To help supervisees determine and enact their contribution to their world – as they define it. Explicitly to act in 'good faith' towards building the 'good society' (Western, 2018).

Normative:

5 To enable wider, deeper and more complex perspectives – especially an understanding of interdependence both their own and their clients' (individual, team, organisation, community, society).

Restorative:

6 To support supervisees to cultivate compassion for human fallibility: to include vulnerabilities and imperfections alongside growing strength and courage to 'do the right thing.'
7 To increase a supervisee's capacity for joy and creativity, as integral to their sense of self, and thereby become more their 'best self.'

In developing these capacities in themselves, supervisees become more able to role model and enable them in their clients. In addition to the responsibilities outlined above, contemporary transpersonal coaching and supervision emphasise two further dimensions as important influences on the client: coach and supervisee–supervisor relationships of today (Einzig, 2017):

- *Global*: in a globalised world, significant events and the current zeitgeist impact us all at both conscious and unconscious levels; and in a

24/7 networked world managing boundaries and anxiety are prominent issues.

- *Spiritual*: in a world of failed leadership, faltering institutions, of fake news and 'alternative truths,' the search for meaning, purpose and the desire for service are ubiquitous and demand attention.

How would you prepare yourself to work congruently with this approach?

The coaching supervisor needs to not only be well versed in transpersonal principles, models and techniques but to also have the capacity to hold a 'transitional space.' This requires a tolerance of not knowing, staying alert to levels of dependency and the emotional state of the supervisee as containing layers of message and meaning. The transpersonal supervisor holds the questions: What is the purpose of this coach bringing this issue at this time? What wider and deeper meaning can we derive from this 'problem'? What is the impact on the broader ecology of this issue? What is the coach a 'messenger' for – from their client, team and organisation?

The transpersonal supervisory relationship is co-creative, enabling development but also allowing space for regression and dependency within a learning process that is not linear but iterative. There is space for both the practical and the mysterious, the known and the unknown. Transpersonal psychology integrates references from art, literature and music so the transpersonal supervisor can prepare themselves by cultivating a rich and wide personal development journey, a grounding in the power of stories and myth, and a trust in the 'will to growth' of all organisms.

How is this way of working useful to the supervisee?

We live and work in a much more volatile world than 40 years ago when coaching first ventured into organisations. Change is constant, fast-paced, volatile and often abrupt. Quiet and peace are at a premium. In this context, transpersonal supervision offers a space to cultivate the counterbalancing forces of stability and stillness.

Transpersonal supervision explicitly allows for the shadow to emerge. Exploring our fear, anger, envy, doubt and shame within the context of an emphasis on the cultivation of joy, creativity and love builds the supervisee's muscle to address the shadow aspects within their coaching relationships. When explored in the context of Love and Will, 'monsters' lose their dominance and power to oppress; compassion and action are available.

Anything else that you need to be aware of before using the techniques which follow?

All transpersonal supervision is held within a framework which supports the fulfilment of human potential as an interdependent part of the health of the wider ecology. The transpersonal approach is a specifically ethical one, seeking to create the conditions for supervisees to consider their values, ethical choices, their sense of meaning and the purpose of their client work. In an age where it is no longer a given to look to our leaders for moral guidance, this approach can strengthen the supervisee's capacity to engage with ethical dilemmas, reflect on and articulate their own values and make informed choices.

Just as coaching is not a neutral occupation, so the coaching supervisor's job is not to support the supervisee without question, but also to challenge them to consider several perspectives and actions in any situation. Coaching supervision can provide the space for robust debate and for the delicate process of figuring out where the supervisee stands on an issue before coming to a choice of action to take forward with courage. The 'mythical journey' concept, articulated most famously by Joseph Campbell (2012), is used to consider the supervisee's development. With this in mind, the aim of the transpersonal supervision journey is one which moves the supervisee towards greater wisdom not just higher performance.

References

Campbell, J. (2012) *The Hero with A Thousand Faces* (The Collected Works of Joseph Campbell). 3rd edition. Novato, California: New World Library.

Caplan, M. (2009) *Eyes Wide Open: Cultivating Discernment on the Spiritual Path.* Louisville, Colorado: Sounds True Inc.

Einzig, H. and Whitmore, J. (2015) Transpersonal coaching. In J. Passmore ed. *Excellence in Coaching: The Industry Guide.* Maidenhead: Kogan Page, pp. 134–146. Ch.9.

Einzig, H. (2017) *The Future of Coaching: Vision, leadership and responsibility in a transforming world.* Maidenhead: Routledge.

Western, S. (2018) *Emancipatory Ethics.* [Online] www.analyticnetwork.com/ [Accessed 26 September 2019].

Further Reading

Assagioli, R. (1974) *The Act of Will.* Wildwood House.

Assagioli, R. (1980 2nd edition) *Psychosynthesis.* Turnstone Press.

Bachkirova, T. (2016) The Self of the Coach: Conceptualization, Issues, and Opportunities for Practitioner Development, *Consulting Psychology Journal: Practice and Research*, 68(2), pp. 143–156.

Ferrucci, P. (1982) *What We May Be: The Vision and Techniques of Psychosynthesis.* Wellingborough: Turnstone Press.

Ferrucci, P. (2014) *Your Inner Will: Finding Personal Strength in Critical Times.* Jeremy Tarcher, Penguin Random House.

Hardy, J. (1987) *A Psychology with a Soul: Psychosynthesis in Evolutionary Context.* Routledge Kegan Paul.

Iordanou, I., Hawley, R., and Iordanou, C. (2017) *Values and Ethics in Coaching.* Sage Publications.

Western, S. (2019) *Leadership, a Critical Text.* 3rd ed. Sage Publications.

~ ~ ~ ~ ~

92. Centring

Paul King

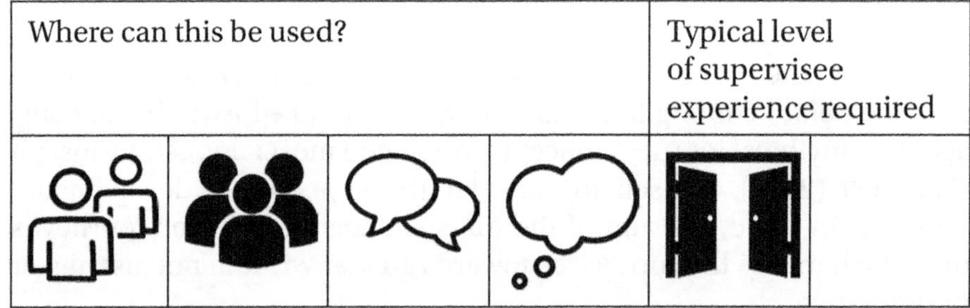

Where can this be used?				Typical level of supervisee experience required	

When is this used?

This technique is used whenever anyone (supervisor, coach or client) desires to be present, resourceful and gain a non-judgemental and fresh perspective. It is particularly useful as preparation for a session or when stuck or stressed.

What is the technique?

Centring can be described as a neutral state that supports an open mind for clear perception, an open heart for compassion to self and other, and a strong and confident core. It is connected to what is often known as a 'flow state' (Huang, 2011). Centring is not a self-contained insolating experience; it is defined as 'placing something in the centre of something else' (Lexico, 2019) and is a relational process.

Centring offers a state change, balancing our nervous system through physical and energetic reorganisation. We all naturally have a sense of what it is to be centred. It is part of our human evolutionary inheritance. Sometimes the mind cannot change the mind. The body can lead the way.

When stressed, stuck or troubled we typically hold increased levels of tension; we are contracted in body and mind and are emotionally negative. Centring is a body-based practice to physically, psychologically and emotionally resource us. When we are centred, we are grounded, uplifted and expanded, connected within and open to all that is around us. The body leads the way towards a shift in state and relationship to the context at hand. The way we organise the body impacts the way we perceive and behave.

Step 1: Sitting with feet fully on the ground and weight evenly balanced, breathe in as if from the base of the spine, up the back and out of the top of the head, giving a sense of lengthening uplift.

Step 2: Breathe out with a feeling of the breath moving down the front of the body and a sense of softening and lengthening downwards. Make the outbreath twice as long as the inbreath. The inbreath is an enlivening breath, activating the sympathetic nervous system, the outbreath stimulates the relaxation phase of the parasympathetic nervous system. Typically, we are 'switched on' by challenging situations. The emphasis on a longer outbreath helps to regulate and balance the nervous system.

Step 3: Expand your awareness from the centre of your being to all directions around you including who and what is within that space.

Step 4: Let your energy settle and quieten as you repeat Steps 1–3. Open, expanded, uplifted and grounded, centred in your core and the space around. Allow a sense of spaciousness outside and inside. Physically and energetically feel your length, breadth and depth.

Step 5: Your centred, open and expanded self can embrace the context with compassion to oneself and to others. You have shifted from being contracted and threatened in some way to a creative relational and resourceful state.

How to work with the technique ...

Centring takes practice for it to be embodied and quickly accessible, especially to be able to do so when stressed or emotionally disturbed. With practice, the process of centring can be streamlined and anchored for an individual to have access to being centred quickly, whenever wanted.

Centring utilises the power of how we organise our breath and body shaping to impact our psychological and emotional state to resource oneself in relationship to the context. Each psychological and emotional state has a uniquely associated physiological pattern of use and shape. Particularly under stress and trauma the deep patterns held in the body win out.

What else might need attention?

Working directly with the body as well as a client's thinking and emotions should be clearly contracted for. Some deep patterns are held in the body out of consciousness awareness.

A word of caution

People are used to wanting quick wins, the body learns slower than the mind, it takes time and practice to embed new patterns.

What other uses are there for this technique?

Centring is a state into which we can invite resources from inside and outside. Inviting a quality that you already have or one you associate with an inspiring source, human or otherwise. Ask yourself what would it be like if you embodied just 2% more of that quality.

Note: The body works best through small changes. When the body experiences big changes it triggers a sense of threat.

References

Lexico (2019) Lexico powered by Oxford. [Online] Available at: www.lexico.com/en/definition/centring [Accessed 4 September 2019].

Huang, C.A. (2011) *Embrace Tiger, Return to Mountain: The Essence of Tai Ji*. London: Singing Dragon.

Further reading

King, P. (2016) Somatic intelligence: Working with and through the body-mind. *Global Perspectives*, 11, pp. 20–22. Association for Coaching.

King, P. (2017) Wellbeing – an energetic perspective. *Global Perspectives*, 13, pp. 36–38. Association for Coaching.

King, P. (2019) Coaching the narrative of the soma. *Global Perspectives*, 22, pp. 24–26. Association for Coaching.

Palmer, W. and Crawford, J. (2013) *Leadership Embodiment: How the way we sit and stand can change the way we think and speak*. CreateSpace.

Van Der Kolk, B. (2015) *The Body Keeps the Score: Brain, Mind and Body in the Healing of Trauma*. USA: Penguin Random House.

~ ~ ~ ~ ~

93. Healthy self-feedback (for group supervisors)

Helen Reuben

Where can this be used?				Typical Level of Supervisee Experience Required	

When is this used?

The supervisor is likely to use this approach immediately after a group session has ended, it offers an additional perspective to more traditional verbal or written feedback.

What is the technique?

This is a method of 'Mindful' self-feedback and can be used to encourage supervisors to tap into their intuitions, 'Spiritual Intelligence', learning and awareness.

Step 1:

- The supervisor calms their mind by placing feet flat on the floor and breathing in – through the nose focusing on calm, presence and self-compassion. Self-doubt and judgement can be released by breathing out – through the mouth and tensions, concerns and limitations

Step 2:

- The supervisor recalls an image of the group and identifies each member and where they were seated; including themselves
- In the moment – almost as a 'fly on the wall' – a distanced perspective helps the supervisor notice feelings and sensations as they focus on the group. What comes to mind? What images can represent the experience as a whole? What physical sensations emerge?
- The supervisor can focus on each group member in turn – almost experiencing the session as that supervisee. What

is noticed? How do they feel? What learning is enhanced/needed? What blocks may be there for that person?

- How is this individual responding to the supervisor, to other group members? How well supported do they feel? What is happening for them in terms of their insights?

Step 3:

- The supervisor may sit in the seat that was occupied by a specific group member and imagine what the experience may have been for that supervisee. When seated – eye closure is recommended to block out any distractions and help to focus the mind. Eventually, when ready, the supervisor moves to the next seat to focus on the next individual.
- The supervisor can make notes before moving to the next chair. They may receive images or colours, symbols or sounds; these may have deeper meaning if the supervisor can trust their instincts and intuitions. Remember, the meaning may not reveal itself immediately to the supervisor and may emerge given time.

How to work with the technique ...

At a practical level it may be helpful for supervisor to create a simple diagram of where each supervisee is seated before starting the self-reflection.

Mindfulness is a state achieved by focusing one's awareness on the present moment, while calmly acknowledging and accepting feelings, thoughts and sensations. It is moment-by-moment awareness through a nurturing lens, paying attention to our thoughts and feelings without judging them. It is essential that supervisor allows self-compassion to support any and all self-feedback and not allow their 'Inner Critic' to dominate. Balanced self-feedback without judgement supports the self-esteem and accessing supervisor's inner wisdom will ensure a positive self-dialogue to maintain healthy self-belief.

Interesting this slowing down of the earlier experience often helps the supervisor notice something that did not hold their attention in the moment of the session.

What else might need attention?

This technique may supplement that which was not said more overtly by the supervisees, perhaps paradoxically therefore the supervisor therefore needs to be careful about whether and how they share their new insight with the group. Perhaps individual supervisees lack awareness or are not ready to voice and process what the supervisor is able to access through using this technique. Differentiate between what insight is useful for the supervisor's development and what might be useful to inform the group's understanding of their dynamics.

A word of caution

The supervisor needs to be practiced and competent in becoming mindful more generally before engaging in this as a feedback review activity.

What other uses are there for this technique?

With permission the supervisor may bring their own noticing that occurred following a session as part of the content for a subsequent session. Like many other techniques by logging what they notice over time, themes and patterns may emerge that hold interesting developmental information – for both supervisees and supervisors alike.

This technique can also be adapted used when coaching – either individual group or team coaching.

Further reading

Wigglesworth, C. (2014) *SQ21: The 21 Skills of Spiritual Intelligence.* Select Books.

Williams, J. (2009) Breath of life: Calm power through natural breathing. [online] 15 December. Available at:< https://visionarybeing.wordpress.com/2009/12/15/breath-of-life-calm-power-through-natural-breathing/> [Accessed 7 September 2019].

Resources

For more information on Mindfulness visit the Oxford Mindfulness Centre. Available at: http://oxfordmindfulness.org/ [Accessed 7 September 2019].

~ ~ ~ ~ ~

94. Ideal model

Hetty Einzig

Where can this be used?				Typical Level of Supervisee Experience Required

When is this used?

This is useful for envisioning the ideal state of any chosen subject, e.g. being the best coach I can be or developing my ideal coaching practice. A strong vision acts like a magnet. It provides the 'north star' that guides the supervisee towards realising their vision. Typically, you would be prompted by the supervisee wishing a situation were different or better, or by the supervisee over-focusing on the negative aspects of a situation, or seeing only problems to be solved. It could also be prompted by the supervisee's desire for self-development or a goal they wish to attain.

What is the technique?

Working with ideal qualities and states taps into the higher unconscious: it draws on the best of our self. It is most powerfully facilitated through co-opting our imagination (through drawing, visualising, bodywork, guided visualisation). It is well known that envisioning something helps us work towards it. Lakoff, 2004 called this 'motor force' – images act like a magnet, propelling us to achieve what we imagine.

Step 1: Contract to use this technique and agree the time frame for the full realisation of this ideal state, as chosen by the supervisee and topic-appropriate, e.g. six months, one year, five years.

Step 2: Invite the supervisee to sit comfortably; do a brief relaxation breathing technique to induce a calm, receptive state.

Step 3: Guide the supervisee to fully imagine the ideal state/model of their topic, e.g. a relationship, their identity as a coach, the achievement of a goal. Here is an example:

a) 'Imagine yourself one year from now. The difficult relationship between you and X is now resolved. In fact, it has flowered into its fully ideal state. See yourself and the other person ... .'

b) Encourage all the senses: 'Where are you? What can you see? What are you hearing? What are you feeling? What are you saying to each other? What is happening? Is anyone else there?' etc.

c) Have the supervisee imagine silently, or talk out loud – whichever suits their style.

d) You might then suggest to the supervisee that they 'helicopter out' and look at the ideal relationship, achieved goal/career from a point of perspective. Ask 'Looking at this ideal state from a distance, what did you have to develop in yourself to get here?' 'What needed to change/happen/be resolved for you to move towards this state?'; and/or further questions related to the steps the supervisee might take to move towards their ideal model.

e) Bring them back to the room in an appropriate and well-paced way.

Step 4: Debrief the learning and insights together. You can invite the supervisee to capture key points in their notebook, or through drawing.

How to work with the technique ...

Transpersonal philosophy holds that just as the acorn has the coding within it to become an oak tree, so each human is born with an emergent life purpose. Working with the ideal model is about realising our highest potential and living congruently with our ideals. Creating an environment where the supervisee is comfortable expressing their most private hopes and dreams is the foundation for using this technique.

Guided visualisation is one way of working. You might also use drawing, movement, or working with clay. It all depends on your personal skills and whether you want to reinforce the supervisee's existing strengths by working congruently or help them develop a new skill by choosing an unfamiliar mode.

What else might need attention?

This way of working can go deep so is best reserved for experienced supervisors. Deep rooted issues may surface so be prepared for this possibility. Make sure you have experienced this technique many times yourself as your confidence will ensure the feeling of safety the supervisee needs to 'travel' in their imagination and envision courageously.

A word of caution

Working with guided visualisation is contraindicated for supervisees who have difficulty grounding (their energy feels speedy, airy, erratic or hyper) or who jump from topic to topic without focus or depth. In these instances the work is about helping them ground in the present and focus on pragmatic action.

What other uses are there for this technique?

With practice this could also be used with coaching clients.

Reference

Lakoff, G. (2004) *Don't Think of an Elephant: Know Your Values and Frame the Debate.* White River Junction, Vermont: Chelsea Green Publishing Co.

Further reading

Assagioli, R. (1965) *Psychosynthesis: A Collection of Basic Writings.* Wellingborough: Turnstone Press.
Campell, J. (2012) *The Hero with a Thousand Faces.* 3rd ed. New World Library.
Einzig, H. and Whitmore, J. (2015) Transpersonal coaching. In: J. Passmore. Ed. *Coaching: The Industry Guide.* Maidenhead: Kogan Page. Ch.9.
Ferrucci, P. (1982) *What We May Be: The Visions and Techniques of Psychosynthesis.* Wellingborough: Turnstone Press.
Murdoch, M. (1990) *The Heroine's Journey.* Shambhala Publications Inc.

~ ~ ~ ~ ~

95. 'Self-preparation' for supervisors

Helen Reuben

Where can this be used?				Typical level of supervisee experience required	

When is this used?

This technique aids the supervisor to increase their focus, self-compassion and presence in order to remain effective. It is therefore useful as part of your preparation for a session.

What is the technique?

This technique allows us to access an appropriate state for being the best supervisor we can be. Some of this approach is inspired by 'Spiritual Intelligence.'

You will need at least five minutes before a session. Find a quiet place, without interruptions.

Step 1: Ground yourself by putting your feet on the floor feeling the ground beneath your feet

Allow your eyes to close. Breathe in through the nose and out through the mouth - breathing 'out' any unwanted tensions, concerns - just let them go. Allow yourself to access peaceful feelings.

Step 2: Now, trusting your imagination, allow yourself to go to a place of beauty and positive change - experience this place in detail (colours, shapes smells, feelings) - be there fully and completely

Wait peacefully, you are about to meet a wonderfully skilled person, this is the best of you, your 'Higher Self' (see pp. 316–317). Perhaps the you connected to a 'higher power'? - Whatever that may mean for you?

See them walking towards you, notice how they walk, move, what they wear.

They wish to offer you guidance and support to help you prepare effectively - when you open your eyes you may want to write this down.

Today, your highest self recognises you may need to let go of something - a belief, thought a feeling that may block your effectiveness. What is that? How will you release it right now?

Take a moment and trust you will gain a sense of how to do this - perhaps you can wash it away in a beautiful waterfall. Perhaps a gentle breeze to blow away this unwanted thought or feeling.

Your 'Higher Self' offers you a gift - a resource that will help you supervise - even more powerfully. What might this gift be? They also offer you words of guidance - what do they tell you about who you really are?

Step 3: Where in your body might you feel blocks or discomfort? Allow these to be released. Breathe away tension in any part of you.

The 'High Self' also asks 'What is diverting your mind right now?' Trust that you will receive a helpful answer. When your answer comes just let it go; like holding a balloon on a piece of string - release it *now*.

Return to the present by listening to any sounds in the room, perhaps your own breathing.

Step 4: Perhaps you will consider an affirmation saying to yourself - 'I am enough' or 'I trust in my supervision abilities'.

Note: an affirmation is a positive statement said as if it is true, now.

How to work with this technique?

Before engaging with this technique consider; what your effective supervisor state would be? Perhaps:

- Being present (your mind focused on the here and now) - not distracted?
- Compassionate, patient?
- Free of the unconscious desire to fix or rescue?

Done regularly - before each session, you will become effective at creating a positive calm and present state. The script given above is an example and over time you will notice what metaphors and cues are most useful to you.

A word of caution

If sharing this, you may want to adjust how you phrase the notion of a 'Higher Self' to reflect the other person's belief system. You may ask, 'When you are the best of yourself who are you?' or 'When you are connected to a positive and powerful energy - what might that be?'

When using this for the first time, and immediately prior to a supervision session, allow ample time to process what emerges. Also, this technique generates a relaxed and reflective energy, so do not practise this directly before driving.

What other uses are there for this technique?

This technique could be of use to both coaches in advance of their session and to their clients in advance of key meetings. Once you are comfortable working with it for yourself, you may offer guidance in its use to others.

Further reading

Wigglesworth, C. (2014) *SQ21: The 21 skills of Spiritual Intelligence*. Select Books.

Resources

For more information on Mindfulness visit the Oxford Mindfulness Centre. Available at: http://oxfordmindfulness.org/ [Accessed 7 September 2019].

~ ~ ~ ~ ~

96. The two dimensions of growth

Hetty Einzig

Where can this be used?				Typical level of supervisee experience required	

When is this used?

This model is used to raise awareness, develop a cogent purpose, harness vision and, critically, ground this in action in the world. In this way we move towards the mid-line, drawn by the magnet of the Higher Self (see pp. 316–317). This is healing and empowering.

What is the approach?

The supervisee plots key life events along the horizontal axis with the line descending or rising according to their perception of the significance of the event. This brings into awareness their sense of being in the world.

Step 1: Contract appropriately for the depth of the work that follows; ensure a degree of safety by reminding the supervisee that you will be guided by them regarding how far and how deep they want to explore.

Step 2: Draw the axes with the supervisee. The horizontal axe represents time, the vertical depth or transcendence. Then explain each dimension along the following lines:

- The horizontal axis is about Quantity: we acquire more knowledge, things, status, money, psychological understanding, cleverness.
- The vertical axis is about Quality: it expresses our spiritual growth, the development of our reflexivity, our compassion, our appreciation of the mystical and the beauty of all life, our wisdom.

Step 3: Give the supervisee time to plot their graph from a point in time of their choice to the present. Facilitate the discussion lightly, start by asking what the supervisee notices about their graph.

Step 4: Note: in transpersonal work we hold the belief that a person needs to develop along both axes. If one or other dominates our trajectory then each axe will hit its own existential crisis.

Step 4 (a): Where there is a dominance of the horizontal/quantitative axis, this could result in the *Crisis of Meaning*, a creeping or sudden loss of meaning and purpose, which causes us to ask: 'Why am I doing this, what for?' With appropriate re-contracting permission, you can help the supervisee acknowledge and explore this, perhaps using imagery, metaphor and drawing to activate the imagination and the Higher Unconscious (see Figure 10.1).

Step 4 (b): Where there is over-development along the vertical/qualitative axis, this could result in the *Crisis of Duality*, when the gap between the vision of wholeness and the messiness of the actual world yawns wider than is bearable, causing loss of 'faith', disgust, self-abnegation or self-destruction, summed up by the question: 'What's the point?' With permission, you can help the supervisee acknowledge and explore this, by using grounding techniques (e.g. bodywork), practical actions and commitments.

Step 5: Check in to see what action the supervisee feels ready to take and how they plan to take it.

Step 6: Agree with the supervisee how they want to close the discussion and check what additional support they need from you or others in their network.

How to work with the approach ...

This work may well generate 'big' questions for the supervisee. It is therefore important to be guided by the pace and capacity of the supervisee in the moment in the room. Occasional re-contracting helps sense check the journey of discovery and helps ensure the supervisee does not stay confused or overwhelmed. Sometimes these discussions stir things up but remain inconclusive so be prepared for the session to feel unfinished and uncertain. However, equally, sometimes powerful insights are generated and something significant shifts, so be prepared for the supervisee to take what may seem like a momentous action – perhaps before you feel ready for them to!

What else might need attention?

The supervisee will almost always need to continue the work outside of the session and so it is important when contracting to differentiate between where the supervisee wants to involve you and where they want to reflect independently.

A word of caution

This kind of deep work should only be facilitated by those who have already engaged and benefitted from similar work themselves. This is as true for the supervisor who wants to use it with their supervisee as it is for the supervisee who wants to use it with clients.

What other uses are there for this approach?

Without specific additional training, no further applications are recommended.

Further reading

Assagioli, R. (1965) *Psychosynthesis: A Collection of Basic Writings*, Wellingborough: Turnstone Press.

Einzig, H. and Whitmore, J. (2015) Transpersonal coaching. In: J. Passmore. Ed. *Coaching: The Industry Guide*. Maidenhead: Kogan Page. Ch.9

Ferrucci, P. (1982) *What We May Be: The Visions and Techniques of Psychosynthesis*. Wellingborough: Turnstone Press.

~~~~~

97. Using the outdoors

Liz Ford

Where can this be used?				Typical level of supervisee experience required	
~~~~~

When is this used?

Coaching outdoors is a wonderfully powerful approach to use when your supervisee is feeling stuck or you sense that movement would be helpful to gain a different outlook. Other times when this technique could be advantageous are when the supervisee has been busy, feels flat and a break is needed or when fresh air and the natural environment might bring a fresh perspective.

What is the approach?

This approach aims to draw on the environment to stimulate new thinking, make connections and provide solutions. It is more than doing what you normally do in an outdoor setting, it involves being mindful of the space around you and what information it might hold. Although often used in countryside or parkland locations, it also works well in inner city locations.

Step 1: Preparation.

- Ask the supervisee if they'd like to work outdoors.
- If arranging this for a future session, ask them to bring suitable clothing and footwear.
- Plan where to go.
- If it's a spur of the moment choice, choose a place that suits the weather and their attire – using the garden or a park can work as well as hills, woods and river walks.
- Before setting off, take time to identify the supervision question or issue to be explored and their desired outcome.

Step 2: Developing insight.

- Hold the supervision question in mind as you walk.
- Encourage the supervisee to stop whenever they want to look closer or take in the view.
- Ask questions to help the supervisee explore their surroundings and how what they notice relates to their supervision question/issue to explore. For example: 'What do you see or hear in this place that connects with your thoughts/feelings about this client?' Then follow up with questions such as 'Is there anything else about … ?' or 'and what do you know from this place here?'
- Encourage the supervisee to also notice how their body feels as they walk, being curious as to what it might be telling them.

For example: 'As we walk, what are you noticing in your body?' or 'And you notice your breathing has slowed and your stride is getting longer, what might that be telling you?'

Step 3: Consolidation.

- Near the end of the walk or back at base, take time to:
  - Reflect on the walk.
  - Notice what's shifted.
  - Explore insights and learning.
  - Capture actions.

How to work with the approach ...

Pay attention during the walk to pace, what is said and not said as well as what the supervisee notices about themselves and their surroundings. Tuning in to this helps the supervisor to decide when to ask questions, when to stop and notice, when to ask the supervisee to choose the way and when to take the lead

Consciously noticing the environment and asking how it relates to the supervision question or issues, helps to maintain focus and stops the session turning into a chatty walk.

Depending on the contract, the supervisor might also ask permission to share what they notice, such as a change in their posture during the walk or a tendency to march onwards without pausing to notice, being curious as to how this might link to the topic of focus.

Walking supervision is easier on an individual basis although groups can also gain from working in a stimulating outdoor environment; it's easier to manage at locations like a park or city square. Encouraging the group to take time to notice their surroundings through a mindful senses exercise can be a good way to draw on the wisdom held by the space.

A word of caution

It is important to keep an eye on the time and ensure you are back at base by the end of the contracted session. If setting off on longer walks ensure one of you knows the area and that you are well prepared and safety aspects have been considered including your fitness and that of the supervisee. Carry a phone just in case any difficulty arises.

What other uses are there for this approach?

This approach works well for individual coaching as well as supervision and can be delivered using the same process.

Further reading

Oppezzo, M. and Schwartz, D.L. (2014) Give Your Ideas Some Legs: The Positive Effect of Walking on Creative Thinking, *Journal of Experimental Psychology*, 40(4), pp. 1142–1152.

Resources

National Trust (2019) A beginner's guide to forest bathing. [online] Available at: <www.nationaltrust.org.uk/lists/a-beginners-guide-to-forest-bathing>[Accessed7 September 2019].

Street Wisdom (2019) Street Wisdom: Answers are everywhere. [online] Available at www.streetwisdom.org/ [Accessed 7 September 2019].

~ ~ ~ ~ ~

98. What's my environmental footprint?

Penny Walker

Where can this be used?				Typical level of supervisee experience required	

When is this used?

If there has been some conversation 'in the margins' about the state of the planet, climate change, plastics, wildlife or similar environmental issues, then the group may be interested to look at their individual and collective 'footprint' and explore what, if anything, they want to do to change it.

What is the enquiry?

Step 1: Before the session, invite the supervisee(s) to self-assess their 'environmental footprint' and bring their results to the session. For the results are comparable, everyone should use the same tool. For example:

WWF's environmental footprint quiz https://footprint.wwf.org.uk/#/

or the eco footprint calculator www.footprintcalculator.org/

or the Berkley Cool Climate calculator. https://coolclimate.berkeley.edu/calculator.

Step 2: Ask supervisees to line up in order of their results, from smallest/lowest to biggest/highest. Anyone who wasn't able to get a result can observe the line and join the conversation.

Optional – create a visual representation of the collective results. For example, an 'instant bar chart'.

Step 3: Debrief the results: What do people see in the line-up? What do they feel about the results? What do they think it means?

Step 4: Explore what they would they like to do as a result. It can be useful to divide this into:

1 Personal life.
2 Professional life (including non-coaching work, how they run their business).
3 As a coach (including whether they see opportunities for working on these issues with clients).

Step 5: For those who would like to take action point them to the resources in 'Further reading'. Invite people to share the sources they have found helpful.

How to work with the enquiry?

Some skilful facilitation can be required to manage not just the content of the discussion, but supervisees' emotional responses to their results. Here are some typical reactions and how you might manage them:

- Critiquing the tool – acknowledge the indicative nature of these tools, giving space for some criticism before exploring their results.
- Get defensive – recognise that our wider society and the economy may have shaped our choices, so point to success stories to illustrate what might still be possible.
- Get despondent – especially likely when most of the group has footprints bigger than the 'one planet' sustainable level. Point them to the Further reading section, which suggests some positive actions.
- Blame others – acknowledge the size of the challenge while encouraging supervisees to become part of the global movement, which is creating change everywhere.

- Argue for a particular solution – affirm the particular passions of those present while also embracing a diversity of views. Remind supervisees that, just as in coaching, people need to discover their own solutions for them to stick.
- Get very angry or sad -bring your restorative skills to help supervisees face their emotions without being overwhelmed by them.

You will need to help the group move beyond these responses, which may otherwise get in the way of looking at their impact, how they feel about it, what it means and what they want to do.

What else might need attention?

It is a good idea to do some background reading on the tool you are using to understand what it shows. Ideally, complete the questionnaire yourself so that you can facilitate from an informed position.

Remember, effective action to reduce emissions and tackle environmental issues includes being an active citizen who engages in political activity and campaigning, as well as directly changing the way we live our lives. People can also support or lead change in their organisations. People may need help reflecting on and researching where they can have the biggest impact.

A word of caution

This enquiry may prompt supervisees to consider working with clients to help them reduce their environmental impact. Indeed, there are coaches who specialise in this and clients who ask for this help. Before raising an issue like climate change with a client, remind yourself of the coaching contract. Is this your stuff or theirs? An open question like 'What are the consequences of that choice?' may lead them to consider environmental impact, but equally it may not. If a coach discovers that their values or views are too far at odds with those of their client, then this may be a reason to discontinue the relationship.

What other uses are there for this enquiry?

This exercise can be adapted for individual use, missing Step 2.

Further reading

Walker, P. (2007) Being the change for climate change leadership, *Organisations and People*, 14(4), pp. 9–14.

Whybrow, A., Cohen, Z., and Aspey, L. (2019) Call for multi-pronged coaching response to the global climate crisis, *Coaching at Work*, 14(5), pp. 12–13.

Resources

Network, C.C. (2019) Start with a quick carbon footprint estimate. [online] Available at: <https://coolclimate.berkeley.edu/calculator. > [Accessed 7 September 2019].

Network, G.F. (2019) *What is your ecological footprint?* [online] Available at: <www.footprintcalculator.org/> [Accessed 7 September 2019].

Ortiz, D.A. (2018) Ten simple ways to act on climate change. *BBC Future* [blog] 5 November. Available at: < www.bbc.com/future/story/20181102-what-can-i-do-about-climate-change > [Accessed 7 September 2019].

Drawdown, P. (2019) Project Drawdown: The world's leading resource for climate solutions. [online] Available at: <www.drawdown.org/≥ [Accessed 7 September 2019].

Walker, P. (2018) Instant barcharts: A safe snapshot of opinion. [blog] 12 September. Available at: <www.penny-walker.co.uk/blog/2018/7/18/a-safe-snapshot-of-opinion > [Accessed 7 September 2019].

WWF (2019) How big is your environmental footprint? [online] Available at: <https://footprint.wwf.org.uk/#/> [Accessed 7 September 2019].

~ ~ ~ ~ ~

99. Wise being guided visualisation

Hetty Einzig

Where can this be used?				Typical level of supervisee experience required	

When is this used?

This guided visualisation is useful when a supervisee wants to connect with the wisest dimension of themselves. It helps enable wise decisions especially at times of dilemma, anxiety, paradox and complexity. It can also help build the supervisee's confidence in their intuition and in their 'Higher Self' (see Figure 10.1, p. 316) as a principal instrument in the coaching relationship.

What is the technique?

The supervisee is encouraged to use their imagination as a route to access their inner wisdom. It is well known that envisioning something helps us work towards it. Images have what we call 'motor force' – they act like a magnet, propelling us to achieve what we imagine (Lakoff, 2004).

Step 1: Contract to use this technique. To guide an appropriate journey for your supervisee, find out where they feel most fully alive, joyous, connected, clear sighted, at peace. Wisdom is generally seen as transcendent, so the typical journey goes towards height and light. e.g. up a mountain. However, for many people wisdom is intrinsic: their journey goes inwards, into the ocean, the mountain's heart, the forest – but still always in connection with Nature.

Step 2: Settle the supervisee with a brief relaxation breathing technique.

Step 3: Guide them on a journey towards their Higher Self. Here is an example:

- 'You find yourself in a beautiful meadow.'
- 'What can you see, hear, feel, smell ... ?'
- 'You will be going on a journey ... what might you take with you ... ?'
- 'You are traversing a wood, the light is dappled, you find your way ... there is a clear pathway ... {or divergent pathways to choose from} ... .'
- 'You see ahead a mountain which you will climb (or descend) ... notice the features of the path you are on ... the view ... the quality of the air you breathe.'
- 'As you climb (descend) you meet {natural obstacles, or magical animals, symbolic of their challenge} ... and you overcome them ... .'
- 'Now you have arrived; what do you see, hear, feel?'
- 'You notice there is someone {perhaps human, perhaps animal} coming towards you, welcoming, benevolent. It is your Wise Being and they have come expressly to meet you and support you.'
- 'You engage in conversation with your Wise Being. You might wish to ask them, e.g. What should I do in this situation? What is my first step? Listen for the answers, which may not come verbally. Trust what comes without judgment.'
- 'Your Wise Being gives you a gift. It is a symbol of your solution to your issue. Note how you feel on receiving this gift. You put it somewhere safe and within reach ... .'
- 'Express your thanks and goodbyes, and take leave of your Wise Being, knowing you can meet with them again at any time.'

Step 4: Bring the supervisee back to the here and now.

Step 5: Invite the supervisee to describe key moments and especially the encounter with their Wise Being. This could be done verbally or through drawing.

Step 6: Capture key points, insights and any actions the supervisee wishes to take. Perhaps source a real object that symbolises their quality of wisdom, represented by the gift.

How to work with the technique ...

While you will craft the journey to suit your supervisee, it is common for the journey to go through similar stages,

1 Start in a safe place.
2 Go on a journey.
3 Make a transition.
4 Meet and overcome challenges.
5 Encounter the Wise Being.
6 Conclude the journey.

In stage 4 guiding them to overcome obstacles helps instil confidence they can do so in real life. Importantly, let them imagine how they overcome them. Be light, be creative and keep the pace fairly brisk; ensure the narrative elements are connected to the supervisee's issue, and encourage them to tap into all their senses.

A word of caution

See 'Ideal model'.

What other uses are there for this technique?

You can also introduce the concept of a wise being into an ordinary conversation without a guided visualisation, e.g. 'What would the wisest person you know do/say in this situation?' It can also be used by supervisors for self-preparation (see pp. 330–332).

Reference

Lakoff, G. (2004) *Don't Think of an Elephant: Know Your Values and Frame the Debate.* White River Junction, Vermont: Chelsea Green Publishing Co.

Further reading

Assagioli, R. (1965) *Psychosynthesis: A Collection of Basic Writings.* Wellingborough: Turnstone Press.
Einzig, H. and Whitmore, J. (2015) Transpersonal coaching. In: J. Passmore. Ed. *Coaching: The Industry Guide.* London: Kogan Page. Ch.9.
Ferrucci, P. (1982) *What We May Be: The Visions and Techniques of Psychosynthesis.* Wellingborough: Turnstone Press.

~ ~ ~ ~ ~

100. Working with emergent purpose

Hetty Einzig

Where can this be used?				Typical level of supervisee experience required	

When is this used?

When your supervisee feels stuck or a failure, or has hit a crisis or painful moment in coaching their client or in their development as a coach.

What is the approach?

The concept of Emergence proposes that every problem, crisis or failure harbours within it an emergent purpose: a clue to the next step on our journey. This is not to make light of the real distress people suffer, but on the contrary to experience and move through any situation with a sense of meaning and intention. The Greek word 'krisis' means decision. Every situation provides creative possibilities for gaining mastery over one's inner states and for transformation. As Assagioli was reported as saying: 'There are no problems, only tasks and opportunities' (Assagioli, 1965).

The working principle derives from Buddhism: while we cannot always change our outer circumstances, we *can* choose our inner response.

Acceptance must be reached before transformation can take place (Assagioli, 1965; Frankl, 1946; Kubler-Ross, 1969). This is not resignation but a true spiritual act of will, a choice to be in the present, eliminating the 'useless acts of rebellion' and 'collaborating with the inevitable,' as Assagioli would say. Acceptance releases energy, new insights emerge and a sense of unity attained.

Step 1: This work may begin when the supervisor sees the supervisee expressing one or more of the typical reactions to problems or crises: fear, denial, anger, blaming, bargaining, self-pity, resistance, rebellion, guilt, shame, paralysis or depression. The transpersonal supervisor helps their supervisee to navigate through the crisis by guiding a different process.

Step 2: Acknowledge the supervisee's pain. Recognition and care will help the supervisee feel seen and heard, and send the message that you are not trying to 'solve' their problem nor 'take away' their pain.

Step 3. Seek permission to work at a deeper level, prepare yourself to work with compassion and curiosity as to the creative potential seeking to emerge, yet without attachment to outcome.

Step 4: Invite the supervisee to explore more deeply. Depending on different processing styles this could be done somatically, cognitively or using other creative approaches (drawing, colours, images, collage, sculpture.)

Step 5: Check the supervisee's readiness to take perspective on the situation and when appropriate explore their understanding in a spirit of compassion and appreciative inquiry. Helpful questions are:

- What may be trying to emerge or unfold?
- What does this mean for you, for your client, for their organization?
- What is the potential in this situation for you or your client?
- What needs to change here?
- What is trying to be born?
- If this situation was sent just for your learning – what are you learning?
- What needs to grow or transform in you, to help my client?
- How does your situation relate to the bigger picture?

Step 6: Your ultimate aim is to help the supervisee reach a state of acceptance and to find meaning and purpose within their situation. The supervisee is likely to feel more empowered to make a conscious choice of next steps - if any. But don't push for this or you will arouse natural resistance.

Step 7: Move the session towards a close by enquiring about feelings, insights or learning.

How to work with this approach …

Observe the dialogue - and also yourself. Take care not to get caught in sympathy or countertransference. Stay away from 'solutionising' - often a result of our own anxiety and discomfort with strong emotion.

What else might need attention?

The depth of this work means that this approach is reserved for experienced supervisors (not just experienced supervisees). It is possible that deep rooted issues may surface (for either person) so vigilance is required. Transparency is encouraged since concealing it would be incongruent with working with emergence.

A word of caution

The supervisor needs to have done a significant amount of personal work before supporting their supervisees to do likewise. To work effectively in this sensitive territory, we need to have had personal experience of how our own dark side manifests and of our capacity to transform 'darkness into light'.

What other uses are there for this approach?

None.

References

Assagioli, R. (1965) *Psychosynthesis: A Collection of Basic Writings*, Winnipeg, Canada: Turnstone Press.

Frankl, V. (1946) *Man's Search for Meaning*. London: Rider.

Kubler-Ross, E. (1969) *On Death & Dying*. New York: Simon & Schuster/Touchstone.

Further reading

Einzig, H. (2017) Darkness and light. In: H. Einzig (ed) *The Future of Coaching: Vision, Leadership and Responsibility in a Transforming World*. Abingdon: Routledge. Ch.6.

Einzig, H. and Whitmore, J. (2015) Transpersonal coaching. In: J. Passmore (Ed.) *Excellence in Coaching: The Industry Guide*. Maidenhead: Kogan Page. Ch.9.

Ferrucci, P. (1982) *What We May Be: The Visions and Techniques of Psychosynthesis.* Wellingborough: Turnstone Press.
Obholzer, A. and Zagier, R.V. (2006) *The Unconscious at Work.* Maidenhead: Routledge.
Whitmore, D. (2004) *Psychosynthesis Counselling in Action,* 3rd ed., London: Sage Publications.

~ ~ ~ ~ ~

101. Working with our sub-personalities

Hetty Einzig

Where can this be used?				Typical level of supervisee experience required	

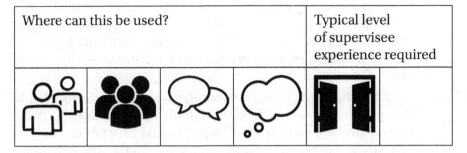

When is this used?

This is a popular and effective approach to deal with dominating emotions or repetitive reactions or tendencies.

What is the enquiry?

The sub-personalities concept was created by Roberto Assagioli (1965) and has been adopted and adapted by several authors since (see e.g. 'mini-selves' Bachkirova, 2016). All philosophies and wisdom traditions recognise the tension between unity and multiplicity: we are unique *and* we have many parts to our 'self'. What we call our 'personality' is not singular but multiple and changeable. Holding the truth of 'both/and' during the supervision work helps us find a more balanced expression and collaboration between the different parts, or 'sub-personalities', within us.

The technique focuses on bringing to life our many 'sub-personalities'. This is a helpful way to work with difficult, over-used, or dominant feelings and behaviours, e.g. my frightened child, my caring helper, my bully, my compassionate self, my warrior, my upholder of justice, my inner-critic. Every sub-personality has its gift and its limitations; its light and its shadow.

Step1: The contract.

Contract appropriately for the depth of work that follows, position the work as an enquiry or experiment. Be light and even playful.

Step 2: The enquiry.

When the supervisee feels dominated by a particularly strong or repetitive response to their client, or especially when they express a dilemma between a 'part' of themselves that feels or wants to do X and an opposing part that feels or want to do Y. We explore by asking for example: 'What part of you feels this?' or 'Whose voice is that saying this?' We might add 'And I hear this other voice which is saying something different' ... You can be light and playful: 'Let's bring this part of you alive: what triggers them, what do they say and do? If this part of you were a person, what would you call them?' and 'Now let's explore the other voice/part - who is this, what are they like?' etc.

We help the supervisee uncover the wants and needs of this 'sub-personality' or 'mini-self' within them. By naming the 'sub-personality' the supervisee is helped to first gain perspective on this part of themselves, to understand it is not the whole of them. The work then focuses on helping the supervisee accept and eventually transform potentially blocking parts of themselves (like their inner critic or anger at their client) into higher expressions through the lens of compassion, or in the case of 'positive' parts (like their caring self) into more nuanced and balanced expressions.

The metaphor of the orchestra is useful as it emphasises the point that no one instrument or part of ourselves is better than another nor should be suppressed. All are inter-connected. The task is to seek to play more harmonious music and to act from a place of choice (the conductor) rather than react to whatever comes at us.

Step 3: The close.

The ultimate aim is to move through the four phases of harmonisation, i.e. Recognition; Acceptance; Collaboration; Integration - with a 'sub-personality'. However, achieving the first two phases can bring about significant changes in attitude and approach. This can have the effect of the supervisee taking a more observational stance and avoid being submerged or over-identified with one aspect of themselves, one approach or a single emotional tone.

How to work with the enquiry …

First get to know the 'sub-personality': you can enquire into how it looks, its name, posture, dress, likes.. Then the key questions we work with are:

- What *triggers* this sub-personality'?
- What does it *want*?
- What does it really *need*?
- What is its *contribution*/gift?
- How does it *limit* you?

Those familiar with gestalt chair work (see pp. 162–165) could can set up two chairs for the supervisee to represent two 'sub-personalities,' which may be in opposition to each other.

A word of caution

Avoid getting rigid with this technique or to press the phases of harmonisation. Often awareness is enough. Acceptance and integration may come later.

What other uses are there for this enquiry?

The capacity to access and integrate our many selves is a marker of maturity and a critical component of both leadership and coaching capacity. Through exploration of the multiple parts of themselves the supervisee gains skill in bringing this technique to their coaching clients.

References

Assagioli, R. (1965) *Psychosynthesis: A Collection of Basic Writings*. Wellingborough: Turnstone Press.

Bachkirova, T. (2016) *The Self of the Coach: Conceptualization, Issues, and Opportunities for Practitioner Development*. Consulting Psychology Journal: Practice and Research. American Psychological Association.

Further reading

Einzig, H. and Whitmore, J. (2015) Transpersonal coaching. In J. Passmore. (Ed.) *Excellence in Coaching: The Industry Guide*. London: Kogan Page.

Ferrucci, P. (1982) *What We May Be: The Visions and Techniques of Psychosynthesis*. Wellingborough: Turnstone Press.

Index

Pages in *italics* and **bold** refer to images and tables, respectively.